Poetics, Rhetoric, and Logic

STUDIES IN THE BASIC
DISCIPLINES OF CRITICISM

BOOKS BY WILBUR SAMUEL HOWELL

Poetics, Rhetoric, and Logic: Studies in the Basic Disciplines of Criticism

Eighteenth-Century British Logic and Rhetoric

Logic and Rhetoric in England, 1500–1700

Fénelon's Dialogues on Eloquence: A Translation, with an Introduction and Notes

Problems and Styles of Communication

The Rhetoric of Alcuin and Charlemagne: A Translation, with an Introduction, the Latin Text, and Notes

Poetics, Rhetoric, and Logic

STUDIES IN THE BASIC
DISCIPLINES OF CRITICISM

Wilbur Samuel Howell

CORNELL UNIVERSITY PRESS

Ithaca and London

International Standard Book Number 0-8014-0945-4
Library of Congress Catalog Card Number 75-6083
Printed in the United States of America

to Harry Caplan
and to the memory of
Lane Cooper and Herbert A. Wichelns

in honor of their brilliant contributions as scholars
and teachers to what their grateful students proudly
regard in retrospect as The Cornell School of Rhetoric

Preface

The essays making up the eight numbered chapters in this volume were first written as self-contained articles for learned journals, or for Festschrifts in honor of two of my esteemed former teachers, or, in one case, for a special conference of scholars.

In bringing them together here, I have not attempted to remove from each those elements which may to some readers seem merely repetitions of elements found in other essays. My excuse is quite unphilosophical and hence perhaps worthy of special consideration. Each of these essays is a particular friend of mine, a companion of some dedicated moment in my career, entitled in a way to live out its life in the form which it had in its beginning. Each may even be considered a child of mine, perhaps underprivileged at birth by reason of its having had an imperfect parent wished upon it, but unwilling, nevertheless, to undergo corrective surgery in its maturity, lest unsuccessful attempts at emendation turn out to be more embarrassing than were the birthday defects. At any rate, I have no heart for changing the original character of any of these essays, and I have not done so. What I have done instead is to write a wholly new essay as an Introduction to them in their present collective capacity, and I have pointed out in that Introduction how especially suited these essays are to be brought together and to be given the opportunity at long last to dwell with each other in the same house. I hope that the Introduction succeeds in carrying out this design. And I hope, of course, that my readers will not blame a given essay too harshly for displaying its family characteristics in the form of repetitions while it is seeking at the same time to say something for itself on the subject that belongs solely to it. All members of a family are entitled in my view to be esteemed on their own even as they are in the process of revealing traits shared with their sisters and brothers, or their mothers and fathers. May my introduction and the essays succeed in evoking sentiments of the same sort from those who come to know them.

I mentioned earlier that these eight essays did not find their way into the present collection from the same set of previous auspices. What these auspices were in each case should now receive brief further comment.

Chapter 1 ("Aristotle and Horace on Rhetoric and Poetics") was published originally in *The Quarterly Journal of Speech,* LIV (1968), 325–339. It is here reprinted with the permission of the Speech Communication Association.

Chapter 2 ("The Arts of Literary Criticism in Renaissance Britain: A Comprehensive View") invites a somewhat longer account of itself. On February 16, 1973, I was asked by Professor L. P. Wilkinson and Dr. R. R. Bolgar, of the Research Centre of King's College, Cambridge, to read a paper at their institution in April, 1974, in connection with a conference to be held at that time on Classical Influences on European Culture, A.D. 1500–1700. In accepting their invitation, I decided to prepare a paper in part involving the history of rhetoric in the Renaissance. As a first step in my specific preparation I wrote an essay of 13,200 words on the interrelations of poetics, rhetoric, and logic in Renaissance literary theory. It is that essay which is now being published in the present volume. As a second step in my preparation, I reduced the

13,200-word text to a 2,500-word abridgment, taking care that the latter would not only represent all strands of my longer argument but would also accommodate itself to the 15-minute time period which I was asked to observe in addressing the conference. I entitled the abridgment "Poetics, Rhetoric, and Logic in Renaissance Criticism," and I presented it at the conference on April 8, 1974. Under the same title the abridgment appears in the proceedings of the conference as edited by Dr. Bolgar and published by Cambridge University Press. Only about 350 words of my original long essay appear in connected sequences in the abridgment. I wish now to express my thanks to Cambridge University Press for permission to use these sequences in the present book.

"Oratory and Poetry in Fénelon's Literary Theory," now Chapter 3 of this book, was first published in *The Quarterly Journal of Speech*, XXXVII (1951), 1–10. The Speech Communication Association has given me permission to reprint it here. It has also been reprinted in *Readings in Rhetoric*, ed. Lionel Crocker and Paul A. Carmak (Springfield, Illinois, 1965), pp. 242–256, hereafter cited as *Readings in Rhetoric*.

Chapter 4 was first published under the editorship of Donald C. Bryant in *The Rhetorical Idiom* (Cornell University Press, 1958), that volume being a Festschrift in honor of my former teacher Professor Herbert A. Wichelns. It is here reprinted with the permission of Cornell University Press. On an earlier occasion it was also reprinted in *The Province of Rhetoric*, ed. Joseph Schwartz and John A. Rycenga (New York, 1965), pp. 292–308.

"The Declaration of Independence and Eighteenth-Century Logic," here making up Chapter 5, was originally published in *The William and Mary Quarterly*, 3d Series, XVIII (October, 1961), 463–484. The copyright for that article was assigned to me on May 27, 1965, by the Institute of Early

American History and Culture. The essay also has appeared in *A Casebook on The Declaration of Independence,* ed. Robert Ginsberg (New York, 1967), pp. 194–215.

"De Quincey on Science, Rhetoric, and Poetry," which makes up Chapter 6, appeared first in *Speech Monographs,* XIII (1946), 1–13. It is here reprinted with the permission of the Speech Communication Association. Like the essay constituting Chapter 3, it was selected for inclusion in *Readings in Rhetoric,* pp. 409–428.

"Literature as an Enterprise in Communication," here presented as Chapter 7, was first published in *The Quarterly Journal of Speech,* XXXIII (1947), 417–426. It was since reprinted in *Contemporary Rhetoric: A Reader's Coursebook,* ed. Douglas Ehninger (Glenview, Illinois, 1972), pp. 98–107. It appears in my book with the permission of the Speech Communication Association.

The essay contained in Chapter 8 invites special comment, as did that in Chapter 2. Here entitled "Kenneth Burke's 'Lexicon Rhetoricae': A Critical Examination," it was called "Rhetoric and Poetics: A Plea for the Recognition of the Two Literatures" when it appeared in *The Classical Tradition,* a Festschrift in honor of my former teacher Professor Harry Caplan, edited by Luitpold Wallach, copyright © 1966 by Cornell University Press. I am indebted to Cornell University Press for permission to reprint it now. Prior to its appearance under the auspices just specified, it had been presented at the University of California in Los Angeles, under the auspices of that institution's Center for Medieval and Renaissance Studies, as a lecture at a symposium on the History and Significance of Rhetoric. I did not know when I prepared the lecture that Kenneth Burke would be one of my listeners, but there he was in the front row as I rose to speak. I thought of flight, but I decided instead to say what I had planned and to trust to his magnanimity to hear me out.

Accordingly I read the essay that now appears under its new title in Chapter 8. Mr. Burke heard me through to the end, and if he felt annoyance, he succeeded admirably in keeping it to himself. When I met him in the corridor later on, I remember his laughing a bit and saying to me, "Ah, I know what you are up to—you are accusing me of revisionism." Revisionism had been, of course, a piece of political jargon since the 1920's to name the efforts of socialists to modify Marxism so as to emphasize the evolutionary rather than the revolutionary character of the latter doctrine. I shall always appreciate having had Mr. Burke in my audience that day at the symposium in Los Angeles. Perhaps he was right. Perhaps I was trying on that occasion to indicate that he had been engaging himself in literary revisionism, and that I for one, as a long-term friend of rhetoric, did not like what he was doing. But I must admit somewhat sadly that my words on that occasion, and my lecture as it was subsequently published, do not seem to have produced either an evolutionary or a revolutionary change in Mr. Burke's theory of rhetoric. They deserve a better fate than that.

WILBUR SAMUEL HOWELL

Princeton, New Jersey

Contents

Poetics, Rhetoric, and Logic

STUDIES IN THE BASIC
DISCIPLINES OF CRITICISM

Introduction

1

Literature may be defined as the general term for all verbal utterances spoken or written in all languages, lands, and times, or, in a more realistic sense, for all verbal utterances which have been recorded in written characters and have somehow managed to survive into history.[1] Speculations concerning the nature of these utterances and the principles or laws which govern or seem to govern their production and evaluation have always attended the utterances themselves and have accumulated over the centuries into an impressively large body of writings about literature. And these latter writings, so far at least as they have been part of the culture of the European community, are generally referred to as literary theory and have been institutionalized during much of their history within such subordinate disciplines as grammar, rhetoric, logic, and poetics.

The last three of these four disciplines are the subject of the present book. Grammar is here excluded, not because the study of classes of words, of inflections, of verbal functions, and of syntax is a nonliterary matter, but because rhetoric,

[1] With a similarly broad definition of literature in mind, Edwin Greenlaw calls literary history "the record of the mind of the past," and he delimits the proper field of literary historians by adding, "Nothing related to the history of civilization is beyond our province." See his *The Province of Literary History* (Baltimore, Md., 1931), p. 29. See also *ibid.*, p. 174.

logic, and poetics, in concentrating upon the study of the
linguistic structures which words may be combined to produce, constitute the essential components of literary theory,
properly so called. And rhetoric and logic are here included
precisely because poetics, if left to stand by itself for all of
literary theory, cannot undertake to explain and evaluate
many eminent literary works which by long-standing agreement lie outside the traditional realm of poetry, yet belong
by long-standing agreement to the traditional realm of one of
the two other disciplines proposed for the present examination. Thus literary theory is defined in the following pages as
the rationale behind the composition and criticism of all the
writings which make up literature in its so-called nonaesthetic
and aesthetic forms—the rationale, for example, behind Milton's *Areopagitica* as well as his *Paradise Lost*.

The exclusion of rhetoric and logic from literary theory is
one of the major current critical attitudes which the present
book is designed to combat. Thus it is designed to combat the
widely-accepted effort of René Wellek and Austin Warren to
equate literary theory exclusively with "imaginative" literature and to insist that "the center of literary art is obviously
to be found in the traditional genres of the lyric, the epic, the
drama." [2] Under the compulsion of this restriction, Wellek
and Warren confine literary theory to those works in which
"the reference is to a world of fiction, of imagination." [3]
Stressing that "the statements in a novel, in a poem, or in a
drama are not literally true," they point to the "central and
important difference between a statement, even in a historical
novel or a novel by Balzac which seems to convey 'information' about actual happenings, and the same information

[2] René Wellek and Austin Warren, *Theory of Literature* (New York,
1949), p. 15. Earlier in the same work (p. 11), these authors say, "The
term 'literature' seems best if we limit it to the art of literature, that is,
to imaginative literature."

[3] *Ibid.*, p. 15.

appearing in a book of history or sociology." [4] Sound as I consider these observations to be as fundamental insights into the nature of literary works composed according to the laws of what I am here calling poetics, I cannot accept them as definitions of the concerns of literary theory in its full legitimate extent. Nor can I endorse the decision which Wellek and Warren make against giving rhetoric and logic any substantial place in the theoretical structure of their own literary universe. [5] The theory of literature must be broad enough to include nonfiction within its whole province, and therefore the natural constituents of that theory in its full traditional extent should include rhetoric and logic as well as poetics.

A second major current critical attitude which this book is designed to combat is illustrated by the practice of allowing rhetorical and logical writings to have a place of honor in the firmament of genuine literature only if they can be shown to differ from their fellows by possessing a quality quite beyond anything to be expected of them as true representatives of their genres. They must in other words have an element of magic in them, and it must be understood that the magical element is not rhetorical or dialectical in its genesis. What

---

[4] *Ibid.*, p. 15.

[5] Neither of these terms finds a place in their Index. Their comprehensive bibliography (pp. 299–387) contains listings (pp. 331–333) of the following major writings on rhetoric: Quintilian's *Institutio Oratoria;* Thomas Gibbons's *Rhetoric;* George Campbell's *The Philosophy of Rhetoric;* I. A. Richards's *The Philosophy of Rhetoric.* As for modern studies involving the place of rhetoric and logic in literary theory, five are listed as follows on the pages indicated: Rosemond Tuve's "Imagery and Logic: Ramus and Metaphysical Poetics," p. 303; Wincenty Lutoslawski's *The Origin and Growth of Plato's Logic with an Account of Plato's Style and of the Chronology of his Writings* (London, 1897), p. 307; Morris W. Croll's "The Cadence of English Oratorical Prose," pp. 325, 367; Hardin Craig's "Shakespeare and Wilson's *Arte of Rhetorique* . . . ," p. 344; Elder Olson's "Rhetoric and the Appreciation of Pope," p. 365.

that element is can perhaps best be indicated by reverting
to the definition bestowed by Wellek and Warren upon true
literature—that genuine literary work must have "reference
to a world of fiction, of imagination." It is obvious, of course,
that rhetorical and logical writings are nonfictional, and that
they could not be judged true literature by the first part of
the definition just quoted. But they might be judged true
literature by the second part of the definition. They might
be called "imaginative prose." This would mean that they
are considered in modern critical circles to be works which,
despite their dialectical or rhetorical origins, have become
worthy of literary study, not on account of any excellence
which could possibly have come to them from their own
genres, but on account of their having an imaginative, say
an aesthetic, dimension quite above the concerns of the nonaesthetic practicality which gave them birth.

A good example of this latter critical attitude is provided
by Laurence Stapleton's treatment of Donne's sermons in her
book *The Elected Circle*. Stapleton holds in effect that sermons cannot be regarded as worthy of critical attention if
they have to be accepted merely as sermons. They become
worthy of critical attention only if they embody the qualities
of "imaginative prose." [6] Donne's sermons assume those qualities under Stapleton's critical analysis, and thus Donne gains
admission to the company reserved by her for the elect. And
what are those qualities? They are a mysterious amalgam
fashioned by Stapleton from the idea that Donne's sermons
were delivered, not to seek "merely for rhetorical effect," and
not to give his congregations at St. Paul's a persuasive vision
of the redemptive power of Christ's teachings, but to identify
Donne himself as a writer whose imaginative prose is "a mode

[6] Laurence Stapleton, *The Elected Circle* (Princeton, N.J., 1973), pp.
4–5.

of art that exalts art." [7] Stapleton expresses many convincing judgments in developing the inner structure of her argument, and her own prose is lucid and imaginative. But she suffers from the twentieth-century malady of literary critics in being unable to see that there is no logical basis for differentiating between the best of rhetorical expression and the best of nonfictional imaginative prose. Donne's sermons are rhetorical because they use the mechanisms of statement to develop their meanings. They use those mechanisms superbly well, and thus they are superb sermons, capable of being admired as imaginative prose and capable also of being respected despite their unashamed affiliations with the literature of rhetoric. They could be treated as poetical only if they had habitually developed their subtle theses by means of the mechanisms of fiction.

If he could have been able to confront the basic vocabulary of Stapleton's argument, Donne might well have been puzzled by it. His older contemporary Francis Bacon had defined poetry as feigned history, and had related it primarily to the faculty of imagination. But Bacon had also defined rhetoric in terms of that same faculty. Thus he made rhetoric into the art of using statements to achieve its goal, and of using those statements in such a way as *to apply Reason to Imagination* for the better moving of the will." [8] Surely Donne would not have been unhappy to have his sermons considered rhetoric in Bacon's sense of the term, particularly when he remembered, as he assuredly would have done, that Bacon had founded his theory of rhetoric upon Plato's *Phaedrus,*[9] and that Plato had given rhetoric a mission connected with the salvation of man's soul and with the attaining of the highest reaches of human capability. In other words, Donne him-

[7] *Ibid.,* pp. 19, 23.   [8] See below, pp. 81–83.
[9] See below, pp. 81–82.

self would have considered his sermons imaginative prose by
virtue of their being sermons in the first place, and he might
have wondered why later criticism would have to take pains to
insist that sermons had to be something more than sermons
before they could be accepted as respectable literary endeavors.

2

Each of the eight chapters in the present volume was written to examine a particular set of circumstances within which
poetics, rhetoric, and logic figure together or separately as
essential components of literary theory. Those circumstances,
and the postures of our three disciplines within them, should
now be made the subject of brief comment, in order to introduce the reader of these pages to the thematic unity of
chapters which might without preparatory explanations seem
from their titles to promise little in the way of central plan-
ning and interconnection.

Chapter 1 presents the views of Aristotle on the interrelations of rhetoric and poetics; and it seeks to question the
assumption of certain modern critics that Horace confuses
the relations of these two disciplines to each other so far as
to have been guilty of creating a rhetorical rather than a
genuinely literary theory of poetry.[10] Aristotle's essential distinction between rhetorical and poetic literature, as all critics
should know, is that poetry accomplishes its purposes by
means of the poetic mimesis or fiction, whereas oratory proceeds to its goal by using statement and proof. Now Horace,
writing also on the art of poetry, makes his observations upon
that great branch of literature conform in essence to Aristotle's poetic theory. Had he written an art of poetry according to the principles of rhetoric, he would presumably have
shown a disposition to conform to Aristotle's rhetorical and

[10] For the identity of these critics, see below, pp. 46–47, 105–110.

dialectical doctrines or to those of Horace's older contemporary Cicero. But he did not do these things. He knew, in short, as did Aristotle, how to keep poetics and rhetoric apart.

Chapter 2 discusses the interrelations of poetics, rhetoric, and logic within the structure of literary theory of the Renaissance in Great Britain. Those interrelations were defined by English critics between 1500 and 1700 in much the same way as they had been defined by Aristotle between 347 and 322 B.C. In other words, logic and rhetoric were confined as disciplines to the literature which consisted in the use of statement and proof, logic being taken as the theory of the learned, and rhetoric of the popular, discourse, whereas poetics was considered as the literature of mimesis, of fable, of fiction. There have been unfortunate tendencies in twentieth-century literary scholarship to see Renaissance poetics as essentially rhetorical, or Renaissance rhetoric as essentially stylistic, or Renaissance logic as a negligible, perhaps even a pretended, factor in the literary theory of that era.[11] The second chapter is designed to correct these tendencies, and if it succeeds, it will help future scholars to see Renaissance literary theory as Thomas Wilson, Sir Philip Sidney, Sir John Harington, Sir Francis Bacon, and Ben Jonson saw it themselves in their magnificently creative epoch.

Chapter 3 explains Fénelon's theory of the relations between rhetoric and poetics, as that theory was stated in his *Dialogues on Eloquence* and his famous *Letter to the Academy*. In their original French texts these two works were first published together at Amsterdam in 1717 and at Paris one year later. Both works in William Stevenson's English translation were very popular in Britain during the eighteenth century. Fénelon's way of differentiating between rhetoric and poetics did not securely rest upon the Aristotelian and Ciceronian bases which had so confidently supported the efforts of Renaissance

[11] For specific illustrations of these tendencies, see below, pp. 74–115.

criticism in that endeavor, but it may be said nevertheless to
have rested in part upon those bases. That is to say, at a
crucial point in his distinction between oratory and poetry,
Fénelon half remembered his Cicero, and half forgot his
Aristotle, with the result that the two literary forms under
his scrutiny were judged by him to be almost alike on Cicero's
authority, and then, on the obvious but unspecified authority
of Aristotle, were judged by him to differ as imitation and
fiction differ from the more direct modes of proof and portraiture.[12] Fénelon's sudden change of mind on this one
point of doctrine is not to be taken as a serious shortcoming
of his theory of rhetoric. On the contrary, his *Dialogues on
Eloquence* are a brilliantly successful attempt to present to
his time the lasting values in the rhetorical doctrines of Plato,
Aristotle, Cicero, and St. Augustine. But the sudden change
of mind just mentioned may be construed as a sign that, by
the early eighteenth century, boundaries securely established
by ancient critics were being obscured and imperfectly remembered, and confused notions of the interrelations of rhetoric and poetics were in the process of becoming the rule
rather than the exception in critical circles.

Chapter 4 discusses in broad outlines the changes that have
taken place in rhetorical theory between the sixteenth and
the twentieth centuries. Poetry does not figure in this chapter,
but logic does. In fact, one theme of the chapter is that logic,
which had been to the Renaissance the theory of scholarly
inquiry and of scholarly communication, began in the 1600's
and 1700's to turn away from the latter interest and to concentrate more and more upon the former, as the new science
became increasingly successful in applying inductive procedures to the understanding of nature. In this situation
rhetoric began to make itself into the theory of learned communication, while keeping alive its ancient interest in the

[12] See below, pp. 134–146.

theory of addressing the popular audience. By the middle of the nineteenth century, when John Stuart Mill proclaimed logic to have as its sole object "the guidance of one's own thoughts," whereas "the communication of those thoughts to others falls under the consideration of Rhetoric, in the large sense in which that art was conceived by the ancients," [13] the partnership between logic and literary theory seemed to have been finally dissolved, and rhetoric appeared in prospect at least to have become the sole representative of literary theory on the nonfictional side. One of the major challenges facing rhetoric in the twentieth century is that of perfecting its theory of scholarly communication even as it enriches its understanding of the process by which speakers and writers transmit ideas to the general public. In perfecting its theory of scholarly communication, rhetoric is being assisted by a series of influential books already published in our time by philosophers and logicians on the subject of semantics,[14] and thus, in a kind of way, logic is reasserting its right to be regarded once more as the partner of rhetoric in literary theory. This latter consideration is not made a major subject of discussion in the fourth chapter, but it is mentioned there, although the chapter is devoted mainly to the subject characterized in the first sentence of the present paragraph.

Chapter 5 analyzes in terms of its logical and rhetorical components the foremost political address of the eighteenth century—The Declaration of Independence. The Declaration reached its original audience in written, not in spoken,

[13] See his *A System of Logic* (London, 1843), I, 5–6.

[14] The philosophical works which modern rhetorical theorists are finding particularly helpful in improving the theory of learned communication are as follows: C. K. Ogden and I. A. Richards, *The Meaning of Meaning* (London, 1923); A. J. Ayer, *Language, Truth and Logic* (London, 1936); Charles William Morris, *Signs, Language, and Behavior* (New York, 1946); Max Black, *The Labyrinth of Language* (New York, 1968).

form, and it was designed to make all interested members of the European community understand the inherent justification of the act of the thirteen united American colonies in absolving themselves from all allegiance to the British Crown, and in proclaiming their right to be free and independent states. Under these conditions, a rhetorical address based upon the still ascendant traditional rules of classical rhetoric would have been expected, if the gifted author of the Declaration and the contemporary audience which he addressed had been largely insensitive to the changes then taking place in rhetorical and logical theory under the influence of the new philosophy of Francis Bacon and John Locke.[15] But Thomas Jefferson was not insensitive to those changes. Thus he fashioned the Declaration, not upon the old concepts of what a public address should be, but upon the concepts that were becoming influential in his time. For example, he did not write the Declaration in the form of a six-part classical oration, complete with exordium, narration, division, proof, refutation, and peroration; but he composed it instead to follow the principles of the synthetic method, which the influential rhetorical theorists of his time had borrowed from logic and were adapting to rhetoric. He himself and his generation would have found this method persuasively outlined in William Duncan's *Elements of Logick,* and there can be little doubt that Jefferson was introduced to Duncan's *Logick* by William Small, his revered teacher, during Jefferson's first college year at William and Mary.[16] However that may have been, the point to be emphasized is that the fifth chapter brings logic and rhetoric to bear upon the problem of literary evaluation and therefore shows these two disciplines to have

---

[15] For an account of those changes, see my *Eighteenth-Century British Logic and Rhetoric* (Princeton, N.J., 1971), pp. 259–263, 360–361, 441–447.

[16] See below, pp. 173–176.

been rightful components of the theory of literature. An incidental point of emphasis might well be that the fifth chapter shows rhetoric to be something more than the neat set of stylistic devices so often made the entire province of rhetoric by twentieth-century literary critics.

Thomas De Quincey's theory of rhetoric and his famous distinction between the literature of knowledge and the literature of power are the subjects of Chapter 6. Charles Sears Baldwin, author of two important pioneering works on the history of the relations of poetics and rhetoric to literary theory, thought that De Quincey's distinction between the two literatures was intended to reinforce what Aristotle had said on that subject;[17] and if Baldwin had been right, then an important aspect of Aristotle's critical doctrine would have had to be acknowledged as a living presence in the poetical theory of the Romantics and their followers. But Baldwin was not right on this occasion. De Quincey's theory of the two literatures does not coincide with that of Aristotle. Nor does De Quincey's theory of rhetoric, as he himself expounded it in an essay which he published in *Blackwood's Edinburgh Magazine* for December, 1828, owe its basic concept to Aristotle's parallel theory, despite De Quincey's avowal that it does.[18] My sixth chapter is devoted in part to showing that the two literatures are what they are in De Quincey's way of thinking, not because one of them is nonmimetic and the

[17] See below, pp. 191–192. Baldwin's two important books are *Ancient Rhetoric and Poetic* (New York, 1924) and *Medieval Rhetoric and Poetic* (New York, 1928).

[18] See "Elements of Rhetoric," *Blackwood's Edinburgh Magazine,* 24 (Dec., 1828), 885. De Quincey took his title on this occasion from a book presumably under review, Richard Whately's *Elements of Rhetoric* (Oxford, 1828). In fact De Quincey pays very little attention in his essay to Whately's work, preferring to expound his own theory of the subject treated by Whately. Had he stuck to Whately, he would have been closer to Aristotle than he manages to be on his own. See my *Eighteenth-Century British Logic and Rhetoric,* pp. 698–699, 707–712.

other mimetic, but because one of them, the literature of
knowledge, is predominantly concerned with conveying subject matter, thought, and reasoned judgments to its readers,
whereas the other, the literature of power, is predominantly
concerned with the public communication of form, emotion,
and intuitive insights. As for the other part of the sixth
chapter, it is devoted to a discussion of the grave limitations
of De Quincey's theory of rhetoric—limitations which reduce
its often alleged originality to a condition best described as
historical naiveté and dialectical confusion. Had the Romantic critics whom De Quincey addressed been really learned
in the Aristotelian rhetorical tradition, which De Quincey
was pretending at the moment to reconstruct from what has
to be regarded as his own partly mistaken and partly muddled
recollections of his study of Aristotle's *Rhetoric* at Oxford,
they would have recognized that De Quincey did not fully
know what he was talking about when he equated some of
his views of rhetoric with those of Aristotle. And they would
have seen De Quincey's rhetorical theory as in the main a
retreat from historical and textual realities into a world of
fantasy and self-deception. De Quincey's essay on rhetoric
has of course been solidly admired. Sigmund Proctor calls it
one of De Quincey's "major critical pieces and perhaps the
most original contribution of modern times to speculation on
the subject." [19] Proctor adds later of the same essay that by
means of it "De Quincey became at once a practicing
rhetorician and a philosopher of rhetoric—almost certainly
the most original one since Aristotle." [20] John Jordan recognizes that opinions about De Quincey's essay on rhetoric
range from laudatory to unfavorable, but, without attempting
himself to decide which of these two points of view might be

[19] Sigmund K. Proctor, *Thomas De Quincey's Theory of Literature*
(Ann Arbor, 1943), p. 228.
[20] *Ibid.,* p. 261.

preferable, he remarks that De Quincey's theory "is interesting as an example of a precept which controlled much of his critical thinking." And, he goes on, "certainly it is original and, with relation to his criticism at least, significant." [21] These tributes by Jordan and Proctor are not questioned by Laurence Stapleton, who admits De Quincey into her elected circle of gifted writers of imaginative prose and discusses his "Rhetoric" as a major essay.[22] To rhetorical scholars, however, that essay represents better than anything else De Quincey wrote the basic problem in rhetorical criticism, and that problem arises whenever content and form in a given work are at war with each other. As a writer, De Quincey had great verbal ease and dexterity; as a scholar he did not always have an anxious concern for accuracy of subject matter. Thus critics who particularly admire his amazing skill with words find his essay on rhetoric delightful, as Proctor, Jordan, and Stapleton obviously do. But what would happen to their feelings of delight if in that essay De Quincey's felicity with language turned out to have been brilliantly expended upon the expression of thoughts not continuously worthy of a reader's serious attention? Can it be that De Quincey's essay on rhetoric is an example of rhetorical literature gone wrong? And, if so, did it go wrong because it violated the Platonic and the Baconian concept that such literature is in the last analysis acceptable only so far as it manages to represent the truth of its subject while succeeding at the same time in its endeavor to win the soul of the reader by discourse? In his theory of rhetoric De Quincey shows no concern for questions like these, and his own rhetorical prose, when tested by questions like these, sometimes falls short of excellence. If we subject Walter Pater's essay "Style" to the

[21] John E. Jordan, *Thomas De Quincey, Literary Critic: His Method and Achievement* (Berkeley, 1952), p. 215.
[22] *The Elected Circle*, pp. 127–130.

same tests, we see it as an example of rhetorical literature adhering itself to the admirable standards which the literary theory expounded within it requires of all writers. And we regretfully see once more why De Quincey does not on all occasions belong in the front rank of rhetoricians or of truly acceptable masters of rhetorical prose.

Chapter 7 was written to explore the possibility of developing a new critical vocabulary in which to express with accuracy and discrimination the principles involved in Aristotle's theory of the two branches of literature. Those Aristotelian principles had of course been eminently viable for many centuries preceding De Quincey's time, and those principles seemed still viable to some in my generation when we first learned to use them. But we knew that their application to modern literature was attended by real difficulties, and we thought that at the heart of these difficulties lay the problem of finding modern terms that would convey to modern ears basic meanings formerly conveyed by quite different ancient terms. Inasmuch as the central concept in Aristotle's theory of poetry is mimesis, or imitation, and inasmuch as the central reality to which that concept refers is as much a part of the procedures of today's writers of fiction, drama, and narrative poetry as it had been a part of similar literary procedures in ancient times,[23] the crucial problem in bringing Aristotelian poetic theory into relation with twentieth-century criticism seemed to be that of finding a word to convey to the modern literary sensibility what the term *mimesis* had conveyed to ancient Greek and Roman critics and to the literary world of the European Renaissance. *Mimesis* is now an English word, but it no longer carries its ancient meaning. It

[23] For a survey of the meanings of mimesis in the history of literary criticism, see Gerald F. Else, "Imitation," in *Encyclopedia of Poetry and Poetics,* ed. Alex Preminger (Princeton, N.J., 1965), pp. 378–381. Else appends to this article a useful list of works dealing with the term it discusses.

now carries with it the notion that it refers to something imitated, mimicked, unoriginal, secondhand, unspontaneous, artificial. Meanings like these had led in the first place to the disappearance of the term *mimesis* from the critical vocabulary of the Romantics, and meanings like these would have to be avoided if modern criticism was to be comfortable with some kind of substitute term. Any substitute term would also have to meet certain other requirements. It would have to be already at home in literary orbits. It would have to avoid limiting poetry to an aesthetic mission alone. That is to say, it would have to allow poetry to be an instrument of communication, an instrument of instruction, and an instrument of persuasion, as well as a source of delight, inasmuch as the Aristotelian mimesis involved all of these capacities. Above all, it would have to be capable of suggesting that a poet's words refer, not directly to incidents in the world of every man's daily experience, but to fictional deputies which can ultimately endow daily experience with new significance. For what is Aristotle's concept of mimesis but a term for the process by which a poet projects some aspect of actual human living into an imagined action and then proceeds so to plot what he has imagined as to make it identify itself with the reality behind it and to reveal by the identification the deeper human significances of that reality? [24] Having in mind this latter requirement, and the other requirements just proposed, and endeavoring always to use them as a test of the acceptability of any modern synonym for mimesis, twentieth-century scholarship might do far worse than to regard *symbol* as the term which we are seeking. As authoritatively defined for modern usage in one of its major meanings, *symbol* is said to be "something that stands for or suggests something else." [25]

[24] See below, pp. 57, 98–100, 104.
[25] See *Webster's Third International Dictionary* (Springfield, Mass., 1966), s.v. symbol.

Certainly a term with this kind of meaning carries the essential freight of the Greek term, and not only is it already at home in literary orbits,[26] but it also meets the other two requirements specified above. Moreover, if we equate the term *literature of symbol* with what Aristotle called *mimetic poetry,* we are in a position to propose that *literature of statement* properly describes the writings produced according to the Aristotelian theories of rhetoric and dialectic. These latter writings contain statements which refer directly, not through an intervening deputy, to some aspect of the world of things behind them. As Aristotle unmistakably indicates in the *Poetics,* statements made to an audience by an author speaking in his own person are nonmimetic, even when they occur in poetry; and in going on to warm poets to keep such statements out of their poems, he says in effect that rhetoric and poetry can be mingled so as to interfere with each other.[27] The terms *literature of symbol* and *literature of statement* would thus seem to be perfectly acceptable modern equivalents of Aristotle's mimetic and nonmimetic literature. Equipped with them, modern literary critics would be able to see that the dividing line between the two literatures is a line between symbol and nonsymbol, and that poetics is in fact the theory of symbols of all degrees and kinds, whereas rhetoric alone, or formerly rhetoric and logic, make up the theory of statement in its entire range from oratory and history to biography and scientific exposition. Rhetoric would no longer need be a term only for style or for works not deemed worthy of literary study. At any rate, the seventh chapter was written in an attempt to impart a degree of precision to our use of rhetoric as a critical term, and the essay must stand or fall by the success it achieves or by the

[26] See Norman Friedman, "Symbol," in *Encyclopaedia of Poetry and Poetics,* pp. 833–836.
[27] *De Poetica,* 1460ᵃ 7–8. Bywater's translation.

failure it risks in setting out so ambitiously toward that goal.

The two terms proposed in Chapter 7 may be defended in part at least by observing that they seem either much less limiting or much more specific than the rival terms offered now and then since the middle of the eighteenth century to separate the poetical and the rhetorical enterprises from each other. In his *Lectures on Rhetoric and Belles Lettres,* Adam Smith declared that amusement and entertainment were the distinguishing aims of poetry, and that the other branch of literature was variously engaged in instruction, conviction, and persuasion.[28] This opinion has been frequently expressed by other critics, but it seems curiously limited, and its severest limitation is that it excludes the possibilty of instruction and persuasion from one of the two literatures, and the possibility of delight from the other, thus separating in theory what cannot be separated in a sensitive reader's experience with either kind of writing. Horace's dictum that poetry both delights and teaches is more sophisticated, and of course it reflects what Aristotle had said himself when he was looking for something more basic then the pleasure-profit dichotomy to explain how poetry really differs from history, science, and oratory.[29] Hugh Blair suggested in his *Lectures on Rhetoric and Belles Lettres* that the line to be drawn to distinguish one literature from the other was that between verse and prose.[30] This opinion has also been frequently expressed by many critics, but it seems so superficial as to warrant no discusssion whatever. It is an example of a falsehood that refutes itself. A much more creative view, indeed a view which, while avoiding the terminology of Aristotle's theory, comes nevertheless close to the inner reality of his meaning, was pro-

[28] Ed. John M. Lothian (London, 1963), pp. 58, 113–123. See also my *Eighteenth-Century British Logic and Rhetoric,* pp. 558–560.

[29] See below, pp. 71, 103–104.

[30] See my *Eighteenth-Century British Logic and Rhetoric,* pp. 667–670.

posed by George Campbell in his *The Philosophy of Rhetoric.*
Campbell indicated that the difference between the figurative or metaphorical mode and the literal mode was at the
base of the distinction between poetry and rhetoric.[31] But he
expressed this opinion more as a suggestion than as a fully
developed critical thesis, and thus he did not convincingly
work out the enlightening possibility that he so promisingly
alluded to. Precisely the same observation applies to what
Walter Pater said in his essay "Style" in distinguishing the
literature of fact from the literature of the imaginative sense
of fact.[32] When he remarked that the standard for the first
of these literatures could be said to be "truth . . . as accuracy," he laid down a principle of great weight and significance for scholarly writing, and there can be no doubt how
the principle applies and what it means. But when for the
other of these literatures he specified that the standard is
"truth . . . as expression, that finest and most intimate form
of truth, the *vraie vérité,*" his explanation did not proceed
far enough to differentiate imaginative prose from the imaginative mimesis, and thus he left the internal divisions of the
second of his two literatures quite vague and indeed unsus-
ceptible of exact determination. T. S. Eliot has done more
than most modern critics to show his awareness of the
separateness of the two literatures, and his views deserve great
respect. But he has thrown them out more as brilliant critical
asides than as major themes in criticism, and thus they leave
unspoken some of their most fertile suggestions. In his essay
" 'Rhetoric' and Poetic Drama," he perceptively recognizes
that a speech in a drama has a double function, and that the
spectator in the theatre should keep that double function in
mind. Had he added that the ability to be aware of that

[31] *Ibid.,* pp. 592–594.
[32] See his *Appreciations, with an Essay on Style* (London, 1924), pp.
8, 32. See also below, pp. 231–232, 245.

double function is at the heart of the ability to distinguish rhetoric from poetry either inside or outside the domain of dramatic dialogue, he would have been very close indeed to Aristotelian doctrine. Here is what he said:

A speech in a play should never appear to be intended to move us as it might conceivably move other characters in the play, for it is essential that we should preserve our position of spectators, and observe always from the outside though with complete understanding.[33]

In other words, the speech in a play is an example of rhetoric to the persons being addressed by it on the stage. It makes direct statements about its subject, whatever that subject may be. But to the spectator in the theatre, the same speech is an example of poetry, by virtue of its being part of the poet's mimesis. That is to say, it carries the spectator to the speaker's subject, and then it brings the spectator to see the speech, and the speaker himself, as deputies of the function of the drama in which they occur. Thus they convey meanings not only about the speaker's immediate topic but also about the implications incidental to having such a speech delivered by such a person within the context of such a situation. But an even better example of Eliot's awareness of the essential differences between the two literatures is provided by his celebrated reference to the "objective correlative." His way of defining that concept is brief, undeveloped, casual. But even so he makes the term a sure analogue of what Aristotle held the poetic method to be when he described it as mimetic. "The only way of expressing emotion in the form of art," declared Eliot in the course of his essay on *Hamlet,* "is by finding an 'objective correlative'; in other words, a set of objects, a situation, a chain of events which shall be the formula of that *particular* emotion; such that when the external facts, which must terminate in sensory experience, are

[33] T. S. Eliot, *Selected Essays, 1917–1932* (New York, 1932), p. 28.

given, the emotion is immediately evoked." [34] There would of course be no need of finding an "objective correlative" in writing a history, a lecture, a critical essay, or an oration. Only the poet qua poet is engaged in such a quest. But Eliot's term for mimesis, however close it is to the tradition that I have been discussing, does not accommodate itself to the task of promising a neat differentiation between poetical and rhetorical literature, and thus it lacks in critical mobility what it possesses in the way of deep critical insight.

Chapter 8 is devoted to an analysis of Kenneth Burke's "Lexicon Rhetoricae." This phrase is used by Burke in his *Counter-Statement* as the title of a chapter in which he codifies, amplifies, and corrects the terminology already used in two of the preceding chapters to develop his basic argument.[35] He himself characterizes the "Lexicon Rhetoricae" as an attempt "to define the principles underlying the appeal of literature." [36] By literature he means primarily what I have been calling poetic writings, that is, fiction, drama, and poetry, but he also has in mind what I have been calling rhetorical writings, as he demonstrates in little asides mentioning such nonfictional genres as the geometrical demonstrations of Euclid, the processional and recessional of the Episcopalian choir, the exordium in Greek-Roman oratory, the political writings of Edmund Burke, and the biography of a historical figure, for instance, the Little Corporal.[37] In short, the term *literature* embraces for Burke all so-called aesthetic and nonaesthetic writings. Burke's thesis in *Coun-*

[34] *Ibid.,* pp. 124–125. For other explanations of the background of Eliot's phrase, see John D. Kendall, "Objective Correlative," in *Encyclopedia of Poetry and Poetics,* pp. 581–582.

[35] See *Counter-Statement* (New York, 1931), pp. 156–232, for the "Lexicon Rhetoricae." The two preceding chapters just referred to are entitled "Psychology and Form" and "The Poetic Process."

[36] *Ibid.,* p. 156.

[37] These are among Burke's continuing references to nonfictional writing. For them, see *Counter-Statement,* pp. 157, 160, 162, 194.

ter-Statement is that the theory of literature has its central
focus in the study of the mechanisms by which literary works
produce effects upon their readers and hearers. Brilliantly
demonstrating as he repeatedly does the presence of those
mechanisms within those works, and pointing convincingly
on many occasions to the effects produced by those mechanisms upon audiences, he comes eventually to the conclusion
that literary theory and rhetorical theory are one and the
same thing. Poetics, logic, and rhetoric thus become a single
discipline to him, and the name which he bestows upon that
discipline is rhetoric.

This conclusion as Burke himself presents it in his own
words is stated for the first time in *Counter-Statement* as
that work is coming to an end; and the manner of its presentation deserves some notice. The conclusion appears to have
originated in Burke's casual and subordinate remark upon
one of the two aspects of conventional literary form. Then
it is suddenly expanded in Burke's next paragraph into the
central theme of his literary philosophy. We can of course
only speculate upon the reasons which led Burke to promote
a peripheral observation into a central theory of literature.
My speculation is that he was prompted to take that step by
virtue of his having discovered a clarifying definition in the
pages of a reference work which he consulted between the
writing of the casual remark and the formulating of his final
theory. Here is the passage in which Burke proceeds from
the opening to the final stages of the evolution of the rhetorical doctrine that has become so characteristically his own:

The reader of modern prose [he says, in commenting upon conventional form] is ever on guard against "rhetoric," yet the word,
by lexicographer's definition, refers but to "the use of language
in such a way as to produce a desired impression upon the hearer
or reader."
Rhetoric. As a final instance of the hazards of convention, we

might with profit examine the history of this word's decay. In accordance with the definition we have cited, effective literature could be nothing else but rhetoric: thus the resistance to rhetoric *qua* rhetoric must be due to a faulty diagnosis.[38]

The historian of rhetoric must interest himself in any definition which that term may chance to receive at any time or place. In particular, the historian wants to know who is responsible for a given definition, and what his credentials are as an authority upon his subject. The lexicographer's definition cited by Burke is no exception to this rule, and it turns out on investigation to have had a curious background.

One part of its background may be indicated by observing that Burke got it from the article on rhetoric in the eleventh edition of the *Encyclopaedia Britannica* (1911). That article begins thus: "RHETORIC (Gr. ῥητορικὴ τέχνη, the art of the orator), the art of using language in such a way as to produce a desired impression upon the hearer or reader."

Another part of its background may be suggested by mentioning that the eleventh edition of the *Britannica* has always been regarded in scholarly circles as having special weight and authority in humanistic and literary matters. It is not surprising that Burke would have accepted its definition of rhetoric in full good faith. In fact, there is nothing on the surface of that definition to hint that it might not be all it should have been.

Another part of its background, and a further proof of its reliability, is that it appears in an article signed with the initials of a distinguished classical scholar of the era just prior to the one in which the eleventh edition appeared. That scholar was Sir Richard Claverhouse Jebb, whose two-volume work, *The Attic Orators,* and whose single-volume translation of Aristotle's *Rhetoric,* had given him great authority on the subject of ancient rhetorical theory and practice.

[38] *Ibid.,* pp. 265–266.

Burke would surely have known of Jebb's reputation, and would have been disposed on that account to accept as reliable any definition of rhetoric apparently coming from him.

Still another part of its background, but one which for the first time raises doubts about its reliability, is that the particular definition in question is not Jebb's own. It is someone else's. Now, why should I say this? Well, I say it because that definition does not appear in Jebb's article on rhetoric in the ninth and tenth editions of the *Britannica*. It is obviously the work of the person who revised for the eleventh edition Jebb's earlier article, Jebb having died in 1905 and being no longer around to supervise the revision himself. The presence of this reviser in the process which produced the eleventh edition is proved by his having inserted an X at the end of the article on rhetoric, after having affixed to the article Jebb's initials to indicate the latter's share in the entire effort. Thus the signature, "R. C. J.; X," at the foot of the article from which he borrowed the definition of rhetoric might well have warned Burke that there could be things in the article which classical rhetoric did not authorize and which might spring from the shaky rhetorical learning that was the rule rather than the exception in scholarly and critical circles of the early twentieth century.

It is interesting to notice that Burke and De Quincey had the same kind of impulse as they were preparing themselves to introduce the term *rhetoric* to the literary theory of their respective eras. De Quincey wanted to write a review of Whately's *Elements of Rhetoric* for *Blackwood's Edinburgh Magazine,* and he decided to prepare himself by consulting the rhetorical tradition as it lingered in his mind from his having read Aristotle's *Rhetoric* when he was at Oxford some twenty-four years before. As I mentioned earlier, he would have done better had he depended upon Whately for his impressions of Aristotle, because Whately was a far more authoritative Aristotelian than De Quincey's imperfect and confused recollections of the *Rhetoric* entitled him to be.[39] But at any rate De Quincey sought to derive his rhetorical theories from the very fountainhead of the rhetorical tradition, and thus he can be credited with having a sense of the past and a desire to make it an influence upon the present. Burke must be given the same credits. When he needed to check his impressions of the meaning of the word *rhetoric* against the definition of a lexicographer, he consulted the *Britannica* in the best edition which it had had up to that moment, and he thought its article on rhetoric had full classical authority. But, alas, that authority turned out to be as undependable as De Quincey's recollections of Aristotle were.

The definition of rhetoric which Burke got from X shows little awareness of the tradition from which it would have emerged had it been the work of a careful and learned lexicographer. To be sure, the definition does call attention to the abiding interest of rhetoric in producing effects upon listeners or readers, and so far, at least, it is completely in line with the most perceptive moments of the history of rhetorical theory. But does not poetry also produce effects upon its audience, and are not its capacities to do so, and the mechanisms by which it works, the chief considerations in its theory? How, then, would poetics and rhetoric differ, if the definition of X is allowed to prevail? It is precisely in its inability to suggest differences between the oration and the poem, after similarities have been properly and duly noted, that X's definition shows itself impotent as an instrument of criticism and completely blind to the realities that a critic must face in seeing the crucial difference between nonfiction and fiction.

Burke was writing *Counter-Statement* at a time when lit-

[39] See above, n. 18.

erary theory was under pressure from two directions. Critics with leanings toward Communism were insisting that literature was a political arm of the state and an instrument for disseminating propaganda by the party in power. Critics with opposite leanings were claiming literature as an end in itself, expressive but never crassly communicative, dedicated only to artistic interests, and forever hostile to materialism and political advantage. Burke wanted to lend the authority of his own gifted analytical insights to the proposition that literature, quite apart from its connection or lack of connection with the class struggle, aimed above all else to produce effects upon mankind. Had he at that moment been lucky enough to stumble upon a definition of rhetoric more sensitive to literary realities than that proposed by X, he might have seen that the problem was not only to accept the production of effects as the aim of all literature but also to account for the ways in which effects as the orator and historian produce them differ in respect to the mechanisms involved from the effects which the dramatist and novelist and poet produce. The recognition of a foundation of that sort for his literary theory would have led Burke to adopt "Lexicon Poeticae et Rhetoricae," not "Lexicon Rhetoricae" alone, as the title of his dictionary of the basic terms of literary theory. Moreover, a foundation of that sort would have spared modern criticism some of its current foolishness about rhetoric, and would have joined the best of ancient literary theory to a helpful new strain in the literary theory of our own era. But in the end X won the battle. Rhetoric became a critical term which meant little or nothing precisely because it was suddenly made to mean too much.

The views of X, thanks to the considerable influence of Kenneth Burke, have had wide currency in modern criticism. One finds them dominating the critical theories of

Wayne Booth, W. Ross Winterowd, Charles Osborne Mc-
Donald, and many others.[40] Perhaps I can best express my
own dissatisfaction with this state of affairs if I point back
to these introductory comments on Burke's "Lexicon Rhetoricae" and forward to the eighth chapter in this volume,
while adding here the following verses for whatever contribution they too can make to an understanding of the plight
of rhetoric in these present times:

> X marks the spot where rhetoric was altered.
> Burke gelded rhetoric at a spot marked X.
> Since then the pace of rhetoric has faltered,
> As yours would too, if you had lost your sex.

3

Walter Pater began his essay "Style" with a sentence which
I should now like to use in closing this Introduction. "Since
all progress of mind," said Pater, "consists for the most part
in differentiation, in the resolution of an obscure and complex object into its component aspects, it is surely the stupid-
est of losses to confuse things which right reason has put
asunder, to lose the sense of achieved distinctions, the distinction between poetry and prose, for instance, or, to speak
more exactly, between the laws and characteristic excellences of verse and prose composition." [41] Writing these words
in the late 1880's, Pater intended them to introduce his own
major contribution to literary theory, and that contribution,
surely one of the finest of its kind in the last hundred years,

[40] See Wayne Booth, *The Rhetoric of Fiction* (1961), Charles Osborne
McDonald, *The Rhetoric of Tragedy* (1966), and W. Ross Winterowd,
Rhetoric: A Synthesis (1968). For articles showing Burke's influence
upon criticism in general, see William H. Rueckert, ed., *Critical Responses to Kenneth Burke, 1924–1966* (1969). Marie Hochmuth Nichols's
"Kenneth Burke and the 'New Rhetoric,'" in the volume just cited,
pp. 270–286, will be found especially helpful as a survey of Burke's
complete rhetorical philosophy.

[41] *Appreciations, with an Essay on Style*, p. 5.

consisted in defining truth as the cardinal principle of all literature, and in showing how that principle has to enter into every sort of verbal utterance.[42] Indeed, the sense that criticism had lost its way by ceasing to emphasize that principle and by failing to take explicit notice of its differing applications to what he called the literature of fact and the literature of the imaginative sense of fact had led Pater in the first place to compose "Style." And there can be little doubt of his success in making that principle convincing and in providing modern critics with many of the necessary tools for applying it to any literary genre.

What strikes me particularly about Pater's words is that they express something as pertinent to the eight chapters in the present volume as to Pater's own "Style." I too feel that modern criticism has lost an achieved distinction, and I too regard the loss as stupid. Moreover, I consider, as Pater did, that the loss is associated with the distinction between the two great branches of literature. As the reader of this Introduction and of the ensuing pages will ultimately see, the loss which I deplore above all others is that connected with the disappearance from modern literary theory of a genuine and deep learning in the ancient discipline of rhetoric and in the interrelations of that discipline with logic and with poetics. If this book calls attention to that loss and perhaps leads to some constructive efforts to make up for it, I shall be happy. I shall of course also be happy if that loss is removed without any help from me and my writings but rather from the personal discovery by present and future scholars that the great classics of the European rhetorical tradition are worth their careful study and are deserving of a more exactly defined place in literary theory than we have been willing to give them of late.

[42] See above, p. 34. Also below, pp. 231, 245.

CHAPTER 1

Aristotle and Horace
on Rhetoric and Poetics

1

According to Bernard Weinberg, the Aristotelian distinction between rhetorical and poetic literature grows out of the difference between the persuasive as distinguished from the aesthetic effect, the actual as distinguished from the hypothetical audience, and internal characteristics dictated by the demands of a specific occasion as distinguished from internal characteristics dictated by the author's resolve to achieve artistic perfection.[1] This way of accounting for the dissimilarities between rhetoric and poetics depends in the last analysis upon Weinberg's own interpretation of what Aristotle said upon those matters in his *Rhetoric* and *Poetics*; but, as Weinberg indicates, it also depends upon the writings of the Chicago school of Aristotelians, among whom he names Ronald S. Crane, Richard P. McKeon, and Elder Olson.[2] From these original and secondary sources, Weinberg draws the conclusion that Aristotle's *Poetics* "concentrates its attention upon those qualities of the work of art itself which make it beautiful and productive of its proper

[1] For Weinberg's own statement of this distinction, see his *A History of Literary Criticism in the Italian Renaissance* (Chicago, 1961), I, 350–352. Cited throughout this book as Weinberg.
[2] *Ibid.*, p. 352 n.

effect"; that "Aristotle is at no time neglectful either of the audience in whom this proper effect is produced or of the natural reality which is represented in the artificial work of art"; that his aim, however, "is neither to analyze audiences nor to study nature," but "to discover how a poem, produced by imitation and representing some aspect of a natural object—its form—in the artificial medium of poetry, may so achieve perfection of that form in the medium that the desired aesthetic effect results." [3] In developing these ideas, Weinberg continues thus:

Statements about the "effect" of which I have spoken may be made either in terms of the kind of reaction within an audience or of the structural particularities within the work which produce that reaction. In either case, the audience is considered in a general way; it is a general and universal one, and never particularized through race, time, place, class, or personal idiosyncracies. It is composed of men sharing the common feelings and experiences of all mankind, having the common conviction that actions spring from character and that events spring from causes, susceptible of enjoying the pleasures afforded by the imitative arts, and capable through their sensitivity and their habits of reading of distinguishing good works from bad. Otherwise, it has no distinctive qualities as an audience. Hence the position of the *Poetics* is not a rhetorical one, because nowhere is the poem made to be what it is in order to have a particular effect of persuasion upon a particular audience; moreover, nowhere does the "character" of the poet enter as a structural element in the poem.

The emphasis in this passage upon the absence of a rhetorical dimension in Aristotle's *Poetics,* even though that work discusses the effect of poetry, the audience which poetry reaches, and the structural particularities which bring that effect and that audience into conjunction, exactly accords with what Weinberg says about the presence of a rhetorical dimension in Horace's *Ars Poetica.* Of the latter work Wein-

[3] *Ibid.,* pp. 350–351, for these quotations and that which immediately follows.

berg observes that it "regards poems in the context of the society for which they are written. It considers above all the dramatic forms, in relation both to nature and to their capacity to please and to instruct an audience of a given kind that would see them in a given age under given circumstances. What goes into the making of any poem will be determined in large part by the expectations, the requirements, the taste of this particular audience." [4] And, after commenting upon the Horatian precepts which are derived from these requirements, Weinberg says:

The fact that, in Horace's theory, the internal characteristics of the poem are determined largely, if not exclusively, by the external demands of the audience brings his theory very close to specifically rhetorical approaches. In theories of this kind, the determining factor in the production of the work is not an internal principle of structural perfection, but rather an acceptance of the assumption that all those elements are included in the work that will be susceptible of producing the desired effect upon the audience envisaged, arranged in an order calculated to achieve the maximum degree of that effect. However, in proper and complete rhetorical approaches, one essential element—absent from Horace—enters at all times into consideration: the character of the orator (or poet) as it really is (Quintilian) or as it is made to appear to be (Aristotle's *Rhetoric*). If Horace's thesis is a rhetorical one, it is incomplete rhetoric because it omits this essential aspect.[5]

Weinberg's interpretation of Horace's *Ars Poetica* and Aristotle's *Poetics* plainly indicates that any given work of literature, regardless of the convention which would classify it in advance as a poem, or a play, or a novel, or an oration, or a philosophical dialogue, or a history, or a treatise on science or art, is to be regarded as a member of the family of rhetorical or of the family of poetical compositions, not by deciding where it would belong by tradition, but by deciding whether

[4] *Ibid.*, p. 71.   [5] *Ibid.*, pp. 71–72.

it conforms to the rhetorical thesis of Horace or to the poetical thesis of Aristotle. Under this interpretation, that is to say, orations would sometimes be classed as specimens of rhetoric and sometimes as specimens of poetry, the difference being that in the one case they would have been designed to have structural particularities to make them capable of persuading a given audience at a given time, and in the other case, to have structural particularities to make them capable of giving aesthetic delight to mankind. The same rule would apply to tragedy. Tragedy, too, would sometimes be classed as a specimen of rhetoric and sometimes as a specimen of poetry, and the same considerations which determine whether an oration belongs to one family or the other would determine to which family the tragedy would belong. And so on throughout the entire range of literary productions. To be sure, an aesthetic oration would probably occur much less often than an oration of the persuasive type, even as the rhetorical tragedy would be more prevalent than the tragedy designed austerely to achieve structural perfection. But Weinberg's system allows for the existence of these and all similar deviant and normal literary forms, and it provides critical standards by which they may all be judged. Thus at first glance it seems comprehensive and promising.

Nevertheless, there is at least one difficulty involved in Weinberg's system, and I should like to devote this essay to an analysis of it. It is an important difficulty. I shall indicate its nature in a preliminary way by observing that Weinberg's system is not authorized by Aristotle's *Poetics* and *Rhetoric,* nor for that matter by Horace's *Ars Poetica,* despite Weinberg's claims to the contrary. Aristotle and Horace, as I hope to show, saw the poetic principle as something which, on the one hand, would never be present as the controlling influence in an oration, even if the orator sought only for perfection of internal form as he composed it, whereas, on the other hand, the poetic principle would always be present in any kind of poem, even if the poet sought to write it only in terms of the expectations, requirements, and tastes of his own era. At the same time, Aristotle, with the silent concurrence of Horace, saw the rhetorical principle as the very essence of the oration and certain other kinds of discourse, but as incapable of application to the poem, except as its presence in a drama or a narrative would be recognized to be a special case in which rhetoric was marching, not to its own independent commands, but to those of the poet. Let us now turn to a discussion of these matters.

2

The basic distinction drawn by Aristotle between the poem and the oration, or in broadest terms between poetical and rhetorical literature, is that poetry is mimetic, and rhetoric, nonmimetic. Aristotle dwells upon this distinction at considerable length in the *Poetics,* and it must be understood with equal emphasis that he silently adheres to it everywhere in the *Rhetoric.*[6] It may be difficult to explain in modern terms what this distinction should mean to us, and it may be presumptuous to claim that we know for sure what it meant to Aristotle. But there can be no doubt in anyone's mind that Aristotle regarded it as the most important and the most fundamental of all the differences between the drama and the oration. Thus it becomes a matter of crucial interest. What I should like to do now is to develop the idea

[6] These two works in excellent English translations are published together in a single volume in *The Works of Aristotle,* ed. W. D. Ross, Vol. XI (Oxford, 1924). The same two translations are reprinted in a single volume as follows: Aristotle, *Rhetoric* (trans. W. Rhys Roberts), *Poetics* (trans. Ingram Bywater), Modern Library (New York, 1954). My present references are to the two works as they appear in the latter volume. For Aristotle's discussion of mimesis ("imitation"), see pp. 223–230, *et passim.*

that this single fundamental distinction between mimetic and nonmimetic literature meant to Aristotle a whole range of cooperating distinctions, and that, by examining those co-operating distinctions, we can equip ourselves to understand what the underlying distinction may have meant to him. It is obvious to any reader of the *Poetics* and *Rhetoric* that the respective contents of these two treatises differ in regard to the types of discourse involved in each, the doctrinal constituents of the theory set forth in each, the quantitative parts of the literary structures described in each, the effects assigned by each to a discourse when it reaches its audience, and the philosophical definitions that have to be formulated in giving each kind of discourse its distinctive character. Let us now examine Aristotle's thinking upon these lines of difference between the drama and the oration, and let us keep in mind as we examine them that they amount to a systematic elaboration of his concept of the nature of mimesis and its opposite, as those concepts reveal themselves in discourses of various sorts.

Aristotle's *Poetics* identifies with great clarity the types of discourse under examination in it, and the same statement can emphatically be made of Aristotle's *Rhetoric.* The types of poetical discourse enumerated in the *Poetics* consist of a series in which tragedy is the highest species, and epic poetry is next in order of importance, with comedy and lyric poetry mentioned but not specifically analyzed.[7] This series omits nothing of note when it is taken as an inventory of the kinds of writing ordinarily accepted as the dominant members of the family of poetical literature. It would have to be under-stood in this connection, of course, that epic poetry in Aris-totle's sense includes what we would call prose fiction, and that satire, pastoral poetry, narrative poetry, and a dozen

[7] *Poetics,* pp. 223–224, 229, 230–256, 257–266.

other literary species are modern names for branches of the main poetical types in Aristotle's catalogue. As for the types of rhetorical discourse enumerated in Aristotle's *Rhetoric,* they consist of a series in which deliberative oratory, forensic oratory, and epideictic oratory are central specimens.[8] But, since Aristotle considers rhetoric to be the counterpart of dialectic,[9] and since dialectical discourse, which includes the whole field of philosophical and learned writing, differs from rhetorical discourse only so far as the requirements for addressing the learned audience differ from those for addressing the populace,[10] we can readily see that the types of non-mimetic discourse as Aristotle enumerates them by implication, comprise all forms of expository, scientific, philosophical, and argumentative prose. Historical works would also have to be included in this large family, as Aristotle plainly indicates in the *Poetics* in his celebrated distinction between history and poetry.[11]

Thus it is to be carefully remarked that, so far as types of discourse are concerned, Aristotle's *Poetics* is a treatise on writings ordinarily allocated to departments of literature in the modern university, whereas his *Rhetoric* and his *Topics* must be called treatises on the writings studied in the modern university in departments of public address, history, philosophy, and the social and natural sciences. And the central distinction between works studied in the department of literature and those studied in other departments would by Aristotle's standard involve the presence in the former, and the absence in the latter, of the influence of the principle of mimesis.

[8] *Rhetoric,* p. 32, *et passim.*   [9] *Ibid.,* p. 19.

[10] Aristotle's *Topics* deals with the subject of dialectical discourse, that is, with philosophical argument and its learned cognates. The *Rhetoric* on two notable occasions specifies that its concern is with discourse addressed to untrained thinkers. See *Rhetoric,* p. 27.

[11] *Poetics,* pp. 234–235.

As for the doctrinal constituents of the theories set forth in Aristotle's *Poetics* and *Rhetoric,* they can be unmistakably identified without departing from the exact terms used by Aristotle to designate the main heads of each treatise. The *Poetics* successively discusses plot, character, thought, diction, melody, and spectacle.[12] These six terms denote the six aspects of tragedy, and the first four of them are applicable as well to narrative poetry and the epic, in which stories are not presented in a theatrical setting and hence do not involve the requirements of spoken melody and a mise-en-scène. The doctrinal constituents of the theory of rhetorical discourse, on the other hand, are invention, arrangement, delivery, and style, as Aristotle himself specifies in the *Rhetoric;* [13] and as a supplement to this observation, we should note that the theory of dialectical discourse, which like rhetoric is non-mimetic, and which differs from rhetoric only by virtue of its concern for the learned as opposed to the popular audience, has as its two doctrinal constituents in Aristotle's *Topics* the procedures of invention and arrangement.[14] The difference between the doctrinal constituents of the art of rhetoric and of dialectic would appear to indicate that in Aristotle's view rhetoric needs to pay attention to style and delivery because of the orator's concern for the popular audience, whereas the dialectician, with the learned audience as his focus, need not bother with attractive phrasing and dramatic utterance. But both rhetoric and dialectic, says Aristotle, must deal as arts with invention and arrangement, whereas poetics must deal, not with these processes, nor with delivery and style, but with plot, character, thought, and the like.

[12] *Ibid.,* p. 231, *et passim.*   [13] *Rhetoric,* pp. 164–218.
[14] The first seven books of this treatise are devoted to the procedures by which philosophical arguments are brought into being. The last book is devoted to the methods of arranging arguments.

Here we may note once again that the differences between the doctrinal constituents of rhetorical and dialectical theory, on the one hand, and of poetics, on the other, invite us to construe them as a part of Aristotle's larger conception of the difference between nonmimetic and mimetic discourse. If plot is the soul of tragedy, then mimesis must have something to do with plot; and if invention is the first constituent of oratory and of philosophical argument, then the processes by which a discourse is kept from being mimetic must necessarily play an important part in rhetorical and dialectical invention.

Aristotle's *Poetics* and *Rhetoric* also spell out the differences between the quantitative divisions of a tragedy and of an oration. From the point of view of quantity, says Aristotle, "a tragedy has the following parts: Prologue, Episode, Exode, and a choral portion, distinguished into Parode and Stasimon." [15] In more expansive terms, this means that the tragic action is made up of a preliminary episode, a choral passage, another episode, a regular choral ode, yet another episode, still another choral ode, and so on, with a final episode or exode following the last song of the chorus. The various episodes, says Aristotle, are arranged so as to constitute a complication, a climax, and a denouement—a gathering tension, a crucial recognition, and a change of fortune. [16] And the quantitative parts of an oration? Well, as every student of Aristotle's *Rhetoric* knows, the oration has two absolutely necessary parts, called by Aristotle the statement and proof; and it also has certain optional parts, to be added as convenience dictates, these being the introduction and the epilogue. [17] Out of these four parts, and various others which Aristotle discusses only to reject, the Latin rhetoricians devised the six-part oratorical structure which every schoolboy

[15] *Poetics*, p. 237.   [16] *Ibid.*, pp. 236–237, 246.
[17] *Rhetoric*, pp. 199–200.

used to be taught, and which hardly needs to be described at this time.[18]

Suffice it to say that the parts of a tragedy and the parts of an oration offer some contrast when they confront each other as I have just tried to make them do; and that this contrast, like the others mentioned in my previous discussion of types of discourse and of the doctrinal constituents of poetical and rhetorical theory, is one more elaboration of the basic concepts of mimesis and its opposite, as those concepts apply to literary effort. With the quantitative parts of a tragedy in mind, mimesis, we might say, means episode and the attendant choral commentary; and the process opposed to mimesis, we might add, means statement and proof, when it relates to oratory. We might say these things, that is, if we keep carefully before us that they are not intended to exhaust the meaning of mimesis or its opposite. They are intended, rather, to elaborate that meaning in one more of its many perspectives.

One of the most memorable differences between Aristotle's *Poetics* and his *Rhetoric* is that each work is quite specific about the effect which its kind of discourse is designed to have upon an audience, and that the effect of the drama is described in terms which do not designate the effect of the oration. The effect intended for tragedy, says Aristotle, is catharsis.[19] He says this only once, and he does not explain what catharsis means, except to remark that the episodes in a tragedy are designed to awaken pity and fear in the spectators and thus to produce a catharsis of such emotions. Much ink has been used to explain what Aristotle means by catharsis, but for our present purposes we need not go into the

[18] For standard discussions of the six-part classical oration, see Cicero, *De Inventione,* 1. 14–56; also the anonymous *Rhetorica ad Herennium,* 1. 3–17, 2. 1–31; 3. 9–10; also Quintilian, *Institutio Oratoria,* 4–6.

[19] *Poetics,* p. 230.

matter further, except to add Aristotle's own later comment that pity is felt when we see a man suffering an undeserved misfortune, and fear, when we identify that man with ourselves.[20] It is not difficult to extend Aristotle's analysis beyond the boundaries of tragedy, and to say that comedy might be expected to produce the effect of laughter, and might seek this effect by painting a picture of the ridiculous or the deformed in such a way as not to cause pain or harm to others. As a matter of fact, Aristotle makes this very point about comedy in one of the few comments which the *Poetics* as it has come down to us devotes to that subject.[21] As against the tragic and the comic effects, the oration, says Aristotle, produces the effect of persuasion, and this term, of course, is not left unexplained. So far as the *Rhetoric* is concerned, Aristotle makes clear that persuasion is a complex human reaction triggered by a rational belief in the truth of the orator's thesis, by an emotional acceptance of the thesis as in some way pleasurable, and by an ethical acceptance of the orator's character as that of a man of good sense, good morals, and good will.[22]

This comparative analysis of the effect of tragedy and of the oration has proceeded far enough, I trust, to bring into sharp focus the Aristotelian theory that tragedy is designed to effect a catharsis of pity and fear, comedy is designed to awaken laughter, and the oration is designed to lead the audience to agree with the speaker's proposal. And with these considerations before us, we must admit, I believe, that the process by which literature becomes mimetic is related to the process by which it awakens pity or fear or laughter, while the process by which it remains nonmimetic is related to its power to achieve rational credibility, emotional acceptance, and moral authority.

Aristotle's definition of tragedy and his definition of rhet-

[20] *Ibid.,* p. 238.   [21] *Ibid.,* p. 229.
[22] *Rhetoric,* pp. 24–26, 90–92, *et passim.*

oric may now be cited to show how the differences between the poem and the oration are bound up with the concept of mimesis and with all the other concepts that we have been discussing here. Tragedy, says Aristotle, "is the imitation of an action that is serious and also, as having magnitude, complete in itself; in language with pleasurable accessories, each kind brought in separately in the parts of the work; in a dramatic, not in a narrative form; with incidents arousing pity and fear, wherewith to accomplish its catharsis of such emotions." [23] Is not this definition not only an assertion of the mimetic character of tragic drama, but also an enumeration of the ingredients that mimesis must have in this particular form of literature? And is there anything in Aristotle's definition of rhetoric that suggests mimesis? "Rhetoric may be defined," says Aristotle, "as the faculty of observing in any given case the available means of persuasion." [24] It would appear from this definition that the orator observes a given case, and seeks in it the available means by which he can secure agreement between himself and his audience upon the most acceptable meaning allowable to that case under the circumstances. The word mimesis does not appear in this definition of rhetoric, nor is there any possibility that it can appear as an independent entity in the orator's procedures. He must state the facts and prove them acceptable to the reason, the emotions, and the moral sense of his hearers. I repeat, he must state the facts and prove them acceptable. His characteristic verbal devices are thus factual statements and their endless shadings as they take on the colorings of emotion and moral sentiments. And those devices by themselves never produce mimesis.

The difference between poetical and rhetorical literature would therefore appear in Aristotle's eyes to be a difference

[23] *Poetics*, p. 230.   [24] *Rhetoric*, p. 24.

between two separate approaches to the realities of human life. Faced with the problem of doing something about a crisis in their society, the poet and the orator respond in different ways. The poet deals with the problem by telling a story or by presenting a dramatic action. Mimesis may be visualized here as the process by which actual life takes the form of story or play, and as the further process by which the story or play, when presented to readers or spectators, changes back into the form of actual life. The steps taken by the poet to superimpose the universals of actual life upon the particular story which he tells, and the steps taken by the audience to extract from the particular story the universals which have been superimposed upon it, are parts of the most intricate system of communication known to mankind, and this system will always have mysteries connected with it, and probably can never be formalized and taught. But it is the system which Aristotle has endeavored to suggest in the *Poetics,* and without his endeavor the poetic communication would be more mysterious than it is now. But how, you will ask, does the orator proceed in the face of the crisis just postulated? The answer is that the orator deals with the problem by making a speech, or by writing an editorial, or by approaching the problem through the more devious ways of biography or history or science. In short, he makes statements about the problem, and his audience sees the problem directly in those statements. How the speaker connects the problem to his statements, and how the audience, hearing the statements, understands the problem, are parts of another system of communication, and this system, while it too has mysteries connected with it, is better understood than the poetic or mimetic system. In fact, modern semantics, with its conception of a world of facts, and of a world of words, and of a world of human consciousness where the facts and the words are fitted together in meaningful relation to each other and to human needs, has made this nonmimetic system of communication the subject of special study, and has clarified many of its darker puzzles. But Aristotle's *Rhetoric* is a special study of this nonmimetic system, too, and in its day it too has clarified many puzzles. It remains one of the classical analyses of the structure and function of nonmimetic literature.

In the light of the entire context of Aristotle's poetical and rhetorical theories as I have attempted to outline them here, what happens to Weinberg's thesis concerning the Aristotelian approach to poetics and rhetoric? Does Aristotle advocate, as Weinberg says, that "the determining factor" in the production of a rhetorical work "is not an internal principle of structural perfection, but rather an acceptance of the assumption that all those elements are included in the work that will be susceptible of producing the desired effect upon the audience envisaged, arranged in an order calculated to achieve the maximum degree of that effect"? [25] Wouldn't it be a more authentic brand of Aristotelianism to insist that the determining factor in the production of a rhetorical work involves the author's acceptance of nonmimetic popular discourse as his own characteristic response to the challenges that turn men into writers and speakers in the first place, and that, once this acceptance has been achieved, he may seek to make his work conform to the principles of internal structural perfection or to make it register the expectations of his actual audience, without changing its essential rhetorical nature in the slightest degree? At the other side of the literary world, wouldn't it be more in conformity with Aristotle to declare that the determining factor in the production of a poetical work involves the author's acceptance of mimetic discourse as his own characteristic response to the compulsions and capacities which ini-

[25] Weinberg, pp. 71–72. Also quoted above, p. 47.

tially make men poets, and that this form of acceptance is broad enough to permit some poets to seek structural perfection in their work, and others to seek to accommodate their work to their own time, without necessarily ennobling their poetical role in the first case or compromising it in the second? Aristotle's *Poetics* and *Rhetoric* would, I believe, support only an affirmative answer to the question just stated and to that which preceded it.

Perhaps a scattering of examples will further clarify what I would regard as the Aristotelian doctrine upon these matters. In writing the essay called "Style," Walter Pater proceeded by statement and proof, while at the same time he strove for perfection in the structure of that essay and for the involvement of his readers in the kind of aesthetic appreciation which that work was at pains to define. Herbert Spencer also proceeded by statement and proof in his essay called "The Philosophy of Style," while at the same time he sought structural arrangements that would induce his mid-nineteenth-century audience to agree with his ideas of good writing. But the point is that, despite the obvious dissimilarities of these two works in respect to their form and their function, both are in fact rhetorical in the Aristotelian sense, inasmuch as both are nonmimetic in their method of presenting their basic themes. On the other hand, Walter Pater's *Marius the Epicurean* and Bernard Shaw's *Back to Methuselah* were written as fables, with episodes, complications, and turning points as their structural essentials. Thus they both are poetical in the Aristotelian sense, inasmuch as they both involve the mimetic method of thematic presentation. At the same time, of course, they differ in the very ways which Weinberg held to be crucial in determining their right to be poetical or rhetorical. That is to say, Pater's *Marius* fuses its theme and structure in such fashion that the truth of the one and the propriety of the other unite to create in

the reader the aesthetic pleasure that is at the same time intellectual acceptance, whereas Shaw's *Back to Methuselah* insists upon making its ideas persuasive through appeals to the
expectations, requirements, and tastes of post-Darwinian man.

As I turn now to discuss Horace's *Ars Poetica* in relation
to Aristotle's theories of rhetoric and poetics, I should like
to pause for a moment to say a few words about two special
cases in which Aristotle's theories would need to be simultaneously applied, if an adequate literary judgment is to be
made.

The first case involves any actual oration which contains
a fable inserted in connection with the orator's nonmimetic
procedure of statement and proof. In the course of Aristotle's
analysis of the use of induction and example as argumentative
devices, he says that a speaker may establish a conclusion by
citing either an actual or an invented instance in support of
it. The invented instance, he goes on, may be an illustrative
parallel, as when the speaker argues that the selection of
public officials by lot is as hazardous as the use of a lottery to
determine which man in a ship's crew should be captain; or
the invented instance may be a fable, as when the speaker
tells a story from Aesop to establish his thesis.[26] The fable
within an oration is of course a mimetic discourse within
the context of nonmimetic verbal procedures, and it has to be
considered, not as the independent mimesis which it was
designed to be, but as a mimesis controlled by nonmimetic
influences. The important problem about a given fable when
it is judged in its own terms is that of ascertaining how accurately it reflects human truth, and how significant that
truth is. But the fable used in the context of an oration is to
be judged in connection with its capacity to prove the orator's case—to offer logical, emotional, and ethical support to
what he is recommending. The orator would normally select

[26] *Rhetoric,* pp. 133–134.

the poetically better fable in developing his argument, and thus he would need to know what makes one fable better than another in poetic terms. But his overriding consideration is to create an effective nonmimetic discourse, and on occasion the poetically inferior fable might serve that purpose best.

The second case in which the poetical and rhetorical standards of Aristotle would be simultaneously applicable involves an address spoken to an audience within the surrounding context of a literary mimesis, as when Brutus and Antony address the Roman mob in Shakespeare's *Julius Caesar,* or as when the fallen angels address each other in the second book of Milton's *Paradise Lost.* So far as speeches of this sort are considered only to be addresses by an orator to the audience before him on the stage or in the narrative setting, they are nonmimetic—that is, they use statement and proof for persuasive effect as an orator in a historical situation would do. On this level they have only a rhetorical dimension, and they are to be judged only by the standards which apply to any nonmimetic discourse. Indeed, on two significant occasions, Aristotle's *Poetics* recommends to the playwright that he go to the *Rhetoric* for advice about the nature and composition of speeches such as these.[27] But these speeches, in addition to being addresses by a speaker to an audience in furtherance of his personal ambitions, are also to be accepted as part of the mimesis which the poet is simultaneously addressing to his readers or hearers in furtherance of the larger and more universal purposes of the poetic art. On this level the problem becomes that of deciding what contribution the nonmimetic discourse makes to the mimetic discourse which surrounds it. Thus a critic might seek to determine how far Antony's speech and the mob's response to him and to Brutus advance Shakespeare's design in picturing the tragic possibilities which arise when a proud republican idealist chooses

[27] *Poetics,* pp. 232, 248.

rather to tolerate with disdain than to suppress with finality any display of Machiavellian cunning by a friend of tyranny. The evaluation of this design falls outside of the capacities of rhetorical analysis, but rhetorical analysis would on this occasion be helpful, nevertheless, in shedding light not only on the quality of Antony's speech as an oration, and on Shakespeare's gifts in the field of nonmimetic discourse, but also on the distinguishing differences between rhetoric and poetry.[28]

3

In speaking of Horace's *Ars Poetica*, Weinberg indicates, as we have seen, that that work represents the rhetorical as distinguished from the poetical approach to literature. I take this statement to mean at least two things—first, that Horace's treatise bears a strong resemblance to the doctrines and the point of view of Aristotle's *Rhetoric*, and secondly, that it offers a contrast to the doctrines and the point of view which Aristotle made memorable in his *Poetics*. These two lines of argument I should now like briefly to explore.

Horace's *Ars Poetica* and Aristotle's *Rhetoric* do not resemble each other in at least one important respect, as Weinberg acknowledges when he points out that Horace's treatise fails to take notice of an author's character as a contributing factor in the influence which his work exerts upon an audience.[29] This factor is often called the ethical means of persuasion to distinguish it from the means supplied by appeals to logic and those supplied by appeals to emotions. Aristotle's *Rhetoric*, which treats each of these three means of persuasion at some length, as I indicated above,[30] lays special stress upon

[28] For a valuable study of the problem of judging the speeches that occur on occasion in tragedy, see Roland Mushat Frye, "Rhetoric and Poetry in *Julius Caesar*," *The Quarterly Journal of Speech*, XXXVII (1951), 41–48.

[29] See above, p. 47.   [30] See above, pp. 55–56, 60.

the ethical means. "It is not true, as some writers assume in their treatises on rhetoric," it declares, "that the personal goodness revealed by the speaker contributes nothing to his power of persuasion; on the contrary, his character may almost be called the most effective means of persuasion he possesses." [31] In the light of a statement as strong as this, Weinberg is quite right in asserting that Horace's *Ars Poetica,* so far as it fails to consider ethical persuasion, is an incomplete rhetoric to the extent in which Aristotle's treatise on the latter subject is accepted as having indicated what a complete rhetoric should be.

But this line of reasoning forces us to go much farther than Weinberg did. For if Horace's *Ars Poetica* is an incomplete rhetoric on this one important score, what can we say of it when we acknowledge, as we must, that it says absolutely nothing about the two other persuasive means so fully analyzed in Aristotle's *Rhetoric?* The logical means of persuasion, as Aristotle explains them, involve distinctions between artistic and nonartistic proofs, between deduction and induction, and between general topics and special topics as sources of rhetorical arguments.[32] The emotional means of persuasion in his view are found not only by studying such dominant human emotions as anger, calmness, friendship, enmity, fear, pity, and the like, but also by remembering as a general precept that "When people are feeling friendly and placable, they think one sort of thing; when they are feeling angry or hostile, they think either something totally different or the same thing with a different intensity." [33] The important thing to notice here is that Aristotle's *Rhetoric* considers the emotional and the logical means of persuasion as indispensable ingredients of the rhetorical approach to literature, and that Horace's *Ars Poetica,* in omitting them, is even more incomplete as a rhetoric than Weinberg would lead us to believe.

[31] *Rhetoric,* p. 25.   [32] *Ibid.,* pp. 24–26, 30–31.   [33] *Ibid.,* p. 91.

Let us now look at the *Ars Poetica* as if it were intended as
a treatise on poetical theory and as a supplement to Aristotle's
Poetics. On this plane of vision it is clear that, while Horace's
theory does not achieve the completeness that Aristotle's did,
its title is fully descriptive of its contents, and its understanding of the poetic principle is thoroughly Aristotelian. For
one thing, Horace discusses the mimetic, not the nonmimetic,
types of discourse. For another thing, his teachings are in-
formally grouped under the headings of the doctrinal constituents of the theory of poetry, not under those of rhetoric.
For still another thing, when he speaks of the constituent
parts of discourse, he mentions those belonging to the play,
not those belonging to the oration. And for a final thing,
when he mentions the effects of discourse upon the audience,
he has the drama and the epic rather than the speech in mind.
At the same time, it should be mentioned that the *Ars Poetica*
is in the form of an epistle addressed to the father and two
sons of a family called Piso, and thus it must be allowed to
have flexibility in its procedures and to omit ingredients required in more formal treatises. Accordingly, if it does not
contain a philosophical definition of poetry (and it does not),
it should not be considered on that account a diminished
treatment of its subject, although Aristotle's *Poetics* sets a
contrary example. A philosophical definition of his true topic
might have helped Horace to dispel the impression that his
interests in the *Ars Poetica* were dominantly rhetorical. But
if we accept him for what he says in connection with the four
propositions laid down earlier in this paragraph, we shall see
that his intention is not to clarify and expound rhetoric but
to shed light on poetical procedures.

While discussing the contention of Democritus that the
madness of genius rather than the sanity of art is the only
badge of the true poet, Horace remarks that "even though
I am unable to write poetry myself, I will teach the duty and

business of the poet—show where his materials can be found; what improves and develops him; what lends grace, what does not; where excellence can lead, and where error." [34] The key word in the Latin text of this passage is "poeta," the poet, and this is Horace's usual term in the *Ars Poetica* for that kind of writer, although he twice designates him by the much older term "vates." [35] And what is the distinguishing mark of Horace's poet? What sort of work does he produce in his own right? How does he differ from the orator? In answer to the contention of Democritus, Horace declares that the distinguishing mark of the poet is not madness but sanity and wisdom. Horace adds at once that the true poet is "the skilled imitator," that is, the maker of mimeses, and that the poet's representative work is a "fabula," that is to say, "a dramatic poem," "a narrative," "a story," "a fiction," "a tale," "a fable." [36] Here is the complete passage in which Horace defines the poet as "imitator" and identifies him with these kinds of poetical structures.

I should advise the skilled imitator [he says] to observe actual life and manners and to draw from them a language true to life. Sometimes a play glittering with commonplaces and having well defined characters (even though it is without real artistic power) will give more pleasure and hold an audience better than empty verses or tuneful trifles.

Horace never differentiates the poet from the orator in any open way. But it is safe to assume that he would not describe

---

[34] *Ars Poetica,* 306–308. Translation by Christopher Smart as revised by Walter and Vivian Sutton in *Plato to Alexander Pope Backgrounds of Modern Criticism* (New York, 1966), p. 80. I quote Smart's translation from this edition throughout the present essay, except as I have noted below; and I accompany these quotations with parenthetical reference to their line numbers in Horace's Latin text.

[35] *Ibid.,* pp. 73, 82. (*Ars Poetica,* 24, 400.)

[36] *Ibid.,* p. 80. (*Ars Poetica,* 318, 320.) Horace's word for "skilled imitator" is "doctus imitator." On a later occasion (*Ars Poetica,* 338) Horace uses the term "ficta" as a synonym of "fabula."

the orator as either a "skilled imitator" or a maker of "fabu-lae." On one of the few occasions when he mentions oratory, he exempts orators from the burden which everyone expects the poet to shoulder—the burden of realizing that mediocrity can succeed elsewhere but never with him. "A counselor and pleader at the bar of middling abilities is a long way from having the eloquence of Messalla or the legal knowledge of Cascellius," remarks Horace in this connection, "yet there is a demand for his services. But neither gods nor men nor booksellers have any use for a mediocre poet." [37] It is worth parenthetical comment to notice at this point that Horace names only four orators in the whole course of the *Ars Poetica,* two of whom figure in the passage just quoted, while the other two, Cethegus and Cato, are mentioned elsewhere.[38] On the other hand, Horace names fourteen poets: the elegiac poet Tyrtaeus; the iambic poet Archilochus; the epic poets Homer, Choerilus, Virgil, and Ennius; the comic poets Caecilius, Plautus, and (by indirection) Terence; and the tragic poets Accius, Aeschylus, Varius, and (by indirection) Sophocles and Euripides.[39] This list of authors is impressive in its own right, but on the present occasion its value lies in its affording strong additional evidence that Horace's approach in the *Ars Poetica* is hardly rhetorical in any ancient sense of that term.

[37] *Ibid.,* p. 81. (*Ars Poetica,* 369–373.)

[38] *Ibid.,* pp. 73–74. (*Ars Poetica,* 50, 56.)

[39] Horace draws Terence, Sophocles, and Euripides into his theory of poetry, not by mentioning them, but by referring to characters in their plays. Thus he refers to Chremes (*Ars Poetica,* 94), a character in two of Terence's comedies; to Peleus (*Ars Poetica,* 96, 104), a character in a tragedy by Sophocles; and to Telephus (*Ars Poetica,* 96, 104), a character in a tragedy by Euripides.

For these items of information, and for other kinds of assistance in interpreting Horace's poetical theory, I gratefully acknowledge my reliance upon H. R. Fairclough's *Horace Satires, Epistles and Ars Poetica with an English Translation,* Loeb Classical Library (Cambridge, Mass., 1936).

As for the doctrinal constituents of the theory of mimetic discourse, and the quantitative parts recommended when a given mimetic discourse is composed for presentation, we find again that Horace's *Ars Poetica* follows in a leisurely and casual way the lines developed in Aristotle's *Poetics*. Horace does not treat plot, thought, character, and so on, in a systematic way, as Aristotle does, nor does he analyze a play or an epic poem by mentioning how the constituent episodes may be arranged. But he has these various considerations in mind. Thus he comments upon traditional plots and original plots; [40] upon stories that begin too far back from the climax, and those that begin in the middle of things; [41] upon stories presented to the eye and those presented to the ear; [42] and upon stories which show scenes of horror upon the stage, and those which present such scenes through indirect means.[43] Thus also he recommends that thoughts voiced by characters in a play or narrative should fit the requirements of the situation,[44] and that the actions of characters should suit their time of life, whether that of youth, maturity, or old age.[45] Thus also he speaks of the problem of poetic diction,[46] of melody,[47] and of events connected with the history and the current practice of staging plays.[48] Not only does Horace honor these topics by giving them various degrees of recognition, but it is also to be noticed that he inserts among them a brief yet memorable comment upon the quantitative parts of the dramatic composition when it is arranged for the

[40] Smart's translation, p. 75. (*Ars Poetica,* 119–135.)

[41] *Ibid.,* p. 76. (*Ars Poetica,* 146–152.)

[42] *Ibid.,* p. 77. (*Ars Poetica,* 179–182.)

[43] *Ibid.,* p. 77. (*Ars Poetica,* 182–188.)

[44] *Ibid.,* p. 75. (*Ars Poetica,* 99–118.)

[45] *Ibid.,* p. 76. (*Ars Poetica,* 153–178.)

[46] *Ibid.,* pp. 73–74, 78–79. (*Ars Poetica,* 46–98, 251–274.)

[47] *Ibid.,* p. 77. (*Ars Poetica,* 202–219.)

[48] *Ibid.,* pp. 77–79. (*Ars Poetica,* 220–250, 275–284.)

stage. "If you would like your play to have appeal and to be repeatedly performed," he says in this regard, "let it have five acts, neither more nor less." [49] As an aside, we might observe that this advice implies a greater interest in the commercial success of a play than in its artistic quality, and of course there are several places in the *Ars Poetica* where a similar note is sounded.[50] Certainly it is true that Aristotle's *Poetics* is more austere in tone, more dedicated to artistic excellence, less given to the counsels of prudence and expediency, than is Horace's similar work. There is even a possibility, indeed, that it is Horace's occasional commercialism which has led modern criticism in a spirit of contempt for the market place to call him a rhetorical rather than an aesthetic critic. But commercialism is not an issue in determining whether an author is a poet or a rhetorician. An author can have commercial inclinations in either company, or for that matter he can in either company be austere and aesthetic. What matters in determining whether he is a poet or not by Aristotelian standards is to decide whether his writing involves or does not involve mimesis. On this count, Horace's *Ars Poetica* deals with the composition of mimetic rather than of nonmimetic literature, as we have repeatedly seen, and thus its status as a properly poetic approach to poetry cannot be assailed.

Before the case against Horace's membership in the company of rhetorical critics is complete, it is necessary, however, to show that his famous comment upon the effects of poetry does not in fact require a poet to assume a rhetorical obligation, even though Horace describes these effects in a terminology somewhat different from that of Aristotle in the

---

[49] *Ibid.*, p. 77. (*Ars Poetica,* 189–190.)

[50] *Ibid.*, pp. 76, 81. (*Ars Poetica,* 153–157, 345, 373.) But see also p. 80 (lines 330–332) where Horace condemns the commercial instinct as hostile to poetry.

Poetics. Let us begin the discussion of these effects by inspecting Horace's own treatment of them. He speaks thus:

Poets wish either to profit or to delight or to utter what is simultaneously both pleasant and proper to life. . . . Fictions intended to please should be close to the real. . . . All gatherings of elders reject poems neglectful of worth; all young men of high birth reject poetry harsh and austere. He has won every vote who marries to pleasure the useful, so as in one stroke to instruct and give joy to his reader.[51]

As these words and Horace's Latin equivalents bear witness, there is one and only one type of author under consideration here, and he is the poet, the "poeta." Moreover, there is only one type of discourse here involved, the fictitious story, the "fictum." This sort of author using this sort of means has three choices in respect to the effect which he may hope to produce upon his readers or hearers—he may present his fiction for their profit, or for their pleasure, or for their pleasure and profit at once. And this sort of author using this sort of means has three possible audiences—those elders who reject all fictions that seem to them empty of moral meaning, those young persons who reject all fictions that seem to them sternly moral, and those others, old, young, and middle-aged, who accept the fictions that are made delightfully significant. Horace's point is that these latter fictions represent artistic excellence at its best. There would always be old men who would find this excellence frivolous; and there would always be young men who would find it forbidding; but also there would always be authors who sought it and achieved it, and audiences who found it more satisfying than anything which lacked one or the other part of it. And so long as those authors used fictions to produce this composite effect, or to produce either of the component effects which make it up, just so long were they makers of mimeses—just so long were they poets.

[51] Translation mine. (*Ars Poetica,* 333–334, 338, 341–344.)

They might produce these same effects by nonmimetic discourse, as when they delivered an oration which offered instruction, or which caused delight, or which, by doing both things together, caused persuasion. In fact, Cicero had these three possible effects of the oration in mind when he said, "The man of eloquence whom we seek, following the suggestion of Antonius, will be one who is able to speak in court or in deliberative bodies so as to prove, to please and to sway or persuade. To prove is the first necessity, to please is charm, to sway is victory; for it is the one thing of all that avails most in winning verdicts." [52] The Latin verb used by Cicero to name the second of these three effects sought in oratory is a form of the word "delecto," and another form of that same verb figures behind the passage which I quoted above to set forth the second of the two effects assigned by Horace to the poet. Since Horace and Cicero both use variant forms of the same verb to describe one of the effects of discourse upon an audience, and since another of these effects is described by Horace with a form of the verb "prosum," and by Cicero with a form of the verb "probo," these two words being not too dissimilar in meaning, it is tempting to conclude that the two authors, by speaking of the same effects, are also speaking of the same cause, and that the cause must in both instances be oratorical discourse, inasmuch as Cicero wrote his most notable works on that subject, and Horace seems more or less to have the same subject in mind. But this sort of argument can only be valid if Horace and Cicero are shown to have meant statement and proof rather than mimesis when they spoke as they did about the effects of discourse. It is obvious that Cicero has statement and proof in mind when he wrote as he did about the effects of eloquence; and it is equally obvious that Horace speaking of similar effects has in mind the story,

[52] *Orator,* 21. 69. Trans. H. M. Hubbell in Loeb Classical Library (Cambridge, Mass., 1939).

the fiction, the fable. Thus it is injudicious to call Horace's interests rhetorical if that term is used to denote Cicero's interests. Moreover, the terms used by Cicero and Horace to describe the effects of discourse upon the audience agree well enough with Aristotle's terms in the *Rhetoric* and *Poetics.* "Persuasion," as used in Aristotle's *Rhetoric,* and "catharsis," as used in his *Poetics,* indicate responses of great complexity, each having ingredients shared by the other to an extent not ultimately definable. Pleasure is an ingredient of both; so are intellectual conviction, emotional acceptance, ethical identifications; so is a sense of having been instructed and enlightened. These complexities being incapable of precise analysis, Aristotle chooses to say that the intent of the orator is to discover the means of persuasion in any given case, and that the intent of the tragic poet is to arouse pity and fear in the spectator so as to purge him of the disturbing effect of these emotions. What differences there are between persuasion and catharsis are implied by Aristotle to be definable only as we concentrate upon the differences which we ourselves can discern between our reaction to an effective mimesis and our reaction to an effective statement and its proof. And this position would seem to be exactly that of Horace and Cicero.

4

Although Weinberg's interpretation of the differences between rhetoric and poetics is not authorized by Aristotle and Horace, it should nevertheless be considered and studied as a promising attempt towards defining in modern terms the nature of rhetoric and its place in twentieth-century criticism. Before his interpretation could be declared a success in this latter enterprise, it would have to be given a close examination, of course, and it would need to be evaluated in relation to the success achieved or the failure incurred in other

modern attempts of the same sort.[53] But these tasks lie well
beyond the limits of my present chapter. Here I have tried only
to show what the ancient opinion of the difference between
rhetoric and poetics was, and how far that opinion gave each
of these arts a distinctive role in literary effort and an honor-
able and precise relation to each other. Perhaps the ancient
opinion loses some or all of its value when it is applied to the
problems which confront modern criticism. Perhaps it still
has great value for us. In either event, it should always be
understood, not for what we wish it to have been, but for
what it actually was.

[53] Among modern works which deal with the relations between rhet-
oric and poetics, the following are of fundamental interest: Charles S.
Baldwin, *Ancient Rhetoric and Poetic;* Herbert A. Wichelns, "The
Literary Criticism of Oratory," in *Studies in Rhetoric and Public Speaking in Honor of James Albert Winans* (New York, 1925), pp. 181–216;
Kenneth Burke, *Counter-Statement;* I. A. Richards, *The Philosophy of
Rhetoric* (New York, 1936; Donald C. Bryant, ed., *Papers in Rhetoric
and Poetic* (Iowa City, Ia., 1965)—cited below as Bryant.
    For an examination of Kenneth Burke's application of the term *rheto-
ric* to criticism, see above, pp. 36, 42, and below, pp. 234–255.

CHAPTER 2

The Arts of Literary Criticism
in Renaissance Britain:
A Comprehensive View

1

Among scholars, philosophers, and literary critics who
flourished in Britain during the sixteenth and seventeenth
centuries, the interrelations of poetics, rhetoric, and logic
were understood in well defined and widely accredited terms.
I propose to explain what those terms were understood to
be. Any attempt in this direction obliges me, of course, to refer directly to the treatises which British Renaissance authors
wrote upon these three subjects, and to draw therefrom the
essential materials of my present argument. I must also have
in mind the ancient Greek and Latin works which guided the
literary theorizing of Renaissance authors, for the classical
tradition was much closer to them than it is to most of us, and
it sheds great light upon what they believed. Moreover, I
must approach my task with the active realization that it has
been of very recent concern to critics and scholars. For example, I myself published some years ago a book entitled *Logic
and Rhetoric in England, 1500–1700* (Princeton, 1956),[1] which
contains an extended account of the interrelations of two of
the subjects of my present discussion. Then too there is Rosemond Tuve's *Elizabethan and Metaphysical Imagery* (Chicago, 1947), and that book is so important a study of the in-

[1] Cited below in this chapter as Howell.

fluence of rhetoric and logic upon Renaissance poetry as to deserve the wide attention which it has received. Much less important, but much more attuned to modern critical prejudices, is the analysis of the relations of Renaissance rhetoric to poetics in Brian Vickers's *Classical Rhetoric in English Poetry* (New York, 1970).[2] In fact, the wide currency of the views expressed by Vickers makes them a convenient starting point, and I shall begin by outlining their major trend.

Vickers argues that classical rhetoric became the ascendant influence in Renaissance poetics and is to be accepted as the key to the composition and the subsequent appreciation of the poetry of that time. By classical rhetoric Vickers means, not the whole of ancient rhetorical theory, but only that part which had devoted itself to the three oratorical styles (grand, middle, plain) and to the enumeration, definition, and illustration of the figures of thought and speech. Thus by rights Vickers should have called his book *The Classical Theory of Rhetorical Style in English Poetry,* for that title designates his true subject, even if it does not have the *chic* which modern literary scholars seem to be seeking when they use the term *rhetoric* in all sorts of pretentious and quite inexact literary connections. Vickers would have us believe that, because the poems of such writers as Spenser, Sidney, Daniel, Shakespeare, and Donne abound in rhetorical figures, and because those figures constituted not only the main subject matter of many English Renaissance rhetorics but also the main ingredient in formal Renaissance schooling in the arts of literary composition and analysis, we must therefore understand the theory of Renaissance literature to have been the theory of figurative language, and we must make every effort to identify the tropes and schemes in Renaissance poetry, if we are to approach it as the great Elizabethans and Jacobeans did.

This interpretation contains a kernel of truth, but as Vick-

[2] Cited below as Vickers.

ers presents it, the true interrelations of Renaissance rhetoric and poetics are lost much more completely in what he omits than in what he says. The fact is, the lore of the tropes and the figures made up only one strand of British Renaissance rhetorical theory. A more important strand, as developed for example by Leonard Cox, Thomas Wilson, Thomas Vicars, Thomas Farnaby, and William Pemble,[3] places rhetoric in a different framework from that proposed by *Classical Rhetoric in English Poetry*. But two of the other omissions of our modern Vickers are even more damaging to an ultimate acceptance of his total view of Renaissance rhetoric. Except for three or four passing references, he does not recognize the existence of the poetics which Renaissance criticism took some pains to define,[4] nor does he bother to explain how that poetics carefully differentiated itself from rhetoric and from logic, too. If modern scholars do not grasp that differentiation, then their study of the tropes and the schemes in, say, the sermons of Donne would be based upon the same assumptions as would prevail in their study of these devices of style in the plays of Shakespeare. Renaissance critics invite us to consider that the use of figures in rhetorical compositions is less complicated than in poetic compositions—that sermons and speeches belong to a different order of literature from that which contains epic poetry, rhymed or unrhymed narratives, and poetic or prose dramas. Moreover, Vickers does not recognize logic as a discipline which in the Renaissance was associated with still a third order of literature.[5]

[3] See Howell, pp. 90–95, 98–110, 320–324.

[4] See Vickers, pp. 62, 64, 67, 80, for brief expressions of his awareness of the currency of a Renaissance poetical theory like that discussed in section 3 of the present chapter.

[5] See Vickers, p. 64: "And whereas there is definite evidence of writers using the expressive resources of rhetoric, the direct connections of literature with logic seem to me few: despite Ramus's reforms, logic had no essentially literary effects or aims."

Only by supplying these omissions, and by recovering the distinctions which Vickers has overlooked, can modern scholarship hope to see the true place of poetics, rhetoric, and logic in sixteenth- and seventeenth-century literary theorizing. To these points I shall now address myself.

2

In his treatise on logic, published in 1551 under the title, *The rule of Reason,* Thomas Wilson differentiated logic from rhetoric in terms which indicate how he conceived of the interrelations of these two arts, and what fundamental characteristics the respective compositions produced by each would have. Said Wilson:

Bothe these Artes are much like sauing that Logique is occupied aboute all matters, and doeth playnly and nakedly setfurthe with apt wordes the summe of thinges by way of Argumentacion. Againe of the other side Rethorique useth gay paincted Sentences, and setteth furth those matters with such fresh colours and goodly ornamentes, and that at large. Insomuche, that Zeno beyng asked the difference betweene Logique and Rethorique, made answere by Demonstration of his Hande, declaring that when his hande was closed, it resembled Logique, when it was open and stretched out, it was like Rethorique.[6]

Without taking any liberties with the meaning of these words, we may say that two literatures are under definition here. One is what we may call the literature of the fist, and the other, the literature of the open hand. Each is said to deal with all subject matters, but after Wilson had noted that similarity, he went on to specify in what respects they parted company. The literature of the fist, as the offspring of logic, sought to convert the sum of things, that is to say, the

[6] Quoted by Howell, pp. 14–15. Zeno's metaphor was widely used in the Renaissance, as in earlier times, to characterize the difference between logic and rhetoric. For details, see Howell, pp. 15, 33, 51, 141, 208–209, 293, 315, 320, 341, 365, 374, 377.

total meanings which man gave things, into statements that would exactly match those meanings; and the matching process, the fitting of language to idea, would involve not only a plain and naked style, but also a method to be called argumentation. On the other side, the literature of the open hand, as the offspring of rhetoric, sought to convert the same total meanings into statements that, while also matching the meanings as accurately as possible, would be amplified, expressed in freshly colored words, and adorned with ornament and painted sentences.

The reason why these two literatures differ in these particular ways is not made explicit by Wilson, but his later contemporary, Francis Bacon, shed great light upon it when he pointed to the indifference of logic, as contrasted with the concern of rhetoric, toward the audience being addressed. In the *Advancement of Learning*, Bacon used Zeno's metaphor to provide an opportunity to suggest that the presence of listeners gave rhetorical discourse a quality which logical discourse did not have.

It appeareth also [he said] that Logic differeth from Rhetoric, not only as the fist from the palm, the one close the other at large; but much more in this, that Logic handleth reason exact and in truth, and Rhetoric handleth it as it is planted in popular opinions and manners. And therefore Aristotle doth wisely place Rhetoric as between Logic on the one side and moral or civil knowledge on the other, as participating of both: for the proofs and demonstrations of Logic are toward all men indifferent and the same; but the proofs and persuasions of Rhetoric ought to differ according to the auditors . . . which application, in perfection of idea, ought to extend so far, that if a man should speak of the same thing to several persons, he should speak to them all respectively and several ways.[7]

---

[7] *The Works of Francis Bacon,* ed. James Spedding, Robert Leslie Ellis, and Douglas Denon Heath (Boston, 1860–1865), VI, 300. Cited throughout as *Works of Bacon.*

In his *Rhetoric* Aristotle had said that he assumed "an audience of untrained thinkers" as the target of the discourses which rhetorical theory taught speakers to prepare; [8] and his *Topics,* which was one of the great ancient sources of Renaissance works on logic or dialectic,[9] obviously postulated an audience of trained thinkers, if we may judge from its concern for a rigorous, scholarly method of argumentation, and from its failure to discuss the audience which it intended to reach. With Aristotle's teachings in mind, Bacon made logic the art of addressing the world of scholars, and rhetoric, the world of laymen. To him this necessary differentiation may have been similar to the modern classification of audiences as specialized or general. Or he may have been thinking of the sense in which one and the same person is an expert on some subjects and a nonexpert on others. At any rate, his essential distinction between logical and rhetorical discourses would consist in drawing a line between uttering truth with the truth only in mind, and uttering truth in the full awareness that it must be accommodated to popular opinions and manners. Scholars who learn to address the scholarly community, in their capacity as men and women of learning, and who must also seek, in their capacity as teachers, to address undergraduate audiences, will recognize this Aristotelian and Baconian distinction as having as much relevance today as it had in ancient Greece or in Britain of the early seventeenth century.

Each one of these two literatures has its central and peripheral genres and to some extent genres which belong partly to logic and partly to rhetoric. The academic disputation—the *disputatio* of the medieval and Renaissance universities—is

[8] 1357ª 10–12. Trans. W. Rhys Roberts, in *The Works of Aristotle,* ed. W. D. Ross, Vol. XI. Roberts's translation is cited throughout this chapter.

[9] Howell, pp. 12, 15, 16–18, 24, 35, 40, 44, 47, 55, 62, 149, 152, *et passim.*

the very model of the discourses produced by Renaissance logic, and logic has to be counted among the academic influences which taught students how to compose and organize these particular writings. The public disputations pronounced in Latin when students took their baccalaureate degrees at Oxford or Cambridge in the sixteenth and seventeenth centuries constitute a large literature, and that literature owed a much greater debt to treatises like Ramus's *Dialecticae Libri Duo* than to works on the tropes and figures of rhetorical style. But the disputation was not by any means the sole product of academic training in logic. Philosophical and theological treatises of the Renaissance also belong to the literature of the fist, and as the new science began more and more to invite transmission from scholar to scholar in the world of learning, what we would now call scientific exposition was absorbed for a time into logic, and became therein a rival of traditional argumentation.[10] Thus Renaissance logic bred several kinds of scholarly compositions. As for the literature of the open hand, its model in that era was oratory in its deliberative, its judicial, and its epideictic forms—three literary subspecies that Aristotle's *Rhetoric,* Cicero's *De Inventione,* and Thomas Wilson's *Arte of Rhetorique* had postulated as the precise discourses which students of rhetoric must learn how to create. During the Renaissance the literature associated most directly with the three kinds of oratory consisted of such specimens of eloquence as the speeches of Sir Nicholas Bacon, William Cecil, Robert Cecil, and Sir Francis Bacon in the British House of Commons [11] and the

[10] Howell, pp. 3–4, 9–11, 23–28, 147–165, 185, 293–317, 346–365.

[11] See George Puttenham, *The Arte of English Poesie,* Bk. III, Ch. 2, for a glowing tribute to the parliamentary speeches of Sir Nicholas Bacon and William Cecil, the latter being identified as "the now Lord Treasurer of England," that is, Lord Burghley, to whom Puttenham's *Arte of English Poesie* was dedicated. See G. Gregory Smith, *Elizabethan*

sermons of Lancelot Andrewes at Whitehall and of John Donne at St. Paul's.

If students taught to compose in these rhetorical forms should turn their skills toward the writing of verse, the Renaissance teacher of rhetoric would not have been surprised. He would simply have regarded it as inevitable that competence in one kind of composition would lead to successful practice in other kinds. And the writing of verse would not be the only additional competence that rhetoric might foster. It might also foster skill in the writing of legal arguments, public appeals of all sorts, histories, biographies, and works in literary criticism. In this last connection we should remember that Sir Philip Sidney's *Defense of Poesy* is in form a near equivalent to a judicial oration—a legal defense, one might say, of a client accused of various perfidies—and that a famous seventeenth-century work, John Milton's *Areopagitica,* was modeled upon a speech composed by the Athenian orator Isocrates. We should also remember that a student's training in Renaissance logic would assist him in rhetorical pursuits, and that some literary works of the nonpoetic variety might partake equally of skills developed by rhetoric and by logic, so as to be in fact joint products, neither fully tightfisted nor fully openhanded, but tight and open at successive moments. Bacon's *Advancement of Learning* might be suggested as a fine example of Renaissance logic and rhetoric in action together—a fine example, in short, of the literature of the fist and of the palm.

In the passage which I quoted just now from the *Advancement of Learning,* Bacon introduced the more important of the typical terms used in the Renaissance to describe the respective functions of the literature of the fist and of the open

---

Critical Essays (Oxford, 1904), II, 1, 144–145, 419. Below in this chapter I cite Smith's edition of *The Arte of English Poesie* as Puttenham in Smith.

hand. Logic creates proofs and demonstrations, said Bacon on that occasion, whereas rhetoric creates proofs and persuasions. Bacon's key distinction, so far as the differences between the functions of logic and rhetoric are concerned, would thus seem to be a somewhat wavering line between persuasions and demonstrations. But earlier in the same work he had clarified exactly what each of these analogous functions involved. Let us let him explain that matter in his own words.

Having declared his intention of stirring the earth a little about the roots of the rhetorical science, Bacon continued by saying of its function that "the duty and office of Rhetoric is *to apply Reason to Imagination* for the better moving of the will." [12] What he said next is one of the most famous of seventeenth-century comments upon the ways in which logic and rhetoric work together and separately as instruments for the control of human conduct:

For we see Reason is disturbed in the administration thereof by three means; by Illaqueation or Sophism, which pertains to Logic; by Imagination or Impression, which pertains to Rhetoric; and by Passion or Affection, which pertains to Morality. And as in negotiation with others men are wrought by cunning, by importunity, and by vehemency; so in this negotiation within ourselves men are undermined by Inconsequences, solicited and importuned by Impressions and Observations, and transported by Passions. Neither is the nature of man so unfortunately built, as that those powers and arts should have force to disturb reason, and not to establish and advance it: for the end of Logic, is to teach a form of argument to secure reason, and not to entrap it; the end of Morality is to procure the affections to obey reason, and not to invade it; the end of Rhetoric is to fill the imagination to second reason, and not to oppress it.[13]

Bacon then recalled the eloquent discussion of rhetoric in Plato's *Phaedrus,* where Socrates had pointed out that virtue inspires men with great love and affection, and that men

[12] *Works of Bacon,* VI, 297.   [13] *Ibid.,* pp. 297–298.

would accordingly follow virtuous courses by inner compulsion if only the human imagination could be brought to recognize virtue concretely for what she is, the human reason being powerless to see her in corporal shape. At that point Bacon developed Plato's doctrine as follows:

> Again, if the affections in themselves were pliant and obedient to reason, it were true there should be no great use of persuasions and insinuations to the will, more than of naked proposition and proofs; but in regard of the continual mutinies and seditions of the affections, . . . reason would become captive and servile, if Eloquence of Persuasions did not practise and win the Imagination from the Affection's part, and contract a confederacy between the Reason and Imagination against the Affections. For the affections themselves carry ever an appetite to good, as reason doth; the difference is, that *the affection beholdeth merely the present; reason beholdeth the future and sum of time;* and therefore the present filling the imagination more, reason is commonly vanquished; but after that force of eloquence and persuasion hath made things future and remote appear as present, then upon the revolt of the imagination reason prevaileth.[14]

In this analysis, we see logic as the instrument of the faculty of reason, capable always of supplying naked propositions and proofs to the faculty of passion and the faculty of imagination; and we see reason itself as having an inherent appetite for goodness through its capacity to see the present under the aspect of the eternal. As for the faculty of affections, it too has an inherent appetite for goodness, but what it sees as present goodness not only impresses it to the exclusion of everything else but also impresses with equal exclusiveness the neighboring faculty of imagination. Thus a powerful alliance between the affections and the imagination is so formed as to threaten to nullify the influence of reason and to dominate the will. At this point in Bacon's analysis, we see rhetoric

[14] *Ibid.*, p. 299.

as the instrument by which the imagination can be won to the side of reason by virtue of rhetoric's capacity to make the eternal as palpable as the present always is, and thus to capture the imagination and solidify a new alliance between it and reason. In other words, persuasion occurs when rhetoric is able to induce the imagination to second reason against the contradictory influence of the affections; and without rhetoric, the human will would be the creature of present preferences for goodness as distinguished from preferences for the goodness that lies at the end of time. Rhetoric takes from logic the naked propositions of the reason's eternal view of things and makes them visible to the imagination as something sensible and immediate. And at once the reason triumphs. In these transactions rhetoric has not played the part of evil minister. Rhetoric has not played upon the passions or deceived the imagination. Rhetoric has not been hostile to logic or to reason. Rhetoric has simply done what needs on many occasions to be done if human conduct is to realize the highest potentialities of the human soul—rhetoric has brought the imagination "to second reason, and not to oppress it." Certainly Lancelot Andrewes and John Donne would have considered their sermons as specimens of rhetoric and of logic in regard to the functions which these arts are declared by Bacon to perform. In fact, in Donne's *Devotions,* written when his career as preacher had already advanced to greatness, he spoke of logic and rhetoric in words which remind us of Bacon's description of the function of these two arts, and of Thomas Wilson's, too. Said Donne:

The *arts* and *sciences* are most properly referred to the *head;* that is their proper *Element* and *Spheare;* but yet the *art* of *proving, Logique,* and the *art* of *perswading, Rhetorique,* are deduced to the *hand,* and *that* expressed by a *hand* contracted into a *fist,* and *this* by a *hand* enlarged, and expanded.[15]

[15] *Devotions upon Emergent Occasions,* ed. John Sparrow (Cambridge, England, 1923), p. 121.

Renaissance treatises on logic were devoted to a description of the procedures to be followed in bringing into existence and then organizing the naked propositions and proofs which made up the literature of the fist. Invention was the name given to the first of these procedures, and the second procedure was called disposition or method. The invention of propositions consisted in subjecting a given debatable question to a systematic analysis in order to determine what could be said in answering it in the affirmative or the negative. The systematic analysis advocated by Thomas Wilson and other traditional humanistic logicians involved a progress through nineteen distinct topics or places, each of which would be expected to provide propositions or arguments upon the point at issue. One of these topics was that of definition; another, of genus; another, of species; another, of property; another, of whole; another, of parts; and so on.[16] An interesting feature of Wilson's *Rule of Reason* is its illustration of the way in which these places, and those not included in the list just given, could each be visited and made to yield subject matter in connection with the development of an argument on the question whether a priest should or should not take a wife.[17] The systematic analysis recommended by Ramistic logicians involved a progress through ten distinct places—causes, effects, subjects, adjuncts, opposites, comparatives, names, divisions, definitions, and testimonies.[18] As for disposition or method as the second main procedure treated in Renaissance logic, it was made up of doctrine connected with the problem of arranging into coherent discourses the materials found in the process of invention. Thus the Ramists discussed disposition under three headings, namely, proposition, syllogism, and method,[19] whereas the traditional humanists like Thomas Wilson assigned to this part of logic a discussion not

[16] Howell, pp. 25–26.   [17] Howell, pp. 26–28.
[18] Howell, pp. 155–156.   [19] Howell, pp. 158–164.

only of the five predicables and the ten categories, but also of such other dialectical procedures as definition, division, method, proposition, and argument.[20] Whether a student followed the Ramists or the traditionalists, the doctrine of arrangement would help him to convert ideas into terms, terms into propositions, propositions into syllogisms, and syllogisms into whole argumentative discourses. Thus disposition in logic, and invention as well, are of concern in Renaissance literary criticism, so far as the form and the function of an argumentative composition are permanent considerations whenever its artistic qualities are to be judged.

Renaissance treatises on rhetoric were sometimes devoted exclusively to the problem of style, as Vickers rightly indicates, and sometimes they were devoted exclusively to style and oral delivery, as the Ramistic treatises uniformly ordained;[21] but in its full development Renaissance rhetoric envisaged five compositional procedures that had to be undertaken by any author in the course of creating a speech of the deliberative, forensic, or epideictic kind.[22] Style and delivery were of course the more elementary of these procedures, in the sense that they could be taught effectively in the lower schools. Memory has also to be counted one of the more elementary of these procedures. The remaining two, always regarded as the more difficult of the steps to be taken in the creation of the literature of the open hand, were called invention and disposition, and in respect to them rhetoric and logic overlapped in the Renaissance as they had in ancient Greece and Rome. But the overlapping was not exact. In effect, to be sure, the Ramists made rhetorical invention and logical invention identical, but the tendency of the less dogmatic theorists was to recognize that the literature of the open hand required a subject matter made up not only of the

[20] Howell, pp. 15–23.   [21] Howell, pp. 116–137, 247–281.
[22] Howell, pp. 66–115.

naked propositions of logic but also of the popular opinions and manners which had to enter into addresses to the people, and that therefore rhetorical invention and logical invention would differ in certain ways. And even the Ramists recognized an ingenious difference between the disposition of materials in a learned discourse and the disposition of materials in an oration. That is to say, the Ramists spoke of two kinds of disposition, one of which they called the method of science, and the other, the method of prudence, and it is obvious to anyone reading their works that the former method was intended to control the organization of a learned discourse, whereas the latter controlled a discourse addressed to a popular audience.[23] This is not the place for a more extended comparison of Renaissance rhetoric with logic in respect to their theories of disposition and invention. Suffice it to say that rhetorical invention, outside of Ramistic treatises, involved the use of topics or places similar to those taught by logic, and that rhetorical disposition recommended the organizing of materials in the form of a classical oration rather than in the form of a scholastic disputation. As for the presence of theories of style and delivery in Renaissance rhetoric, and the absence of those theories in Renaissance logic, we need no abstruse speculations to account for that particular state of affairs. After all, a persuasive style and an effective delivery were vitally important to the success of discourses bent upon winning the people's imagination to the side of reason against the powerful beguilements of the people's passions, and thus Renaissance rhetoric, like its ancient counterpart, had to treat these two compositional procedures in some depth. But Renaissance logic, like ancient dialectic, had concern primarily for discourses addressed to reason, with the result that it did not regard style and delivery as urgent topics, so far as its theorizing about its own doctrine was concerned.

[23] Howell, pp. 160–164.

3

Although Zeno's metaphor characterizes to perfection the spirit of the relations between logical composition and rhetorical composition as Renaissance critics saw these two literatures, the contrast between fist and palm cannot be made to shed light upon what was then understood to be the fundamental nature of poetical composition. Those critics never said, for example, that poetry stated the tightfisted truths of logic in the openhanded style of rhetoric. For them, such a statement could not have finally differentiated poetry from oratory. What they did instead was to envisage poetry as a particularly gifted way of revealing truth through the linguistic forms of stories or fictions, whereas oratory and learned argument revealed truth through statement and proofs. The key idea of Renaissance critics is that poetry is fable, and fable, poetry. To them fable was equivalent to the Latin word *fabula,* and it meant primarily a narrative of imagined characters taking part in imagined events.[24] The characters could be gods, or heroes, or kings, or nobles, or knights, or commoners; they could also be monsters, or animals, or even inanimate things, speaking and acting like human beings. The events could be mythical, or legendary, or fictitious, or quasi-historical, or historical. The imaginings could be conducted in realistic terms, or in terms of romance, or allegory. The end sought could be amusement with or without barbs of meaning capable of pricking the ordinary conscience or the conscience of a hearer-king. A fable could be presented in any of these guises, or in a guise in which its plot remained so latent in a lyric outburst as to seem to have no episodic structure at all. But regardless of its particular guise on a given

[24] For an account of the various meanings assigned to the word "fable" in the British vocabulary of the fourteenth, fifteenth, sixteenth, and seventeenth centuries, see the entry for it in *OED.*

occasion, the fable was understood to be as it were the principle which made poetry what it is and which distinguished it basically from all other literary kinds, that is to say, from all compositions falling within the two literatures just discussed.

For example, this principle was taken for granted by Thomas Wilson in his *Arte of Rhetorique*, first published in 1553, as he was discussing the uses of poetry in rhetorical amplifications. On that subject Wilson spoke thus:

> The saying of Poetes and all their fables are not to be forgotten, for by them we may talke at large, and win men by perswasion, if we declare before hand that these tales were not fained of such wisemen without cause, neither yet continued vntill this time, and kept in memorie without good consideration, and therupon declare the true meaning of all such writings. For vndoubtedly there is no one tale among all the Poetes, but vnder the same is comprehended some thing that parteineth, either to the amendment of maners, to the knowledge of the trueth, to the setting forth of Natures work, or els the vnderstanding of some notable thing done.[25]

These words can only be construed to mean that, so far as the nature of poetry is concerned, it is the fable which makes the writer a poet, the writing, a poem. In illustrating the character of the truths figured forth in tales, Wilson went on to say that the *Odyssey* was "a liuely picture of mans miserie in this life"; and he would have us understand thereby that the tale of Odysseus was more than a one-dimensional narrative of particular events about particular persons—it was a picture of human experience, of the particular as universal. At this point Wilson laid his own interpretation of Homer alongside those of Plutarch and Basilius Magnus, and it is obvious that

[25] Fol. 104[R]. See also p. 195 of the edition by G. H. Mair (Oxford, 1909). Mair's edition reproduces the text of 1560, to which my quotation conforms. The same quotation, however, is in the edition of 1553. My subsequent quotations from Wilson throughout this book are based upon Mair's text. Cited as Mair.

those two ancients, the one a pagan historian, the other, a Christian archbishop and saint, were authorities for the poetical principle which Wilson was here expounding.[26] But Erasmus was a more recent authority than they. Wilson had quoted one of the letters of Erasmus as an example of the deliberative oration, and in the course of that letter, Erasmus had used a fable to substantiate one of his points, indicating at the same time that fables and poems were one and the same thing. "The olde auncient and most wise Poets," said Erasmus, "doe feigne (who had euer a desire vnder the colour of fables, to set forth precepts of Philosophie) that the Giauntes, which had Snakes feete, and were borne of the earth, builded great hilles that mounted vp to heauen, minding thereby to bee at vtter defiance with God, and all his Angels." [27]

The best and most authoritative examples of the identification of poetry with fable in English Renaissance criticism occur in Sir Philip Sidney's *The Defense of Poesy*. On one occasion, speaking of what the crucial factor is in differentiating the poet from other kinds of writers, Sidney remarked, "For

[26] Plutarch's comment on Homer would have come to Wilson from an essay by Plutarch generally known in Wilson's time by its Latin title, *Quomodo Adolescens Poetas Audire Debeat* [How the young man should study poetry], or *De Audiendis Poetis* [Concerning the study of poetry]. As for the source of Wilson's other reference, it was a work by St. Basil generally known in the Renaissance by its Latin title, *Concio ad Adolescentes, Quomodo ex Gentilibus Authoribus Sit Utilitas Capienda* [Address to the young men on how profit may be derived from Gentile authors]. For a convenient English translation of these two works, see Frederick M. Padelford, *Essays on the Study and Use of Poetry by Plutarch and Basil the Great* (New York, 1902). Cited as Padelford. For Plutarch's influence on Renaissance poetics, see J. W. H. Atkins, *English Literary Criticism: The Renascence* (London, 1947), pp. 14, 27, 51, 160, 184, 188–189, 194, 208, 275, 324, 349. Cited as Atkins. See Atkins, p. 14, for a reference to what Atkins calls St. Basil's *De Legendis Gentilium Libris*.

[27] Mair, p. 47. Wilson quotes this passage from "An Epistle to perswade a yong Gentleman to mariage, deuised by Erasmus." For the entire letter, see Mair, pp. 39–63.

that wise Solon was directly a poet it is manifest, having written in verse the notable fable of the Atlantic Island which was continued by Plato." [28] Lest this statement be taken to mean that Sidney was making verse no less than fable the true line of demarcation between poetry and the two other literatures discussed above, we should remind ourselves of Sidney's explicit statement elsewhere in the *Defense* that the presence or absence of verse in any literary composition had nothing whatever to do with its being true poetry, "since there have been many excellent poets that never versified, and now swarm many versifiers that need never answer to the name of poets." [29] On another occasion, in one of the most attractive passages in the whole of his *Defense,* Sidney pictured the poet coming to his readers not only "with words set in delightful proportion, either accompanied with, or prepared for, the well-enchanting skill of music," but "with a tale, forsooth,"—"with a tale which holdeth children from play, and old men from the chimney-corner." [30] And on still another occasion, Sidney openly contrasted the poem with the philosophical argument and the oration, leaving no doubt that the essence of poetry was fable, while the essence of both of the other literatures consisted in their being directly declarative. This contrast occurred as Sidney was relating an incident involving Menenius Agrippa, a Roman consul of the sixth century B.C. Menenius, who was counted a brilliant orator, had once confronted a rebellious mob bent upon destroying the Roman senate and bringing an end to the government of Rome itself. In that crisis, what was Menenius to do? As an orator he could have urged the mob to reconsider their contemplated action, calling their attention to its folly in direct, forceful,

---

[28] Sir Philip Sidney, *The Defense of Poesy,* ed. Albert S. Cook (Boston, 1890), p. 3. I refer to this edition through the present chapter and cite it as Cook.

[29] Cook, p. 11.   [30] Cook, p. 23.

imaginative words. As a master of the literature of the fist, he could have sought to change their ill-considered conduct by contrasting it with the wiser courses recommended to them by the weighty maxims of philosophy. But he did neither of these things. He decided instead to play the role of poet. And he played the role of poet, not by versifying, but by speaking to them through a fable. Here are the words used by Sidney to relate this episode:

Menenius Agrippa, who, when the whole people of Rome had resolutely divided themselves from the senate, with apparent show of utter ruin, though he were, for that time, an excellent orator, came not among them upon trust either of figurative speeches or cunning insinuations, and much less with far-fet maxims of philosophy, which, especially if they were Platonic, they must have learned geometry before they could well have conceived; but, forsooth, he behaves himself like a homely and familiar poet. He telleth them a tale.[31]

The tale which Menenius proceeded to tell concerned a revolt of all members of the human body against the belly. The complaint of these members was that the belly got all the food which they produced, and they decided to solve the problem by practicing against the belly the tactics of starvation. But they soon found that, in punishing the belly in this way, they punished themselves in this way as well. We are told by Sidney that the story of Menenius had a remarkable effect in quieting the mob and making them resolve not to destroy the senate after all. But for us the story illustrates in a particularly authoritative context a recurring theme in Renaissance poetics—that the poet and the story-teller are one and the same person, and that the story may have on occasion a greater persuasive effect than the oration or the argument, without becoming in the light of that particular result any the less a poem. A literary sensitivity that is capable of seeing these ap-

[31] Cook, p. 25.

parent contradictions as in fact not ultimately contradictory must be admired for its depth, its sophistication, and its ultimate wisdom.

Sir John Harington's *A Brief Apology for Poetry* was published in 1591, four years before Sidney's *Defense* appeared in print. But the latter work had been written in or around 1583, and it was widely circulated in manuscript before it became a book, one of its admiring early readers having been Harington himself.[32] Thus it is not surprising that the thoughtful Harington would agree with Sidney's view of poetry as in essence fable or fiction. Harington's endorsement of this view came as he was answering the familiar charge that poets were liars. Poetry "is but an imitation (as *Aristotle* calleth it)," said Harington; and in this connection he noted that, "by the rule of *Poetica licentia*," poets "are allowed to faine what they list."[33] But Harington realized, of course, that this answer did not get to the heart of the problem, and so he went on to assert that the poet by virtue of his exercise of the principle which made him what he was could not be accused of telling lies. "For in my opinion," he declared, "they are said properly to lye that affirme that to be true that is false: and how other arts can free themselues from this blame, let them look that professe them: but Poets neuer affirming any for true, but presenting them to vs as fables and imitations, cannot lye though they would: and because this obiection of lyes is the chief, and that vpon which the rest be grounded, I wil stand the longer vpon the clearing thereof."[34] True to this promise, Harington proceeded to show that any fable could be analyzed in three distinct ways and that each way would establish not so much a truth as a possibility of

[32] Cook, pp. xii–xv, xxxix.

[33] Harington's *Apology* is printed in G. Gregory Smith's *Elizabethan Critical Essays*, II, 194–222. My references are to that edition, which I cite as Harington in Smith. The quotation given here is on p. 200.

[34] Harington in Smith, p. 201.

truth. In line with an ancient tradition, he called these three
ways the literal sense, the moral sense, and the allegorical
sense, illustrating each by applying it to the story of Perseus
slaying the Gorgon.[35] He concluded this explanation by affirming that Plato, despite his having found fault with the
abuses practiced by comic writers of the time, had nevertheless "kept still that principall part of Poetrie, which is fiction
and imitation; and as for the other part of Poetrie which is
verse, though he vsed it not, yet his master *Socrates* euen in
his old age wrote certaine verses, as *Plutarke* testifieth." [36]
These words, and all of this part of Harington's argument, indicate with unmistakable clarity that the poet, in embodying
truths in the fictions which he creates, does not proceed by
statement and proof, as the logician and rhetorician would,
but by indications shadowed forth but never made explicit
in an arrangement of characters involved in plots and counterplots. And Harington's analysis of the three ways in which
these plots and counterplots are to be interpreted is itself an

[35] The four senses in which his *Commedia* could be construed (literal,
allegorical, moral, and anagogical) were explained by Dante in his
famous letter to Lord Can Grande della Scala (Epistola X of Dante's
Latin works). But the practice of interpreting a text, whether poetical
or biblical, in these four ways, or in fewer or more, was of course much
older than Dante. Plutarch mentioned allegories as having been called
of old "hidden meanings." See Padelford, p. 62. Padelford refers his
readers to August Schlemm, *De Fontibus Plutarchi Commentationum
de Audiendis Poetis et de Fortuna* (Göttingen, 1894), pp. 32–36, and to
George E. B. Saintsbury, *A History of Criticism and Literary Taste in
Europe* (London, 1900–1904), I, 10–12, for details concerning early
allegorical explication. For an authoritative discussion of the application of the four senses of interpretation to the theory of preaching in
the Middle Ages, and for indications of the distant historical background of this method of literary analysis, see Harry Caplan, "The
Four Senses of Scriptural Interpretation and the Mediaeval Theory of
Preaching," *Speculum*, IV (1929), 282–290. This important study is reprinted in its author's book, *Of Eloquence*, ed. Anne King and Helen
North (Ithaca, N.Y., 1970), pp. 93–104.
[36] Harington in Smith, p. 204.

affirmation that poetry has characteristics not shared by the literatures of the fist and the palm. The method of interpretation to be applied to these latter would always be characteristically literal, and their truth or falsehood would emerge thereupon. But a poem can be subjected to three different readings, and its truths emerge, not as a single proposition, but as a set of possibilities—a set capable of expansion or contraction as different critics at different times see different meanings in the work under examination.

Francis Bacon, whom all students of the English Renaissance would regard as an impressive figure indeed, was cited earlier in the present essay as having made an important contribution to the theory of logical and rhetorical compositions. Now he must be cited for an equally important contribution to the theory of poetry. Like the contributions mentioned earlier, this one was made in the *Advancement of Learning*, where it is stated in two forms, one a passage of 1,290 words in the edition of 1605, and the other, a passage of 9,700 words in Spedding's English translation of the expanded Latin version of 1623.[37] Each of these passages is devoted to "Poesy," and this subject in Bacon's total plan stood as the second of the three major parts of human learning, the first major part being History, and the third, Philosophy. These parts of learning, said Bacon, had reference to the three parts of the human understanding. That is to say, History was primarily conversant with man's Memory, Poesy with his Imagination, and Philosophy with his Reason.[38] Bacon added later that Poesy became a major division of learning, not because of the verse forms in which it is char-

[37] The longer version of the *Advancement of Learning* is called *De Dignitate et Augmentis Scientiarum*. For Bacon's shorter discussion of poetry in these two surveys of the learning of his time, see *Works of Bacon*, VI, 202–206; for Spedding's translation of the more extensive discussion of poetry, see VIII, 439–469.

[38] *Works of Bacon*, VI, 182.

acteristically expressed, for these are merely its outward traits, but because it has "a matter" peculiar to it. He then described that "matter" by calling Poesy an imitation of History. As one of the principal portions of learning, he said, Poesy "is nothing else but Feigned History, which may be styled as well in prose as in verse." [39] And he made it clear at once that feigned history was imagined narrative, with characters and events created out of the poet's mind, not out of his recollection at first or second hand of characters once actually existing and of deeds once actually performed.

In one of the most eloquent paragraphs in the whole body of Renaissance writings about poetry, Bacon explained what his definition of that literary form involved. I shall quote in part what he said, inasmuch as it lends interesting detail to the idea that poetry differs from history as fable from fact.

The use of this Feigned History hath been to give some shadow of satisfaction to the mind of man in those points wherein the nature of things doth deny it; the world being in proportion inferior to the soul; by reason whereof there is agreeable to the spirit of man a more ample greatness, a more exact goodness, and a more absolute variety, than can be found in the nature of things. Therefore, because the acts or events of true history have not that magnitude which satisfieth the mind of man, poesy feigneth acts and events greater and more heroical; because true history propoundeth the successes and issues of actions not so agreeable to the merits of virtue and vice, therefore poesy feigns them more just in retribution, and more according to revealed providence; because true history representeth actions and events more ordinary and less interchanged, therefore poesy endueth them with more rareness, and more unexpected and alternative variations. So as it appeareth that poesy serveth and conferreth to magnanimity, morality and to delectation.[40]

With these principles clearly formulated, Bacon proceeded to speak of "Poesy Narrative, Representative, and Allusive." "The Narrative," he said, "is a mere imitation of history, with

[39] *Ibid.*, pp. 202–203.   [40] *Ibid.*, p. 203.

the excesses before remembered; choosing for subject commonly wars and love, rarely state, and sometimes pleasure or mirth. Representative is as a visible history, and is an image of actions as if they were present, as history is of actions in nature as they are, (that is) past. Allusive or Parabolical is a narration applied only to express some special purpose or conceit." [41] This third kind of poetry received a much more detailed treatment by Bacon than did the other two kinds, perhaps because it had a special appeal for his subtle intellect so far as it consisted as much in the telling of obscure and almost indecipherable fables connected with the mysteries of religion, policy, or philosophy as it did in the presenting of fables to demonstrate or illustrate a less weighty enigma. But this is not the place for a further exposition of Bacon's theory of poetry. Enough has surely been said about him here to convince everyone that he regarded poetry as fiction, whether versified or not, and that, in his opinion, the oration, which might occasionally use fiction as a device for clarifying one of its statements, was essentially nonfictional even so, as were historical writings and philosophical arguments, of course.

Ben Jonson adds his own approval to this same conception of poetry, and thus one of the greatest playwrights and critics of the late sixteenth and early seventeenth centuries joined Bacon, Harington, Sidney, and Thomas Wilson in affirming the generic connection between poetry and fable. Jonson's *Timber, or Discoveries,* usually thought to have been composed between 1620 and 1635, but not published until 1641, six years after Jonson's death, is made up of materials based upon, extracted from, or suggested by his daily reading and by his own current literary interests and observations.[42] Thus the content of *Timber* has to be accepted as doctrine which

[41] *Ibid.,* p. 204.
[42] See *Ben Jonson Timber or Discoveries Made Upon Men and Matter,* ed. Felix E. Schelling (Boston, 1892), pp. xiv–xxi.

Jonson largely borrowed from others; "but in selecting and thus endorsing that material" remarks J. W. H. Atkins, "he has not only recalled some of the wisest teaching of antiquity, but has also incidentally revealed what he regarded as some of the guiding principles of the literary art." [43] Atkins's judicious words apply with special force to the remarks which Jonson entered in *Timber* under the caption, *"What is a Poet?"*

A *Poet* is that, which by the *Greeks* is call'd κατ' 'εξοχὴν, o' Ποιητὴs, a Maker, or a fainer: His Art, an Art of imitation, or faining; expressing the life of man in fit measure, numbers, and harmony, according to *Aristotle:* From the word ποιεῖν, which signifies to make, or fayne. Hence, hee is call'd a *Poet,* not hee which writeth in measure only; but that fayneth and formeth a fable, and writes things like the Truth. For, the Fable and Fiction is (as it were) the forme and Soule of any Poeticall worke, or *Poeme.*[44]

Critics trained in twentieth-century habits of thought would probably be unwilling to accept Jonson's conception of poetry as a contribution to the understanding of modern poetic forms. But if the modern critic denied the existence and reality of Jonson's conception as a pervasive theme in Renaissance criticism, he would be guilty of reading that criticism, not for what it said to its own time, but for what modern prejudices have made it say to us. In other words, the evidence just now presented proves beyond doubt that the principle which makes poetry and fiction one and the same thing is a conspicuous truism of Renaissance literary theory, and if that truism had been questioned at that time, it would have been justified by the very authority which Jonson, Harington, and Sidney had in mind. It would have been justified, that is to say, by an appeal to Aristotle's discussion of mimesis

[43] Atkins, pp. 314–315.
[44] *Ben Jonson,* ed. C. H. Herford, Percy and Evelyn Simpson (Oxford, 1925–1952), VIII, 635. Cited below in this chapter as *Ben Jonson.*

and mythos in his *Poetics,* and by that work's highly revealing account of the differences between poetry and history. Let us look for a moment at what Aristotle said on these matters.

Mimesis as Aristotle used it is usually considered the equivalent of the Latin term *imitatio* and of the English term *imitation.* Jonson rightly equates it with feigning, and by this he meant that a thing was feigned when it was transformed into an imagined structure within somebody's mind. A human face would be feigned when it was transformed by an observer into a mental image of itself; and if that particular image were converted by the observer into lines and colors upon canvas, it would become a portrait. Sequences of human action would be feigned when they were transformed into an imagined structure in someone's mind, and if that structure were converted by that someone into words spoken or written, it would become a narrative. "Epic poetry and Tragedy, as also Comedy, Dithyrambic poetry, and most flute-playing and lyre-playing," said Aristotle in the opening chapter of his *Poetics,* "are all, viewed as a whole, modes of imitation." [45] And, in explaining this statement, Aristotle went on to show that imitation always found a means by which to realize itself, an object toward which to direct its procedures, and a manner in which to present its results to outward view.[46] The means could range from color and line to rhythm, harmony, and language. The objects could be human agents, human actions, human experience, as represented in human awareness. The manner, so far as the literary arts are concerned, could be narrative, dialogue mixed with narrative, or dialogue alone. With these distinctions established, Aristotle took up the dis-

[45] 1447ᵃ 14–16. Trans. Ingram Bywater, in *The Works of Aristotle,* ed. W. D. Ross, Vol. XI. Bywater's translation is cited throughout this chapter.

[46] *Ibid.,* 1447ᵃ–1447ᵇ, 1448ᵃ 1–24.

cussion of tragedy and epic poetry. He defined tragedy as "the imitation of an action that is serious and also, as having magnitude, complete in itself; in language with pleasurable accessories, each kind brought in separately in the parts of the work; in a dramatic, not in a narrative form; with incidents arousing pity and fear, wherewith to accomplish its catharsis of such emotions." [47] Later he defined narrative poetry, or to use his alternate term, epic poetry, by saying in part that it resembles tragedy in the construction of its stories.[48] It too, that is to say, must aim to create from its materials an imagined structure that represents in an organically unified way human beings taking part in human actions. Aristotle's discussion of the structure of a drama and an epic led him to speak of mythos, of plot. Human actions being the important object of imitation in either case, "it is the action in it, i.e. its Fable or Plot, that is the end and purpose of the tragedy," whereas in epic poetry, "the construction of its stories should clearly be like that in a drama." [49] Elsewhere Aristotle observed with some emphasis "that the first essential, the life and soul, so to speak, of Tragedy is the Plot"; and of epics he remarked that "they should be based on a single action, one that is a complete whole in itself, with a beginning, middle, and end, so as to enable the work to produce its own proper pleasure with all the organic unity of a living creature." [50] These words on the subject of plot or fable, coupled with what Aristotle said about imitation as that term applies to poetry, would lead us to conclude that the poet qua poet had a double responsibility. First, he must take human actions as his materials and transform them into an imagined structure within his own mind. And secondly, he must see to it that the

[47] *Ibid.*, 1449^b 23–28.   [48] *Ibid.*, 1459^a 17–29.
[49] *Ibid.*, 1450^a 22–23, 1459^a 18–19.
[50] *Ibid.*, 1450^a 37–38, 1459^a 18–22.

imagined structure is organized into a sequence capable of arousing powerful emotions in the mind of a reader or hearer when it is presented to them as a story or a play.

How, then, does the poet, whose subject matter consists of carefully plotted imagined actions, differ from the historian, whose subject matter also consists of human actions and agents, and whose manner is also narrative? The answer is that the historian narrates actions that have actually occurred, whereas the poet narrates what he imagines to have occurred. Thus there is no feigning in history, at least in the poetic sense. Nor can there be a plot in connection with the structure of a history. The structure of a history is determined by the structure of events that make it up. The structure of a feigned history is determined by what the poet calculates to be needed in giving a sequence of imagined events the power to arouse specific emotions and a sense of general pleasure. Here is what Aristotle himself said on the differences between poetry and history:

The distinction between historian and poet is not in the one writing prose and the other verse—you might put the work of Herodotus into verse, and it would still be a species of history; it consists really in this, that the one describes the thing that has been, and the other a kind of thing that might be. Hence poetry is something more philosophic and of graver import than history, since its statements are of the nature rather of universals, whereas those of history are singulars.[51]

By poetic statements Aristotle would seem here to mean a set of general truths or insights rarely articulated in direct terms but almost always figured forth in the tensions among imagined events and characters acting within a unified plot envisaged by the poet to be conducive to the arousal of emotions that reinforce and deepen his story's implied insights

[51] *Ibid.*, 1451^a–1451^b.

and truths. By historical statements Aristotle would seem here to mean specific truths openly tied to the personages and events which accompany them within a given history. Aristotle would seem here also to reinforce what I said a moment ago—that no mimesis and no mythos are involved in history, whereas poetry is what it is because of its accomplishments when mimesis and mythos, imitation and plot, are involved in its narratives. And if we extended these principles to the literatures of the palm and fist, Aristotle would seem to invite us to conclude that they, like history, are nonimitative and not plotted as poems are. In other words, the difference between the oration, as a nonimitative verbal structure dedicated to the understanding of reality, and the tragedy, as an imitative verbal structure having an analogous and sometimes a profounder dedication to the same end, can be construed as the difference between carrying out a dedication by means of direct statements and carrying out a dedication by fictions. As for philosophical discourse, it is on the side of oratory in respect to its basic method—it carries out its dedications by statements, not by fictions, and hence it, too, is nonmimetic, nonimitative.

Jonson's use of the word fiction in his definition of the nature of poetry should remind us that Aristotle's *Poetics* has most appropriately been retitled in one of its latest English versions so as to emphasize the very concept which Jonson, as well as Thomas Wilson, Sidney, and Harington, had in mind. I refer to the translation of the *Poetics* by L. J. Potts, published at Cambridge at the University Press in 1953, and reprinted there at least twice. Potts gave his translation the general title, *Aristotle on the Art of Fiction*. He deserves to have his translation widely read and respected for what it sets out to do. I should like to add, however, that he deserves credit, too, for paying tribute to the high quality of Jonson's grasp of the central idea of Aristotle's *Poetics*. His words in this connection should not be forgotten by any modern student of Renaissance criticism. Here they are:

Jonson himself was a conscientious scholar, inclined more than any of our other great writers to be guided by critical principles in his own poetry and drama, and he came as near to a correct interpretation of Aristotle's general theory of poetry as any of them has. He saw clearly that by poetry Aristotle meant *fiction:* the embodiment of a philosophy of life in stories or situations such as we meet in the real world except that they are more consistent, being free from both the inert superficialities that signify nothing, and the occasional contradictory happenings that appear for the moment to invalidate general truths.[52]

4

In defining the artistic function of the literature of fable, Renaissance critics made use of Horace's *Ars Poetica* rather than Aristotle's *Poetics*. That is to say, they repeatedly stated Horace's formula that the end of poetry is to afford instruction and pleasure to its readers. Thus Sidney declared that the aim of the poetic mimesis and mythos was "to teach and delight." [53] And Harington, in praising poetry for its capacity to please the scholar and to make fools wise, spoke of its embodying within itself "both goodnesse and sweetnesse, Rubarb and Sugarcandie, the pleasaunt and the profitable." [54] With very explicit reference to the origin of these ideas, William Webbe confirmed his own opinion about the function of poetry by quoting Horace's formula in Latin and by paraphrasing it as having meant "that the perfect perfection of poetrie is this, to mingle delight with profitt in such wyse that a Reader might by his reading be pertaker of bothe." [55] And

[52] This quotation is from the paperback edition of Potts's work (Cambridge, England, 1968), pp. 6–7.
[53] Cook, p. 9.   [54] Harington in Smith, pp. 207–208.
[55] William Webbe, "A Discourse of English Poetrie," in Smith's *Elizabethan Critical Essays,* I, 250.

then, too, Thomas Nash remarked "that true things are rather admirde if they be included in some wittie fiction, like to Pearles that delight more if they be deeper sette in golde," [56] while Ben Jonson made reference some thirty years later to the same theme, saying of comedy and tragedy that "they both delight, and teach." [57]

These critics would not have considered Horace's words to be inconsistent with Aristotle's conception of poetry. They would have accepted the obvious fact that the Horatian formula and Aristotle's as well were specifically applied only to the literature of fable, the literature, that is to say, which owed its very identity to the processes of mimesis and mythos. Thus they would have understood Horace's formula to include what Aristotle had said in assigning an emotional function to tragedy and a pleasurable function to epic poetry; and they would have seen that Horace had then advanced beyond the Aristotelian position and added the teaching function to the mimesis, on the theory that the instruction of hearers and readers is a necessary consequence of their emotional involvement in the poet's fable. In other words, the didactic element and the aesthetic element in poetry or in any of the arts were not considered hostile to each other in the eyes of Renaissance critics. They would have regarded the didactic aim as an extension of the aesthetic aim, and they would have said that the latter is intensified, not destroyed, when the former comes into operation in the consciousness of those who consider art capable of producing profound, many-sided human responses. To be sure, they would have admitted that the didactic element in the mimesis could become so obtrusive, and be so ineptly handled, as to cause the judicious to grieve; and when that happened, they would have deplored

[56] See his *The Anatomie of Absurditie,* as excerpted in Smith's *Elizabethan Critical Essays,* I, 329.

[57] *Ben Jonson,* VIII, 643.

that brand of didacticism. But they would have regarded it as a flawed didacticism, and they would have insisted that the occasional unhappy occurrence of a flawed didacticism in a mimesis was not proof that skillful didacticism should be denounced as an intruder in mimetic literature in general. As for the literatures of the fist and the palm, they too were didactic in Renaissance eyes, as we have seen. But their didacticism, if managed with finesse, was quite capable of giving a reader or hearer a sense of delight as well as a sense of profit. In the *Orator* Cicero said that "The man of eloquence whom we seek, following the suggestion of Antonius, will be one who is able to speak in court or in deliberative bodies so as to prove, to please and to sway or persuade." [58] This wise observation, which attributes an aesthetic no less than a didactic and a persuasive capacity to oratory, would not have seemed to Renaissance critics to bring mutually antagonistic functions together. Indeed, what Cicero said with oratory in mind echoed what Aristotle in the *Poetics* had said with poetry in mind, when he was seeking to explain why it is "natural for all to delight in works of imitation." "The explanation," he declared, "is to be found in a further fact: to be learning something is the greatest of pleasures not only to the philosopher but also to the rest of mankind, however small their capacity for it." [59] To Aristotle, to Cicero, and to Horace, however, the crucial distinction to be recognized between delight and didacticism in poetry, on the one hand, and delight and didacticism in oratory, on the other, was that the poem accomplished these ends by fictions, the oration by statements.

[58] 21.69. Trans. H. M. Hubbell, in Loeb Classical Library. Cicero's words in Latin are as follows: "Erit igitur eloquens—hunc enim auctore Antonio quaerimus—is qui in foro causisque civilibus ita dicet, ut probet, ut delectet, ut flectat."
[59] 1448b 8–15.

5

This crucial distinction has been overlooked by twentieth-century students of Renaissance literary theory. Their thesis has been that rhetoric assumed control over poetics during the years which we have been examining here, and their arguments in support of this thesis have made it apparent that poetics becomes rhetoric whenever it asserts its capacity for didacticism or persuasiveness, or whenever it shows concern for its audience, or whenever it makes open use of the teachings of rhetoric in regard to the thought content or the style of poetry. But these arguments must be dismissed by insisting that didacticism, and persuasiveness, and concern for audience, and concern for thought content, and concern for style must not be regarded as purely rhetorical. They must be regarded as the common properties of rhetoric and poetics. They must be regarded as the properties which rhetoric has to consider in evolving an adequate theory of statement, and which poetics has to consider in evolving an adequate theory of fiction. With this distinction to guide us, let us examine some of the twentieth-century attempts to represent the Renaissance as embarrassingly rhetorical in its conception of literary art. The truth of the matter will turn out to be, not that Renaissance critics were embarrassingly rhetorical in their approach to poetry, but that modern scholars who concern themselves with such subjects are embarrassingly wrong in their approach to Renaissance criticism.

The notion that poetical theory becomes rhetoric whenever it acknowledges the didactic and persuasive capabilities of a poem is widespread in modern criticism, and it is also widespread among modern judgments of Renaissance poetics. Two examples of the latter will have to suffice at this time.

In his article on rhetoric and poetics in an authoritative reference work, Marvin T. Herrick says that "Sidney's *De-*

fense of Poesy was mainly rhetorical." [60] This judgment is
to be understood in a context in which Herrick had previously commented on the Renaissance idea that poetry should
be didactic. In that earlier connection Herrick speaks as follows:

> There was no explicit statement in Aristotle that the poet is a
> teacher, but Horace, whose rhetorical *Ars Poetica* was enor-
> mously influential for centuries, had said that the poet should
> teach as well as delight. Consequently most critics after Horace
> believed that poetry and rhetoric had a common end, didacti-
> cism, which is usually identical with persuasion.[61]

Another example of a modern judgment which makes
Renaissance poetics prevailingly rhetorical appears in M. H.
Abrams's highly regarded study of the Romantic theory of
poetry and the European critical tradition. In a discussion
of pragmatic theories of poetry within that critical tradition,
Abrams has this to say:

> The perspective, much of the basic vocabulary, and many of
> the characteristic topics of pragmatic criticism originated in the
> classical theory of rhetoric. For rhetoric had been universally re-
> garded as an instrument for achieving persuasion in an audience,
> and most theorists agreed with Cicero that in order to persuade,
> the orator must conciliate, inform, and move the minds of his
> auditors. The great classical exemplar of the application of the
> rhetorical point of view to poetry was, of course, the *Ars Poetica*
> of Horace.[62]

In a footnote appended to his reference to Cicero, Abrams
points to the latter's *De Oratore*, 2.28.121, as the source of
the requirement that the orator should conciliate, inform,
and persuade.[63] Thus, if I read Abrams's argument correctly,
he is saying that persuasion is a recognized function of rheto-

---

[60] *Encyclopedia of Poetry and Poetics*, p. 704.   [61] *Ibid.*, p. 702.
[62] *The Mirror and the Lamp* (New York, 1953), pp. 15–16.
[63] Cicero's prescription is phrased, "ut et concilientur animi et
doceantur et moveantur."

ric, and that any attempt in a poetical theory to claim the same function for poetry automatically makes the latter theory rhetorical. More specifically Abrams is saying that Horace gave his *Ars Poetica* a rhetorical character simply by taking the word "inform" out of Cicero's three-part prescription for oratory and incorporating it into his own two-part prescription for poetry. Herrick obviously has the same line of reasoning in mind. But isn't this dialectic flimsy? Can the word "inform," even if Horace borrowed it directly from a treatise on rhetoric, make his own *Ars Poetica* rhetorical? Is there a law which says that this particular word converts into a treatise on rhetoric any work in which it happens to be used to designate the effect of an art upon the public? What about the word "delight"? Would its presence in a treatise on rhetoric make that treatise poetical, and the art which it treated, poetry? If so, then Cicero's *Orator* and Thomas Wilson's *Arte of Rhetorique* are poetical rhetorics, inasmuch as delight is said by Aristotle and Horace to be an aim of poetry, and both Cicero and Wilson declare that an oration should be designed not only to teach and persuade, but also to delight.[64] But enough of such nonsense. The truth is that oratory and poetry are both able at best to give delight and to persuade or teach. But the oration conveys its delights and its persuasions by the methods of statement and proof, the poem, by the methods of fiction. Each can be didactic and persuasive; each can also be delightful. Indeed, if either fails in the two former objectives, it is difficult to see how it could ever succeed in the latter. But one thing for the student of Renaissance criticism to keep in mind is that each maintained its independence of the other during the early modern centuries, despite its acceptance of these three objectives as aims common to itself and its literary companion.

Still another common property shared equally by the ora-

[64] Mair, p. 2. See also above, n. 58.

tion and the poem in Renaissance literary theory is what I just now called concern for the audience. We remember that this concern was said by Francis Bacon to be of great importance to the orator, and of course it is of equal importance in Renaissance drama and narrative poetry. As a theme in classical criticism, the concern either of poet or of orator for his audience or reader is respectively recognized in such works as Horace's *Ars Poetica* and Cicero's treatises on rhetoric; but in Aristotle's *Poetics* and *Rhetoric* it is given its most authoritative ancient formulation. Aristotle's *Rhetoric* shows the orator how to investigate the means of persuasion in any given case and what to do in working those means into the content, structure, and style of the statements which carry them to the audience. Aristotle's *Poetics* shows the poet or critic that imagined narratives, whether presented as drama or story, have the capacity to stir an emotional and pleasurable response in hearers and readers, provided that those narratives deal with basic human aspirations and failures and are so structured as to make the audience see their own predicaments displayed in the feigned situation unfolding before them. Thus concern for the audience overwhelmingly dictates the content and form of oratory and poetry, and it is given explicit attention in ancient and Renaissance poetics and rhetoric. But the modern idea is that concern for the audience is exclusively a rhetorical concern, and that it gives a rhetorical cast to any poetical theory in which it is embodied or implied. By this reasoning, Horace's *Ars Poetica* and Renaissance poetics in general become rhetorical, and the distinction between rhetoric and poetics vanishes. As expressed by a recent historian of criticism, this reasoning takes the following form:

> The fact that, in Horace's theory, the internal characteristics of the poem are determined largely, if not exclusively, by the ex-

ternal demands of the audience brings his theory very close to specifically rhetorical approaches.[65]

Weinberg goes on to draw a line between a writing produced from an author's attempt to achieve structural perfection in his work and a writing produced from an author's desire to make it arouse a predetermined response in the audience. The latter attempt Weinberg declares to be rhetorical, the former, poetic. And he also declares that the tenor of Aristotle's *Poetics* "is not a rhetorical one, because nowhere is the poem made to be what it is in order to have a particular effect of persuasion upon a particular audience." [66] We can agree with Weinberg, of course, that the *Poetics* cannot be accused of making a rhetorical approach to tragedy or epic poetry. But we cannot agree with the reasoning which he used to support that judgment. For Aristotle emphasized that a poem is to be made with the specific purpose of arousing emotion and giving pleasure to particular spectators and particular readers, and he would be the last to say that these effects were so specialized as to preclude all possibility of their being extended into that other effect called persuasion. The true reason why Aristotle's *Poetics* cannot be said to make a rhetorical approach to poetry is that to him the poem involves the fictional representation of reality, whereas the oration involves reality directly presented in propositions and proof, as his *Rhetoric* fully demonstrates. He would doubtless have admitted that the concern for audience is more visible, more on display, in some fictions than in others, and we could supply him with the example of *Candide* for the former, as against *Madame Bovary* for the latter.[67] And he

[65] Weinberg, I, 71–72.

[66] *Ibid.*, I, 351. For a longer analysis of Weinberg's interpretation of Horace's *Ars Poetica* and Aristotle's *Poetics,* see above, pp. 45–72.

[67] In an endeavor to clarify his theory that the presence or absence of a concern for the audience on the part of the writer determines

would perhaps add that the concern for an audience is almost always more visible in oratory than in poetry, even if
it could be pointed out to him that Emerson's Lectures, which
were distinguished rhetorical achievements, show less concern
for the audience than does Milton's famous *Areopagitica*.
But the fact is that concern for the audience is always present in oratory and in poetry, and it cannot fairly be called
an exclusively rhetorical matter.

Thought and style are the most conspicuous of all the
properties which poetry and rhetoric had in common in Aristotle's time; and these two things must now be taken into
account for their bearing upon certain important modern
misconceptions of their status in Renaissance criticism. In

---

whether the work is to be judged rhetorical or poetic, Weinberg points
to *Candide* as an example of rhetoric, and to *Madame Bovary* as an
example of poetry. He argues, of course, that the structure of *Candide*
is dictated, not by internal narrative necessity so distinctive in poetry,
but by Voltaire's desire to speak to the suspicions, the likes and dislikes, and the sense of enjoyment and mischief, in the audience which
he intended to reach. On the other hand, Weinberg declares that the
structure of *Madame Bovary* is dictated by Flaubert's desire to create
a story in which successive episodes, participating characters, particular
actions, and particular speeches blend into "an effective artistic whole."
See Bernard Weinberg, "Formal Analysis in Poetry and Rhetoric," in
Bryant, pp. 41–44.
It would seem to me, however, that *Candide* cannot fairly be called
an illustration of the rhetorical principle, and that both *Madame
Bovary* and *Candide* are genuine examples of the poetic principle.
Both present imagined sequences of events. Both are mimeses. *Candide*
is an excellent example of the comic, *Madame Bovary* of the tragic,
plot. Voltaire's story is meant to engage its readers in the delighted
appreciation of the forms of intellectual folly. Flaubert's story makes
us identify ourselves with the tragic implications which Emma Bovary's
life holds for all of us. It is true, of course, that Voltaire is much more
open than Flaubert in showing a concern for his audience, but that
concern is an obvious factor in the artistic plans of Flaubert, nevertheless. What is not present in Voltaire's work, or in Flaubert's either, is
the rhetorical principle. Neither work is nonfictional. Neither work
proceeds directly by statement and proof.

Aristotle's *Poetics,* thought and style are two of the major constituents of the theory of tragedy and epic poetry, the other constituents being plot, character, and melody, with spectacle included for its special relevance to dramatic performances. The thesis of the *Poetics* is that the tragic and epic poet must imagine men and women in action, making choices between this or that line of conduct, justifying those choices by speaking back and forth to each other, and keeping, as they converse, to the linguistic rhythms of their station in the plot. The justifying of a person's choices is called thought, the use of appropriate linguistic rhythms, style, in Aristotle's terminology.

Thought he defined as "the power of saying whatever can be said, or what is appropriate to the occasion." "This is what, in the speeches in Tragedy," he added, "falls under the arts of Politics and Rhetoric." [68] Later, when he brought up the topic of thought for analysis as one of the major constituents of poetic theory, he dismissed it from consideration in the *Poetics* by saying, "we may assume what is said of it in our Art of Rhetoric, as it belongs more properly to that department of inquiry." [69] Aristotle plainly meant that the poet, writing feigned speeches for the personages in his fictions, would find in one of the best available treatises on rhetoric the principles governing the preparation of actual speeches and would be able to make use of those principles in composing the kind of fictional speeches that would have the rhetorical effects which the poet imagined for them. Milton may not have composed from a textbook on rhetoric the brilliant speeches which he had the fallen angels deliver at their council in *Paradise Lost,* Book II, but these speeches conform to the principles of rhetoric, nevertheless, and Aristotle's *Rhetoric* would obviously help a critic of Milton's epic to decide whether, in their content, structure, and style,

[68] *Poetics,* 1450^b 4–8.   [69] *Ibid.,* 1456^a 33–36.

the speeches were to be thought capable of producing within
the council of fallen angels the rhetorical effect which Milton
ascribed to them. At the same time, however, these speeches
must be taken as part of the plot of *Paradise Lost*—as part
of the vast mimesis outlined by Milton in Book I and carried
out thereafter into the whole poem. In this latter capacity
they are addressed to the audience of Milton's readers, and
they are to be judged as part of what Milton wanted those
readers to understand from what the poem ascribed to him
in his own person and to him through his fictitious agents.
Aristotle's *Poetics,* but not his *Rhetoric,* would help in this
second judgment. In others words, the critic may go from
the *Poetics* to the *Rhetoric,* at Aristotle's express invitation,
if he would judge the poetic speech in its purely rhetorical
capacities; but if he would then judge it in its poetical capacities, he must return to the *Poetics* and come to understand how far the particular speech intensifies the meaning
of the plot in which it occurs.

Precisely the same line of analysis should be used in re-
constructing the doctrine of style, as Aristotle would have it
understood in its application to poetry and to oratory. In approaching the subject of style in the *Poetics,* Aristotle said
that "the theory of such matters, however, belongs to Elocution and the professors of that art." [70] By elocution he meant,
not flamboyant declamation, as modern usage might suggest,
but what the Latin rhetoricians were to call *elocutio* and
were to consider as the third part of classical rhetoric, the
other parts being invention, disposition, memory, and delivery, as I mentioned above. Elocution, or style, as I also mentioned above, was the heading under which the three kinds
of style and the lore of the figures of thought and speech
were elaborately treated by Renaissance critics, and, we
might add, by the *Rhetorica ad Herennium,* by Cicero, by

[70] 1456^b 10–12.

Quintilian, and by many other writers, ancient and medieval. When Aristotle sent the readers of his *Poetics* to the professor of rhetoric for information about stylistic matters, he knew that they would be introduced to those matters as understood in an oratorical situation, that is to say, in a situation where a speaker was stating truths directly to an audience and was interested in getting the audience to see those truths with their imagination and their feelings as well as their reason. Once the uses of the figures of thought and speech were mastered in the oratorical situation, the prospective orator might have to carry his studies of style no further, but the prospective poet would not be able to stop there. He would have the problem of using those figures as part of his feigned narrative, where he would be addressing his readers or hearers through the speeches which his imagined characters would make to each other. Each imagined character would use figures of speech in an oratorlike way as he addressed his audience within the story or drama. But the poet would see to it that the use of those figures by the imagined character would also make a contribution to what the plot of the story was trying to say in poetic terms. Thus the figures in a poem would often have the kind of double function that poetic dialogue has. When Satan in his third speech in *Paradise Lost* said to Beëlzebub, "Better to reign in Hell than serve in Heaven," [71] the antithesis within his words portrays the clash of cosmic opposites and sets the theme of his own attempts as speaker to inflame the smouldering defiance of the fallen angels. An antithesis of this sort has great value within the rhetorical situation confronting Satan. But Milton is simultaneously using it as a poetic instrument for suggesting to his readers the continuing antitheses in his epic—between ruling and serving, Hell and Heaven, hatred and love, loss and gain, defeat and victory, evil and good, rebellion

[71] Bk. 1, line 263.

and obedience. In Milton's view these opposites are timeless and implacable. Man's destiny, he would say, must be worked out in terms of them; and, in working out his destiny, man has the singular gift, if he would use it, of being able to differentiate between the semblance and the substance of worth in each member of each pair of opposites.

The treatment accorded in Aristotle's *Poetics* to diction and thought as important constituents of the theory of tragedy and epic poetry has led one modern scholar to the conclusion that the whole history of poetics from classical antiquity to the end of the neoclassical era in English letters shows poetics to be subservient to rhetoric, and rhetoric to be the lawgiver, not only for the oration and its affiliates, but for the poem as well. That scholar is P. W. K. Stone, and the conclusion just ascribed to him is contained in his book, *The Art of Poetry 1750–1820*.[72] Chapter I of that book, entitled "Rhetoric and its Relation to Poetry," summarizes his conception of the history of this subject as follows:

> The theory of poetry as an "art" had, during the Renaissance, borne a very close resemblance to the theory of rhetoric. The reasons are not far to seek. Though Aristotle maintained that rhetoricians had originally learnt their skills from the poets, it was in fact the former who took the lead in analyzing and rationalizing what might be called the "artistic" use of language. It was rhetoric from the first that legislated in this field. Hence Aristotle does not find it necessary to discuss "thought" and "style" in the *Poetics:* he refers the reader to his companion treatise. The situation in the sixteenth century is no different.[73]

This argument has value only so far as it indicates once more how very unsatisfactory modern literary scholars are when they handle subjects requiring a genuine learning in classical, medieval, and Renaissance rhetoric. As we have just now seen, Aristotle did send the readers of his *Poetics* to his *Rhetoric* for an analysis of thought and style when these two sub-

---

[72] (London, 1967). Cited as Stone.   [73] Stone, p. 10.

jects came up for discussion in relation to his analysis of tragedy and epic poetry. But he never intended anyone to conclude that rhetoric made all the laws for poetics, or that poetics was to be called rhetorical whenever it discussed topics which rhetoric also discussed. What he did intend was that we see rhetoric as the theory of a very basic kind of non-fictional literary composition, and that we see poetics as the theory of literary fiction. He intended us to see orations, historical writings, and philosophical arguments as nonmimetic. He intended us to see tragedy, comedy, epic poetry, and prose narrative, as mimetic. He would have us understand that the literature of the fist and the literature of the palm accomplish their purposes by means of verbal statements and proof, whereas the literature of fable accomplishes its purposes by means of imagined characters and events. And he would also have us understand that thought and style are common to all three literatures.

6

"But it is time that rhetoric regained its place in our literary criticism," [74] said Brian Vickers on the penultimate page of his *Classical Rhetoric in English Poetry*. I agree wholly with this opinion. I also agree with Vickers when he adds that his own book represents "an attempt to rewrite 'the whole story,' or at least to provide a means of so doing." But I cannot say that I believe his attempt successful. In my opinion his book has not given anything like a complete account of classical rhetoric in the literary theory of Renaissance England. On the contrary, the story that it tells seems to me to be distressingly incomplete in its failure to reckon adequately with logic, and to be distressingly distorted in its insistence that the doctrine of the three styles and of the figures of thought and speech represents what Renaissance crit-

[74] Vickers, p. 166.

ics understood rhetoric and poetics to be in the full range of
their interrelations.

In seeking to define the subject of his book, Vickers makes
a historical approach to Renaissance rhetoric, picturing himself indeed as the first modern writer to offer "a history of
rhetoric across its whole period." [75] Such an approach ought
to have provided him with a reasonably full acquaintance
with the rhetorical theories of Plato, Aristotle, Cicero, Quintilian, and their later followers, and to have introduced him
to many lesser figures. But Vickers deals in the main with
these classical authors through modern accounts of them,[76]
and thus his conclusions are not always what they would presumably have been if he had relied upon the opinions expressed by classical authors themselves. For example, he
remarks of Aristotle's *Rhetoric* that it gives all of its authority to judicial oratory, to the neglect of the deliberative and
the epideictic kind; [77] but he neglects to modify this assertion so as to acknowledge that Aristotle, while giving some
26 pages to judicial oratory, as against 22 pages to the deliberative, says that the latter is "a nobler business" than the
former for its connection with "wider issues," and that the
former, for its concern with "the relations of private individuals," is beneath the latter as a subject of interest to the
citizenry.[78] For another example, also connected with Aristotle's *Rhetoric,* Vickers says that "Aristotle was not over-
explicit in his connection of rhetoric with feeling," [79]—an
odd remark, indeed, in view of Aristotle's discussion of the
emotions through 31 pages of Book II, where, among other

---

[75] *Ibid.,* p. 11.   [76] As he acknowledges, p. 11.   [77] *Ibid.,* p. 69.
[78] *Rhetoric,* 1354^b 23–26, 30. Aristotle's 22 pages on the subject of
deliberative oratory begin at the start of Bk. 1, Ch. 2, and continue to
the end of Bk. I, Ch. 8; his 26 pages on judicial oratory begin with the
opening words of Bk. 1, Ch. 10, and end with the closing words of Bk. 1,
Ch. 15.
[79] Vickers, p. 95.

things, he speaks of the emotions of pity and fear in terms that shed great light upon what his *Poetics* says of the effects of tragedy. But what is of most concern to anyone interested in an accurate account of Renaissance rhetoric is that Vickers allows his obvious scholarly awareness of the whole sweep of ancient rhetorical doctrine to be uncritically superseded by his unflagging determination to deny to Renaissance criticism the value of all elements of the ancient scheme except the element of style.

Invention and disposition, the first two elements in the ancient scheme, involved the would-be speaker in questions of rhetorical content and form, as I noted above. The problem of content involved the discovery of logical, emotional, and ethical proofs, as Aristotle pointed out; and logical proof involved decisions concerning the truth and probability of the arguments which the speaker might use. Truth and probability are messy and difficult problems, of course, but the speaker, or indeed any writer of nonfiction, cannot avoid them if he would. Aristotle recognized them when, to the speaker searching for the means of persuasion, he said that "things that are true and things that are better are, by their nature, practically always easier to prove and easier to believe in." [80] And Plato in *Phaedrus* had memorably demonstrated this same principle of persuasion, as Bacon emphasized in the passage which I quoted above from him. As for disposition in rhetoric, Aristotle said that it must involve two processes, statement and proof, as its essential ingredients, and that it can on occasion involve such other ingredients as those designed to make hearers receptive and to move them.[81] But disposition, with ambitions as complex as these, is, like invention, a messy and difficult problem. And what does Vickers's historical sketch of rhetoric do to rhetorical inven-

[80] *Rhetoric*, 1355ᵃ 37–38.   [81] *Ibid.*, 1414ᵃ 30; 1414ᵇ 5–10.

tion and disposition, when he comes to define the place of classical rhetoric in Renaissance criticism?

The answer is, of course, that, while adequately recognizing invention and disposition as important ingredients in classical rhetoric,[82] Vickers finds them intruders within the ideal rhetoric which he constructs for himself, and he dismisses them with the disparaging implication that they are mere philosophical concerns, and that rhetoric regains its true identity when it ignores them and embraces style as its primary interest. Vickers articulates this implication by referring at one point to "the tacit agreement in many countries at many times that rhetoric was properly a literary art which could get along quite well without the aid of the philosophers."[83] "What it needed to concern itself with," he adds, "was not general issues but particular examples, the details of style, literary language." Thus the ideal rhetoric is to him what he repeatedly calls "literary rhetoric."[84] It deals only with the kinds of style and the figures of thought and speech. If it deals with the messy problems of content and form, it becomes illegitimate.

And who made the law which denies to rhetoric a concern for content and form? Well, the law seems from Vickers's account to have been made by a "tacit agreement in many countries at many times." But I suspect that the true lawgiver for Vickers is Ramus. In fact, he openly proclaims himself a Ramist for having found in poetry his illustrations of the figures of rhetoric, as Ramus's English adherent, Abraham Fraunce, once also did.[85] Ramus, as I mentioned earlier, had laid down a law that logic was to concern itself only with the problems of invention and disposition in literary composition, while rhetoric was to concern itself only with

[82] Vickers, pp. 60–73.   [83] Vickers, p. 21.
[84] *Ibid.,* pp. 22, 41, 43.   [85] *Ibid.,* p. 43.

style and delivery. But Ramus's law does not have divine sanction. It stands or falls on its merits. It had great vogue in Britain from 1574 to 1681, but it was not the sole influence in that period among British writers on rhetoric, and by the late 1600's it had become obsolete.[86] It perhaps became obsolete because questions of content, form, and style are so closely interrelated as simultaneously to require the attention of the writer or speaker as he deals with his own particular subject on a given occasion, and any suggestion that these questions may be settled successively, one after the other, invites an artificial separation of processes best kept together. The tendency within the field of rhetoric to divorce style from content and form leads to a separation of expressive energies from inventional and dispositional energies, with the result that the expressive energies have nothing to express, and the exclusive pursuit of them becomes what Francis Bacon called "the first distemper of learning, when men study words and not matter." [87] At any rate, Vickers's willingness to follow Ramus and to isolate rhetoric from its classical concern for content and form leaves him in the position of not being able to live up to the requirements of the title which he has given to his book. In short, his rhetoric is not classical rhetoric, but only a part of it.

Vickers points to George Puttenham's *The Arte of English Poesie* as an example of the literary rhetoric which he esteems, and he explicitly ranks Puttenham with "the greatest rhetoricians and critics" of the sixteenth century.[88] Like Harington, Puttenham recognized imitation, fiction, multidimensional interpretation, disguise, indirection, feigning, and fable, as traits of poetry, and he gave these terms passing mention in his poetical theory.[89] But his master distinction

[86] Howell, pp. 178–179, 247–281.   [87] *Works of Bacon,* VI, 120.
[88] Vickers, p. 37.   [89] Puttenham in Smith, II, 3, 29, 32–34, 42–44.

was between speech by meter and speech without meter, the essence of poesy being "a skill to speake & write harmonically." [90] In fact, he made it clear at one point that only the common people paid heed to the "matter" of poetry, that is, to the truth being feigned or imitated, while by implication the upper classes, those in the know, paid heed "to the cunning of the rime." [91] Thus the common people, Puttenham added at once, are "as well satisfied with that which is grosse, as with any other finer and more delicate." It will be remembered that Puttenham devoted the second book of his poetics to verse forms, and the third book to the figures of rhetoric. Thus he seems partly to confirm Vickers's thesis that poetics in the Renaissance yielded up its proper spheres of influence and became rhetoric. But on the basis of his adequate yet by no means distinguished treatment of the figures of rhetoric, Puttenham certainly does not deserve to be classed with "the greatest rhetoricians" of his time; nor does he deserve either to be hailed as one of the best critical minds or best poetic theorists of the period of Sidney, Harington, and Ben Jonson. His *Arte of English Poesie* has as its main subject what Harington, without specific reference to Puttenham, called "The other part of Poetrie, which is Verse, as it were the clothing or ornament of it." [92] And Harington, while conceding that verse "hath many good uses," and that Puttenham's treatment of it has the merit of giving new terminology to the figures of rhetoric,[93] is obviously more interested himself in "that principall part of Poetrie, which is fiction and imitation." [94] Thus Puttenham is open to the charge that his *Arte of English Poesie,* in Harington's eyes at least, treats the externals rather than the inner realities of his subject, and that same charge would have been endorsed by Francis Bacon. Bacon, it will be remembered, said of the word *poesy*

[90] *Ibid.,* p. 67.   [91] *Ibid.,* p. 86.   [92] Harington in Smith, p. 206.
[93] *Ibid.,* p. 196.   [94] *Ibid.,* p. 204.

that "it is taken in two senses, in respect of words or matter"; [95] and when he added that, "In the first sense it is but
a character of style, and belongeth to arts of speech, and is
not pertinent for the present," he indicated most plainly that
he did not consider poetry in its stylistic aspect alone to be
of the highest significance. In fact, it is only when poetry is
considered in respect to its matter, that is, in respect to its
character as feigned history, that it receives explicit recognition by Bacon as "one of the principal branches of learning." [96]

My own conviction is that, if rhetoric is to regain its true
place in Renaissance criticism, it must be recognized, not
only in its stylistic aspects, but in its full range; and it must
in the latter capacity be treated as the theory of that branch
of nonfictional writing or speaking which is addressed to the
general public and which performs such functions as exposition and persuasion, enlightenment and exhortation, education and conviction. At the same time, logical theory, as
presented by Thomas Wilson and the British Ramists, must
be recognized as the theory of that branch of nonfictional
writing or speaking which is addressed to the world of learning, as scholars, philosophers, and scientists speak to each
other and seek to advance learning by disputation, controversy, argument, and exposition. As for poetics, it cannot be
made to coincide with the theory of rhetorical style, although
the poem and the oration and the disputation all have stylistic interests in common. Renaissance poetics must be treated
as the proper term for fictional literature of all kinds, whether
in prose or verse. And if the figures of thought and speech
are studied in respect to their function within fictional literature, they must be treated as having a double purpose, one
of which concerns their bearing upon the audience within
the writer's plot, and the other, their bearing upon the writer's

[95] *Works of Bacon*, VI, 202.   [96] *Ibid.*, VIII, 439.

own audience on the outside of his story. These are some of the considerations which will make truly fruitful and productive the continuing endeavor of twentieth-century literary scholarship to come to terms with Renaissance criticism.

CHAPTER 3

Oratory and Poetry in Fénelon's Literary Theory

1

Fénelon is believed to have written his famous *Dialogues on Eloquence* in the year 1679.[1] At that time he was twenty-eight years old, and his career as priest of the parish of Saint-Sulpice in Paris had just been terminated by his appointment as Superior of the "New Catholics," an institution designed to strengthen the orthodoxy of young women newly converted from Protestantism to Catholicism. Thirty-five years later, his life almost at an end, he composed his *Letter to M. Dacier, Permanent Secretary of the French Academy, on the Occupations of the Academy*. Between those two epochs in his literary career, he distinguished himself in various ways: he served for ten years as preceptor of Louis XIV's grandson, heir presumptive of the throne of France; he became a member of the French Academy and wrote his best-known work, *The Adventures of Telemachus;* he was named Archbishop of Cambrai; and he identified himself with the doctrine of Quietism as advocated by Madame Guyon. This doctrine, with its emphasis upon the annihilation of self and the passivity of the soul as the conditions necessary to achieve

[1] C. Revillout, "Un problème de chronologie littéraire et philologique: date présumable des 'dialogues' de Fénelon 'sur l'éloquence.'" *Revue des Langues Romanes*, XXXIII (1889), 5–30, 194–216. See also E. Carcassonne, *Etat présent des travaux sur Fénelon* (Paris, 1939), p. 109.

a mystical union between man and God, cast a shadow across the last two decades of Fénelon's life. His support of Madame Guyon when she fell from favor at court led to the termination of his productive friendship with the great preacher Bossuet, and caused such other misfortunes as his dismissal from his preceptorship in the royal household and the condemnation of one of his works by Pope Innocent XII. These events occurred during the last three or four years of the seventeenth century. Thereafter Fénelon lived at Cambrai and devoted himself to his duties as Archbishop and his pursuits as writer.

His *Letter to the Academy* was first published at Paris in 1716, the year after his death, and it achieved immediate recognition in intellectual circles. At Amsterdam in 1717 it was printed in company with the *Dialogues on Eloquence,* which up to that moment had lain in manuscript.[2] Upon these two works Fénelon's reputation in the field of aesthetics and rhetorical theory pretty largely depends.[3] At no place in the whole body of his writings is oratory analyzed with the care and brilliance that he bestows upon it in the *Dialogues,* where he also has things to say about historical and philosophical composition, poetry, music, dancing, painting, and architecture. The *Letter to the Academy* is concerned with much the same subject matter. It begins by recommending that the Academy complete its dictionary of the French language. It then proposes a grammar and a rhetoric as projects of immediate concern. Next it furnishes a detailed plan for treatises on poetics, tragedy, comedy, and historical writing. It concludes with a contribution to the controversy between ancients and moderns, and with an indication that

[2] A. Cherel, *Fénelon au XVIIIe Siècle en France (1715–1820)* (Paris, 1917), p. 269.
[3] For an enumeration of other works by Fénelon on these subjects, see Carcassonne, pp. 73–74.

Fénelon had not lost his earlier preference for Greek architecture as against Gothic.

The *Letter to the Academy* has received more praise than have the *Dialogues,* no doubt because the predominance of aesthetic interests in the former turned out to be more congenial to subsequent taste than did the predominance of rhetorical interests in the latter. But it should be emphasized that Fénelon himself did not in either of these works take the part of the aesthetic interests against the rhetorical. He makes no invidious assumptions about the superiority of poetry to oratory. Nor does he give more care to one than to the other, as if they were of unequal value and deserved unequal kinds of intellectual effort from the theorist who chose to write upon both. He does not see them as so disparate in quality that oratory has to be patronized for claiming a persuasive function and a concern for a practical method, whereas poetry has to be exalted for its capacity to give delight by means veiled in the higher mysteries of genius. He does not account for the differences between the oration and the poem by postulating that they stand in relation to each other in the kingdom of letters as commoner stands to aristocrat in the monarchy of the Bourbons. The fact is, Fénelon sees oratory and poetry as instruments of similar value in human affairs. But he is aware that there are differences between them, and he devotes productive attention to the formulation of these differences.

In this chapter I should like to state what Fénelon's conception of these differences is. I shall not attempt to handle my subject in terms of everything Fénelon had to say upon all matters pertaining to critical and aesthetic theory. My discussion instead will be limited to his analysis of oratory and poetry in the *Dialogues* and the *Letter to the Academy.*[4]

---

[4] For other studies bearing upon Fénelon's theory of aesthetics, criticism, and rhetoric, see F. Brun, *Fénelon, critique d'art* (Meulan, 1899);

These two works, as I have already indicated, represent in concentrated form the essential principles of this aspect of his thinking. This aspect is worthy of attention for three reasons. First, it illustrates a specific application of the views of Plato, Cicero, and St. Augustine to the problems of the seventeenth century. Secondly, it raises issues similar to those involved in the modern question of the relations between propaganda and art. Thirdly, it indicates the frustrations that attend even the most promising distinctions between the rhetorical and the poetic branches of literature.

2

The basic principle in Fénelon's conception of the relations between oratory and poetry is that these two arts, in common with all the others, are persuasive in function. By this he means that the various arts cannot be logically grouped to one side or the other of a dividing line between that which gives pleasure and that which influences thought and action. His belief is that, if there seems to be a class of artistic works devoted wholly to the giving of pleasure, the critic should deal with it, not as something fundamentally unpersuasive, but as a case of concealed persuasion. He insists, in short, that all works of art act to influence the conduct of mankind, pleasure being an intermediate aim, a way station on the road to ultimate persuasiveness.

This view is applied to oratory early in the *Dialogues on Eloquence*. One of the spokesmen, who is called *A*, and whose importance suggests that he expresses Fénelon's own ideas, demands of another spokesman, *B*, the definition of eloquence. *B* replies that eloquence is the art of speaking well. *A* wonders whether men speak simply to speak well,

---

P. Bastier, *Fénelon: Critique d'art* (Paris, 1903); G. Landolf, *Esthétique de Fénelon* (Zurich, 1914); E. B. O. Borgerhoff, *The Freedom of French Classicism* (Princeton, 1950), pp. 220–234.

whether talk has no design except that of achieving the status of refinement. This observation leads *B* to declare that men speak in order to please and in order to persuade. Thus are two rival aims of oratory brought into focus, the former being no doubt intended by Fénelon to represent the prevailing conception of rhetoric as derived from the teachings of Peter Ramus,[5] while the latter is the conception of Fénelon himself. What *A* says in reply to *B* is not only a denial that these two aims were in any final sense mutually exclusive, but also a fresh approach to the pleasure-persuasion dichotomy in artistic theory. *A* remarks at once that a careful distinction should be made between "to please" and "to persuade." Then he states how orators proceed in practice:

They speak to persuade—that is what they always do. They also speak to please—that is merely what they too often do. But when they seek to please, they have another, a more distant, aim, which is nevertheless the principal one. The good man seeks to please only that he may urge justice and the other virtues by making them attractive. He who seeks his own interest, his reputation, his fortune, dreams of pleasing only that he may gain the bow and esteem of men able to satisfy his greed or his ambition. Thus, even his case can be reduced like that of the good man to persuasion as the single aim which a speaker has; for the self-interested man wishes to please in order to flatter, and he flatters in order to inculcate that which suits his interest.[6]

Later in the *Dialogues, A* reverts once more to the thesis that pleasure is an effect to be striven for only because it lies

[5] See below, section 5. The relation between Fénelon's *Dialogues on Eloquence* and the dialectical and rhetorical doctrines of Peter Ramus is discussed at some length in my *Fénelon's Dialogues on Eloquence: A Translation, with an Introduction and Notes* (Princeton, 1951). A brief summary of that relation appears in the concluding section of this chapter.

[6] *Oeuvres de Fénélon* [ed. J. -E. -A. Gosselin and A. -P. -P. Caron] (Versailles and Paris, 1820–1830), XXI, 9. All quotations from the *Dialogues on Eloquence* and the *Letter to the Academy* in this chapter are referred to this edition, the translations being by the present author.

athwart the road to persuasion. He demands of *C*, Fénelon's
third character, whether anything in a discourse can have any
function except that of influencing the hearer. *C* replies that
certain things in discourse will contribute to the hearer's
pleasure. *A* observes:

Let us distinguish, if you will. That which serves to please in order to persuade is good. Solid and well-expounded proofs are un-
questionably pleasing; the lively and natural movements of the
speaker have much charm; faithful and animated portraitures en-
chant. Thus the three things which we make essential to eloquence give pleasure; but they are not limited to this effect. It
is a question of knowing whether we shall approve of thoughts
and expressions which have no purpose but to please, and which
cannot in any way have a more substantial purpose. These I call
conceits. Of course, you are always to keep well in mind, if you
will, that I praise in discourse all the pleasing traits which minister to persuasion; and that I reject only those wherein the author, full of self-admiration, has sought to exhibit himself and
to amuse the listeners with his wit, rather than to absorb them
utterly in his subject.[7]

Oratory in Fénelon's scheme is not the only art that has
persuasion as its principal function and pleasure as an intermediate effect. He puts poetry and the other fine arts in the
same class. In the *Dialogues C* observes: "But if true orators
are poets, it seems to me that poets are also orators, because
poetry is by rights persuasive." And *A* replies: "Unquestion-
ably they both have the same end." [8] These statements are
made in connection with Fénelon's attempt to differentiate
poetry from oratory, and later we shall see what that differentiation amounts to. Just now, however, we need perhaps

[7] *Ibid.*, p. 50. Lines 26–27 read, "je ne rejette que celles où l'ora-
teur. . . ." The first Paris edition of the *Dialogues* (Paris, 1718), p. 102,
lines 13–14, reads, however, "je ne rejette que celles où l'Auteur. . . ."
At this particular point the translation follows the first Paris edition,
which is ordinarily regarded as the most authoritative of the texts of
the *Dialogues*.

[8] *Ibid.*, p. 49.

only to notice that, whatever differences he has in mind, he insists at least upon the complete identity of these two arts in respect to persuasiveness. In the *Letter to the Academy* he attributes the same function to the other fine arts, emphasizing again that pleasure is an auxiliary effect:

Plato does not permit in his republic any music with the effeminate pitch of the Lydian style. The Lacedaemonians excluded from their republic all the highly complicated instruments which were able to weaken the spirit. Harmony which goes only so far as to flatter the ear is merely an amusement of weak and idle folk. It is unworthy of a well-governed republic. It is good only so far as the sounds of it agree with the sense of the words, and the words of it inspire virtuous sentiments. Painting, sculpture, and the other fine arts, ought to have the same end. Without question eloquence ought to enter into the same design. Pleasure ought to be mingled in it only to form a counterbalance against evil passions and to make virtue attractive.[9]

The words just quoted echo a passage in the *Dialogues* upon the subservience of pleasure to persuasiveness in ancient art. In the course of a panegyric upon the serious intent of the art of the early Greeks and Hebrews, *A* remarks:

All the arts which consist in melodious sounds, or in movements of the body, or in the use of language—in a word, music, dancing, eloquence, poetry—were devised only to express the passions and to inspire them in the very act of expressing them. By such means as these, mankind wished to impress great thoughts upon the human soul and to bring to men lively and striking pictures of the beauty of virtue and the ugliness of evil. Thus all these arts appeared to be for pleasure, but were in reality among the ancients a part of their deepest striving for morality and religion.[10]

Thus does Fénelon admit pleasure and persuasion into artistic theory without making these effects mutually exclusive or using them as keys to the difference between the fine and

[9] *Ibid.*, pp. 176–177.   [10] *Ibid.*, p. 18.

the practical arts. He recognizes, however, that throughout the entire domain of art, practical as well as fine, pleasure may receive more emphasis than persuasion, even though when this happens the effect must still be counted persuasive in the final analysis. In fact, one of his critical principles is that pathologies in the world of art appear as the product of a persuasive intention which is limited on the one hand to the promotion of the artist's personal fortunes and on the other to the excessive exploitation of the spectator's fondness for pleasure. This principle receives some development in the *Dialogues* and the *Letter to the Academy*. I should like to examine it now in order to show that it underlies Fénelon's distinction between health and disease in art rather than his distinction between the poetical and the rhetorical branches of literature.

3

Interpreted in the broadest sense, Fénelon's view of good and bad art, whether oratorical or poetic, stresses the concern of the artist for the interests of mankind as opposed to the interests of himself. If someone were to object that this principle belongs more to the realm of morality than to aesthetics, Fénelon would doubtless answer by denying the desirability or possibility of separating these two realms. Indeed, this phase of his critical thinking derives special support from the theological doctrine of Quietism, which, as I indicated earlier, strives for the annihilation of self as one condition of spiritual perfection. Good art in Fénelon's sense of the term is that which inspires men in the quest for wisdom, good laws, justice, and individual betterment, whereas bad art inspires men to favor their flatterers, to follow their private inclinations, to give rewards on the basis of something less than merit, or to seek personal power, wealth, reputation, at no matter what expense. It is in this latter kind of art where pleasure tends to be the most visible of the possible effects, seeming at times to be the artist's only aim, and at other times to be the aim which but partly masks his desire for personal advancement.

Many passages in the *Dialogues* and the *Letter to the Academy* illustrate this principle. For example, when *A* is mentioning the degeneracy which followed the period of Athenian rule in ancient Greece, he characterizes it as one wherein "pleasure, which ought only to be the means to inculcate wisdom, usurped the place of wisdom herself." [11] Thus is the concept of social decadence linked with the concept of art as mere diversion. The same spokesman had earlier borrowed the Socratic manner and the Platonic doctrine to get *B* to consent to banish from the ideal republic "any of the sciences or any of the arts which serve only for pleasure, for amusement, and for curiosity." [12] And why are they to be banished? Because, as *B* finally concedes, they are not merely indifferent to the struggle between good and evil, but actually are on the side of evil. His words are:

If anything can assist the cause of virtue, the identification of virtue with pleasure can do so. On the contrary, when you separate them, you strongly invite men to abandon virtue. Besides, everything that pleases without instructing beguiles and softens merely.[13]

But the principle is not developed only in terms of abstract moral precepts. It is made highly concrete in its application to oratory. *A's* unfavorable opinion of Isocrates, a recurrent theme of the *Dialogues,* shows that orator to typify an art devoted, not to national ends, but to self-exhibition, with ostentatious ornaments the artist's means, and amusement his principal, almost his only, goal.[14] Again, a concern for his own fortune, as distinguished from the fate of the

[11] *Ibid.,* p. 19.   [12] *Ibid.,* p. 16.   [13] *Ibid.,* pp. 19–20.
[14] *Ibid.,* pp. 10–13, 74–76.

Roman republic, is alleged by the same spokesman to be a visible blemish in the works of the youthful Cicero.[15] *A* also remarks that a selfish concern vitiates Pliny's eulogy of Trajan.[16] And in the course of constructing his own theory of oratory, he lays great stress upon the necessity for complete disinterestedness on the part of a speaker both as a matter of good morality and good oratorical strategy.[17]

The issue of preoccupation with self as opposed to preoccupation with the interests of mankind has the same application to poetry as to oratory. *A* cites the *Aeneid* as being open to the charge, if one cared to press it, of showing somewhat more interest in flattering Augustus and his family, and thus in advancing Virgil's own fortune, than in giving the Roman people an unmixed image of their national destiny.[18] This charge against Virgil *A* does not regard seriously. On the contrary, he emphasizes in the same breath that the *Aeneid* is an example of high poetic excellence. But the charge, as a possible line of attack upon Virgil, embodies a precise principle by which criticism may separate good poetry from bad, and that principle is given a general formulation by Fénelon himself in the following words from the *Letter to the Academy:*

Just in the same degree as one ought to despise bad poets, so ought one to admire and cherish a great poet, who does not make poetry into a play of wit to attract unto himself a vainglory, but uses it to transport men in favor of wisdom, virtue, and religion.[19]

Fénelon's distinction between good and bad art rests upon the teachings of Plato and St. Augustine. He leaves no doubt upon this score, not only because he probably thought it simple honesty to acknowledge his philosophic debts, but also

---

[15] *Ibid.,* pp. 45–46.   [16] *Ibid.,* p. 25.   [17] *Ibid.,* pp. 27–41.
[18] *Ibid.,* p. 26.   [19] *Ibid.,* p. 186.

perhaps to suggest that his theory cut across the boundaries between paganism and Christianity, and thus could not be called merely parochial. At any rate, he has *A* emphasize that one does not have to be a Christian to believe in the self-forgetfulness of the artist as the precondition of great art, inasmuch as Socrates and Plato had taken the same position.[20] *A* documents this statement with a lengthy analysis of Plato's *Gorgias* and a shorter reference to the *Phaedrus*.[21] As for St. Augustine, who figures preponderantly in the Third Dialogue by virtue of his authority in the field of sacred rhetoric, he too is used to support Fénelon's view that the aesthetic stature of a work of art is determined by the stature of its selflessness of purpose. In a passage in the First Dialogue made up of borrowings from two separate chapters of St. Augustine's *De Doctrina Christiana, A* declares:

For what do a man's beautiful speeches serve, if fine as they are they contribute no benefit whatever to the public? Words are made for men, as St. Augustine says, and not men for words.[22]

4

Thus far we have seen that Fénelon does not use the distinction between pleasure and persuasiveness as a means of separating poetry from oratory. He uses it instead to show that there is a kind of bad art devoted seemingly to pleasure but actually to the inculcation of attitudes which suit the artist's material interests. He sees poetry and oratory as alike persuasive in their healthy forms. He sees pleasure as normally common to both in the sense that this effect accompanies persuasion. He sees good oratory and good poetry as kinds of discourse which contribute primarily, and in the first instance, to the public benefit. What, then, is his dis-

---

[20] *Ibid.*, p. 30.   [21] *Ibid.*, pp. 30–37.
[22] *Ibid.*, p. 23. See *De Doctrina Christiana*, 4. 10. 24, and 4. 28. 61.

tinction between the rhetorical and the poetic branches of literature?

His answer to this question is that oratory is almost poetry. This is the simplest way to state his distinction. This is also the way he himself follows when he comes in the *Dialogues* to the problem of maintaining on the one hand that poetry as well as oratory is persuasive and on the other that the well-established habit of thinking these two arts to be somehow different must receive attention in criticism. Let us hear what he says on this matter.

The conversation in the Second Dialogue has paused upon the question of the difference between the genuine and the false ornament of style. *A* has been insisting that persuasion is the end of oratory, and that oratory deserves to be called eloquence only when it really succeeds in persuading men to virtue. Now persuasion, *A* explains, requires that discourse prove something and excite strong feelings toward what it proves.[23] To prove, he goes on, is to convince the auditor that a proposition is true. The method by which this is done is characterized by exactness, dryness, bareness; by an adherence to the forms of good argument; by a sense of order similar to that followed in geometry; and by a speculativeness similar to that found in metaphysics.[24] To excite strong feelings is to be forced to do two things beyond proof: to portray and to strike. "To portray is not only to describe things," remarks *A*, "but to represent their surrounding features in so lively and so concrete a way that the listener imagines himself almost seeing them." [25] The term "to strike" is defined later, after *A* has identified it with "movement" as distinguished from "proof" and "portraiture." [26] "Movement" turns out to be not only the stylistic variation of the speech,

[23] *Ibid.*, pp. 42, 44, 47.   [24] *Ibid.*, pp. 43–44.   [25] *Ibid.*, p. 47.
[26] *Ibid.*, p. 50.

as the speaker's linguistic patterns move in accordance with his inner patterns of thought and emotion, but also the physical swing of speaking, as the speaker's voice and body respond to his mind and will.[27]

Of these three elements in persuasive discourse or eloquence, portraiture is of central importance in persuasion; and it is thus a common feature of the oration and the poem. *A* sees a difference in degree, however, between the portraiture produced by the orator and that produced by the poet. Upon this difference in degree he founds his distinction between the two arts. To illustrate portraiture at its best, he points to Virgil's account of the death of Dido. Then he says:

I have given you an example drawn from a poet, in order to make you better understand the matter; for portraiture is still more lively and stronger among the poets than among the orators. Poetry differs from simple eloquence only in this: that she paints with ecstasy and with bolder strokes. Prose has its paintings, albeit more moderated. Without them one cannot heat the imagination of a listener or arouse his passions.[28]

Versification, *A* proceeds at once to remark, has nothing to do with the question of distinguishing the poetical from the nonpoetical discourse. In either form, genuine effectiveness is the product of portraiture. "If one does not have this genius to portray," insists Fénelon's chief spokesman, "never can one impress things upon the soul of the listener—all is dry, flat, boring." [29] A moment later the whole matter is summed up in this exchange between *A* and *C*:

A: The entire difference [between oratory and poetry] consists in that which I have set forth to you. Over and above orators, poets have ecstasy, and this makes them still more elevated, more lively, and more daring in their utterances. You well remember what I told you yesterday from Cicero?
C: What! Is it . . . ?

[27] *Ibid.,* pp. 51–61.   [28] *Ibid.,* p. 48.   [29] *Ibid.,* p. 49.

A: That the orator ought almost to have the diction of the poet. That "almost" tells the whole story.[30]

Thus poetry and oratory in Fénelon's basic view turn out to have persuasion as their end and portraiture as a common means, the distinction between them being that portraiture in poetry has about it an ecstasy, a heat of genius, not found in oratory. In short, as I suggested before, oratory is almost but not quite poetry. Fénelon himself points out in the passage last quoted that the "almost" comes from Cicero. To be more precise, it comes from *De Oratore,* 1. 28. 128, where oratory, comprehensively defined, is said to demand not only a dialectician's acuteness, a philosopher's knowledge, a lawyer's memory, a tragedian's voice, and an accomplished actor's gesture, but also a diction almost that of the poet.

We might in passing note the relations established by Fénelon among the other traditional kinds of discourse. He strongly intimates that philosophical discourse or learned writing in the field of the scientific disciplines differs from oratory as proof isolated from portraiture and movement differs from proof combined with these things.[31] He also says in effect that historical writing differs from poetry as a moderated and impartial portrait of events and personalities differs from a bolder, more inspired, portrait.[32] But it is only against the background of his concept of eloquence that these distinctions have their full meaning. According to that concept, any discourse which actually succeeds in improving men deserves alone to be called eloquent; and no discourse can have that effect without portraiture. Hence poetry, which is in essence inspired portraiture, becomes eloquent when it acts to make men more perfect. Hence history, which is moderated and impartial portraiture, becomes eloquent when it pro-

[30] *Ibid.,* pp. 49–50.   [31] *Ibid.,* pp. 43–46.
[32] *Ibid.,* pp. 47–48, 228–229, 232–233.

duces the selfsame result. Hence oratory, which combines proof and movement with a portraiture almost poetic, becomes eloquent when it achieves no different goal. Of the four conventional types of discourse, only philosophy, which has no concern with image-making as a necessity of its own style, fails to achieve the full stature of eloquence. But its emphasis upon conviction as effect and proof as means gives it a primary concern for truth; and thus, when it succeeds in presenting things as they are, it induces knowledge, which is not least among the preconditions of virtue.

5

Three aspects of Fénelon's theory of the relations between oratory and poetry call for attention by way of conclusion.

First of all, his insistence upon the persuasiveness of oratory is in line not only with the best classical and modern emphasis but also with the tendency of the late seventeenth century to abandon the rhetorical teachings of Peter Ramus. At the time when Fénelon wrote the *Dialogues on Eloquence,* the influence of Ramus upon logical and rhetorical theory in France (and in England) was still pronounced, despite the fact that Ramus had died as long before as 1572. One of Ramus's key doctrines was that one art could not claim any function or subject matter belonging to another art. Accordingly, if logic professed to offer to writers and speakers the theory of invention and arrangement, and thus to provide the means of convincing audiences, rhetoric must abandon these subjects and confine itself to other aspects of composition. As a consequence of this doctrine, Ramus's colleague, Talaeus, created a rhetoric limited to style and delivery, and copiously elaborated in terms of all the figures of speech and all the ornamental contrivances of style. This sort of rhetoric, with its emphasis upon antithesis, paradox, word-play, conceit, and epigram, came to have the reputation of being exclusively devoted to amusement. Against the theory that men spoke only to give pleasure, and that they used as means only the conceits of style, Fénelon leveled his heaviest guns. To some extent he also leveled his guns against Ramus's theory that a work on rhetoric could include nothing pertaining to logic or the other liberal arts, although Fénelon's contemporary, Antoine Arnauld, had effectively attacked this aspect of Ramus's doctrine in the famous *Port Royal Logic,* published seventeen years before Fénelon wrote the *Dialogues.* In Fénelon's emphasis that oratory is primarily an instrument of persuasion, and that the orator is an honored partner of the logician and the historian in the enterprise of learning and communication, we see a wholesome restoration of Ciceronian doctrine as well as an imaginative anticipation of modern interests.

The same reminiscence of a classical attitude, the same foretaste of a modern conviction, is visible in a second aspect of Fénelon's theory of the relations between oratory and poetry. This aspect emerges in his insistence that delight is the intermediate and contributory, persuasiveness the ultimate, object of both of these arts. So far as poetical theory is concerned, Fénelon is here suggesting the impossibility of divorcing expression from communication or aesthetics from rhetoric and logic. He is assuming instead that man's response to a work of art springs from a complex of adjustments, some of which are aesthetic, others, intellectual. He sees no point in treating such a response as if one could unerringly separate its pleasurable from its intellectual phases. No doubt he felt that knowledge of either phase by itself would not be the same as knowledge of both phases in all their complicated interactions. At any rate, at one point in the *Dialogues* he has *C* observe: "As for myself, I wish to know whether things are true before I find them beautiful." [33] If this statement seems to give priority to logic above aesthetics in an act of literary evaluation, Fénelon might have explained his real intention by saying that, in an age which gave the latter more emphasis than the former, counterexaggeration was the approved way to restore the balance between the two.

The third aspect of Fénelon's distinction between oratory and poetry involves a complication which I did not mention earlier for fear of emphasizing it more than our author does. This complication appears both before and after the passages in which he says that poetry differs from oratory only in the superior vividness of its portraiture. There is no doubt that he is convinced of the validity of this major difference; but he seems to realize that it does not completely exhaust the subject. Thus he introduces two terms which suggest that poetical and oratorical portraiture differ not so much in degree as in kind. These two terms are *imitation* and *fiction*. In the *Dialogues,* as *A* is comparing a historian's portrait of the death of Dido with that in the *Aeneid,* he says of the latter: "There one sees the power of imitation and of portraiture." [34] Later, after he has dismissed versification from the list of qualities that poetry must have, *A* remarks: "In the last analysis, poetry is nothing but a lively fiction which portrays nature." [35] In the *Letter to the Academy,* speaking in his own person, Fénelon declares: "Poetry is without doubt an imitation and a portraiture." [36] These passages make it clear that, although Fénelon is insisting upon portraiture as an element in poetry, he half doubts whether oratorical and poetic portraiture differ only in degree, and in his hesitancy he resorts to the terms *imitation* and *fiction,* perhaps to satisfy his subconscious realization that poetry, at least in its epic, dramatic, and narrative forms, portrays situations dif-

[33] *Ibid.,* p. 7.   [34] *Ibid.,* p. 48.   [35] *Ibid.,* p. 49.
[36] *Ibid.,* p. 198.

ferent from those handled in oratory and history. Had he gone on to show that portraiture in poetry is usually the lifelike representation of an imagined situation, whereas portraiture in oratory and history is usually the lifelike representation of a real situation, he would have been able to preserve his emphasis upon portraiture as an essential characteristic of these three literary forms, and at the same time to preserve his emphasis upon fiction and imitation as the distinguishing conditions of portraiture in poetry.

Without some recognition of the difference between actual and imagined situations, it is hard to see how Fénelon's account of the difference between oratory and poetry can explain distinctions taken for granted by the literary critic on the one hand and the rhetorical and historical critic on the other. The literary critic, speaking of portraiture in a play, a novel, or a narrative poem, uses as a matter of course the machinery of oppositions between the romantic and realistic, the naturalistic and symbolic, the allegorical and nonallegorical, the classical and Gothic, to indicate changing fashions in poetic portraiture. The theory that oratory and history differ from poetry only as the moderated portrait differs from the inspired appears to suggest that the same machinery and the same fashions apply to rhetorical and historical criticism. But do they? Except in a pejorative sense, is there a romantic as opposed to a realistic oratory or history? Is there a school of symbolist and another school of naturalist orators and historians? Hardly. And this answer suggests that some concepts applicable to poetry are not applicable to oratory and history, despite Fénelon's apparent indication to the contrary in the basic phase of his distinction between the oration and the poem.

CHAPTER 4

Renaissance Rhetoric and Modern Rhetoric: A Study in Change [1]

1

The Renaissance is a most convenient period with which to begin a discussion of the modern concept of rhetoric. That period, which may be roughly dated from 1450 to 1700, witnessed the last years of medieval civilization in Western Europe and the first years of modern civilization. Thus if we take our stand in the early Renaissance and examine the theory of communication which prevailed at that time, we are face to face with arrangements that counted almost two thousand years of history behind them and had changed only in detail in that double millennium. At the same time, as we look around in the Renaissance, we begin to see that things are changing in the theory of communication as in politics and theology and science, and that those changes have a familiar look, as if they would not be out of place among the similar arrangements of our twentieth-century world. In other words, the Renaissance is the one point in the history of Western Europe where the communication theory of ancient Greece and Rome and that of modern Europe and America are ranged side by side, the older one still alive but losing ground, the younger one still immature but growing.

[1] This chapter represents a further development of ideas outlined in my *Logic and Rhetoric in England, 1500–1700,* and it foreshadows the major argument of Chapter 6 of my *Eighteenth-Century British Logic and Rhetoric.*

What better place could be found for the beginnings of a study of what rhetoric has lost and gained in the transition from medieval to modern times?

During the Renaissance, the theory of communication, exclusive of its poetical dimension, was made up of grammar, rhetoric, and dialectic or logic. These three liberal disciplines, which had been the trivium or lower group of liberal arts in the medieval universities, assumed most of the responsibility for training Renaissance students to speak and write. Latin was the language which those students were asked in grammar school and university to master as the universal basis for all kinds of communication, although as the seventeenth century drew to a close the emphasis upon vernacular languages became more and more pronounced.[2] That the trivium was actually regarded in the Renaissance as a group of studies expressly dedicated to the theory of communication is shown in Francis Bacon's great treatise, the *Advancement of Learning,* where Bacon, speaking of "the fourth kind of Rational Knowledge," proceeds not only to describe this knowledge as "transitive, concerning the expressing or transferring our knowledge to others," but also to term it "by the general name of Tradition or Delivery" and later to analyze it as made up in large part of grammar, logic, and rhetoric.[3]

---

[2] In 1660 Charles Hoole, a writer on education, reflected the classical orientation of the grammar school education of his century when he said that *"speaking Latine is the main end of Grammar."* See "The Usher's Duty," in his *A New Discovery of the Old Art of Teaching Schoole,* ed. E. T. Campagnac (London, 1913), p. 50. The italics are Hoole's. Some years later an educational reformer named John Newton in the Dedicatory Epistle and Preface to his *Introduction to the Art of Logick* (London, 1678) reflected the newer tendencies of the century in asserting that young people should be taught all the sciences in their own tongue and that Latin should be reserved only for those who wished to enter a learned profession.

[3] *Works of Bacon,* VI, 282–303.

Bacon's discussion of these three basic liberal arts as three branches of the great science of transmitting knowledge from man to man, from place to place, and from age to age involves a more rational plan, a more fully developed overview, than one finds in the usual Renaissance treatise on education. But this does not mean that Bacon's ideas on the trivium were different from those of his time. On the contrary, although the precise content of any one member of the trivium was defined in different ways by different schools of thought during the Renaissance, Bacon's *Advancement of Learning* is in harmony with his era in treating the three liberal arts as offshoots of the theory of delivery or communication.[4] In all sectors of Renaissance opinion grammar was regarded as the study of the medium of communication, whether the medium was Latin for learned discourse or English for popular address. Similarly, dialectic or logic was for the most part regarded as the study of the means and methods of reaching the learned audience, whether in scholastic Latin sermons, lectures, and disputations, or in vernacular treatises like the *Advancement of Learning* itself. As for rhetoric, most segments of Renaissance opinion accepted it as the study of some or all of the means of making a discourse palatable and persuasive to the popular audience.

To be sure, the Ramists, whose system of dialectic and rhetoric became very popular in England between 1574 and 1620, did not divide dialectic from rhetoric by orienting the one predominantly toward the learned audience and the other predominantly toward the people.[5] But even they, in making rhetoric consist exclusively of style and delivery while dialectic assumed absolute control over invention and arrangement, tended in fact to relegate rhetoric to those crafts which popular discourse needs in more generous measure than does learned discourse. And it should be observed

[4] See my *Logic and Rhetoric in England,* chs. 2–5.   [5] *Ibid.,* ch. 4.

that dialectic and rhetoric were parts of the theory of communication in Ramus's scheme, as in the medieval synthesis, although Ramus explained the relation of these parts to each other in a different way from that used by scholastic logic or Ciceronian rhetoric.

Five changes in the ancient theory of communication began to appear during the Renaissance, and by and large these changes help to explain why modern rhetoric is as it is. I should like to mention these changes here and to indicate what seems to explain them. Then I should like to suggest some of the benefits or disadvantages they have brought to the modern academic study of communication.

2

Perhaps the most significant change that has come over the theory of communication during the last four hundred years is that logic has dissolved its alliance with the communication arts and has aligned itself instead with the theory of scientific investigation. Descartes in his famous *Discours de la méthode* indicated the need for a logic of inquiry to replace the older logic of communication.[6] By and large, his summons proved to be prophetic. Logic has become the interpreter of scientific and philosophical method, whereas it had been the interpreter of the method of transmitting knowledge from expert to expert. In an academic sense, this means that logic has affiliated itself with the department of philosophy and has ceased to have any primary connection with the department of rhetoric. Of course, certain fragments of logic have continued to appear regularly in all treatises devoted by rhetoricians to argumentation and persuasion; but those fragments, which usually concern the forms of reasoning and fallacies, have not represented the

[6] René Descartes, *Discours de la méthode,* ed. Etienne Gilson (Paris, 1935), pp. 62–63.

full emphasis of the new logic and usually, indeed, have been conspicuous for their perfunctory character, their lack of originality, and their seeming dedication to the appearances rather than the essentials of the tradition they reflect. Meanwhile, logic has studied the sciences and mathematics, has formulated the canons of induction, has denied the priority of the syllogism, and has sought politely to disavow those who wanted to use the study of logic as a practical means of making themselves logical writers and speakers.

There can be little doubt that, since the Renaissance, the major intellectual energies in Western Europe have been devoted to the discovery of new truth, and the greatest reputations in the world of learning have been made by the scientists. At the same time, emphasis upon the communication of new truths across the barriers between persons, specialties, nations, language groups, and generations has been a diminishing study within the universities, although not a diminishing need in the practical world. Thus logic shifted its allegiance from communication to inquiry at an advantageous time. Higher academic rewards lay in the direction of an association with science, while communication could offer its academic devotees little more than a servant's wage. It may seem strange that rhetoric, contemptuously associated with the arts of promotion and self-aggrandizement, should have remained loyal to the unpopular and unprosperous cause of communication, while logic, the aristocratic disdainer of profitable enterprises, should have chosen to go where the academic profits were greatest. But so it was, at least within English and American universities of the late nineteenth and early twentieth centuries.

I do not mean to argue seriously that a shrewd self-interest was the real motive behind the attachment of logic to science. Instead, the attachment was a natural consequence of man's success in studying his physical environment. It has

been more important since the Renaissance to devote oneself
to the search for new knowledge than to the exposition of
that knowledge to others, and logic has accepted this value
as its guide. A few modern authors like Whately and Bain
have continued to write on both logic and rhetoric after the
example of Aristotle, Cicero, Thomas Wilson, Ramus, and
others. But in the main the two disciplines have parted company, and the logicians have outclassed the rhetoricians in
the eyes of the learned community, the favorable verdict for
logic being decisive if not always founded upon an impartial
examination of the evidence on both sides.

The renunciation by logic of its alliance with the theory of
communication has been a serious blow to modern rhetoric.
As I mentioned a moment ago, it has led to an obvious and
fatal superficiality whenever rhetoricians have affixed to their
own works an abbreviated version of traditional logical theory. It has also led to a counterrenunciation of logic by
rhetoric, as in the elocutionary movement of the nineteenth
century, where rhetoric became completely absorbed in delivery, not in the Baconian sense of the full act of communication but as the vocal and physical components of that act.
Perhaps as philosophers and rhetoricians develop their present interest in semantics, a way will be found to create a
new logic for the process of communication and to bring
logic and rhetoric together in a more significant companion-
ship than any they have enjoyed since the days of Thomas
Wilson. Until this happens, however, rhetoric will be de-
tached from some of the impulses that have accounted for its
greatest past glories. When Aristotle began his *Rhetoric* by
defining his subject as the counterpart of dialectic, he meant
to ally his logical treatises, and in particular his *Topics,* with
the work he was about to write. We might say that, until
modern rhetoric helps to create a modern equivalent of Aristotelian dialectic and contributes vitally to its development,

it will continue to lack what the best ancient rhetoric had—
a sense of indissoluble kinship with the philosophical aspects
of the enterprise of communication.

3

Another significant change that has occurred in the theory
of communication since the Renaissance is that rhetoric has
attempted to expand its interests so as to become the theory
of learned discourse while remaining the theory of popular
discourse. As I indicated above, logic had jurisdiction over
the former theory in the ancient scheme as interpreted by
the Renaissance. Indeed, Renaissance logicians and rhetoricians had a favorite image to describe the relation of logic to
rhetoric, and that image associated logic with the closed fist,
rhetoric with the open hand. According to Cicero and Quintilian, this image originated with Zeno the Stoic, and if you
had asked a learned man of the Renaissance to explain it, he
probably would have given you Cicero's interpretation as set
forth in these words of the *Orator:*

> The man of perfect eloquence should, then, in my opinion
> possess not only the faculty of fluent and copious speech which
> is his proper province, but should also acquire that neighbour-
> ing borderland science of logic; although a speech is one thing
> and a debate another, and disputing is not the same as speaking,
> and yet both are concerned with discourse—debate and dispute
> are the function of the logicians; the orator's function is to speak
> ornately. Zeno, the founder of the Stoic school, used to give an
> object lesson of the difference between the two arts; clenching
> his fist he said logic was like that; relaxing and extending his
> hand, he said eloquence was like the open palm.[7]

Debate and disputation, as used in this passage, stand for
all the types of philosophical or scholastic discourses that one
finds in the world of learning; eloquence stands for the open,

---

[7] *Orator*, 113, trans. H. M. Hubbell, p. 389. See also Quintilian,
Institutio Oratoria, 2. 20. 7.

popular speech to political meetings, juries, and gatherings at public ceremonies and celebrations. As logic in the ancient scheme taught the young expert to communicate with his peers while rhetoric taught him to communicate with the populace, so in the modern scheme has rhetoric attempted to teach both functions, inasmuch as logic is no longer available for the purpose it once served.

The advantage of the ancient scheme was that it kept everybody reminded of the two worlds in which communication takes place, of the two types of discourses flowing from speaker to audience, and of the broad differences between the scholar and the popularizer. By his studies in logic and rhetoric a student would get an impression of the differences between dialectical and rhetorical invention, dialectical and rhetorical arrangement. He would also get a sense of the similarities between these procedures as dialectical and as rhetorical operations. Even the duplication between his classroom assignments in dialectic and those in rhetoric would have some value in reminding him of the essential unity of his various subjects. The same lesson studied from two points of view is often better than two lessons studied without reference to each other. And when the same lesson is studied under two teachers, one a rhetorician and the other a logician, the prestige of each increases that of the other, and the student feels a comfortable reassurance in the very fact that his teachers differ only in approach, not in aim.

Of course, when two subjects are adjusted to as narrow a distinction as that between the learned audience and the populace, there is danger that the distinction will seem relatively empty and that one of the two subjects will begin to appear nonessential. This danger was not acute in ancient Greece and Rome, where democratic political institutions and unhampered philosophical debate made rhetoric and logic necessary disciplines in the educational system. But later societies in Western Europe went through a long period of empire and monarchy, during which rhetoric and logic flourished as instruments inherited from the past, although the actual need for the functions discharged by rhetoric was not as pressing as was the need for ability in disputation and learned controversy.[8] Thus rhetoric occupied a somewhat uneasy position in the trivium during the Middle Ages, as grammar and logic were successively the dominant study.[9] It was partly to guarantee rhetoric a firmer standing in education and partly to prevent rhetoric and logic from repeating each other's doctrine that Ramus, as I said before, assigned the entire theory of invention and arrangement to logic and made rhetoric consist wholly of style and delivery. This reform tended to abandon the open emphasis upon the distinction between the learned and the popular audience and to substitute for it a more tangible means of differentiating logic and rhetoric. But neat and practical as it was, Ramism proves that rhetoric becomes a meaningless study unless it is sustained by its ancient concern for the popular audience, even as the Middle Ages show that rhetoric becomes the inferior discipline of communication in any society where the popular audience has no economic and political power.

Modern democratic society would appear to offer rhetoric a greater opportunity than it has had since ancient times; for the popular audience in a democracy is the true source of authority, and the learned community has great need for the technique of learned communication. Rhetoric has grasped that opportunity, so far as its concern for the popular audience goes. Departments of rhetoric and speech are the focus

---

[8] For a discussion of the effect of absolutism upon Roman eloquence of the early Empire, see Harry Caplan, "The Decay of Eloquence at Rome in the First Century," in *Studies in Speech and Drama in Honor of Alexander M. Drummond,* ed. Herbert A. Wichelns *et al.* (Ithaca, 1944), pp. 295–325.

[9] See Baldwin, *Medieval Rhetoric and Poetic,* p. 151.

of study of the ways and means by which the modern speaker reaches the people. But rhetoric has not made much of a show in supplying a theory of learned communication that can compare with Renaissance dialectic. Where, for example, is there an attempt in modern rhetoric to provide a common vocabulary in which the learned men in one field can communicate with the learned men in another? Renaissance dialectic fashioned such a vocabulary from the ten categories of Aristotle and from the ten places of Ramus. Perhaps those vocabularies have completely lost their power to serve modern science. Still, a study of the circle of modern learning might reveal that the barriers between one specialized knowledge and another could be broken down by the use of certain common learned concepts. It would require great scholarship to develop those concepts, and great scholarship is one of the challenges that modern rhetoric has not met. Inspiration might come from the reflection that Aristotle developed his categories from a study of the circle of learning of his time and that a similar enterprise might be undertaken today, perhaps not by one individual scholar, but certainly by an interested group of specialists. Added inspiration might also come from our modern conviction that, unless our learned men can be taught to speak to each other and to the people, we shall create on the one hand a set of Balkanized knowledges and on the other a schism between the people and the intellectual classes. That sort of schism will make the demagogue our master, even as a Balkanized learning will destroy the unity of our culture and the meaning of our spiritual life.

4

A third great change in the theory of communication since the Renaissance concerns what I have been calling invention. To people untrained in the history of rhetoric, invention means either a mechanical device for the saving of labor or the act of discovering something new. In a contemptuous view of rhetoric, invention often means a falsehood, a deceit, an irresponsible utterance, a cynical departure from the truth for purposes of fraud. But invention to the rhetorical scholar means the devising of subject matter for a particular speech and, by extension, the providing of content in discourse. Lest this definition sound as if subject matter comes only from the speaker's mind, and not from the external realities of his environment, it should be emphasized that subject matter comes from external realities as seen and interpreted by the speaker and thus is not on the one hand the result of his fancy nor on the other the mere equivalent of bare facts. Inventional theory conceived in these terms has greatly changed since the Renaissance.

Perhaps the best way to describe this change is to say that nowadays rhetoric in the quest for a theory of subject matter emphasizes external realities somewhat more than mental interpretation, whereas in the Renaissance, and for a thousand years before, mental interpretation was emphasized somewhat more, at times considerably more, than external realities.

Mental interpretation in the ancient scheme consisted in taking the basic facts in a given case and subjecting them to an armchair examination that had three main phases. The first phase supplied large elements of the speaker's actual arguments, and while in this phase he classified his case in relation to its standing or position in the world of cases. The world of cases was made up of positions of fact, of definition, of quality, and of procedure, according to the youthful Cicero's *De Inventione;* and these four positions were supplemented by five others that applied only to disputes involving written documents.[10] The second main phase of invention supplied materials for the ethical aspects of a discourse.

[10] *De Inventione*, 1. 8. 10–18; 2. 4–51.

These were found when the speaker classified his coming speech in relation to its kind in the world of speeches, there being three kinds, the deliberative, the forensic, and the epideictic, to which were respectively attached the ethical considerations of advantage, justice, and honor.[11] The third main phase of invention supplied materials for the structural parts of discourse, so far as these parts had not been stocked by the two other phases. Cicero listed these parts as six in number: exordium, narration, division, proof, refutation, conclusion. These six parts required various kinds of content, which Cicero describes at length.[12]

A similar explanation of the three main phases of rhetorical invention appeared in Thomas Wilson's *The Arte of Rhetorique* in 1553. In fact, Wilson used Cicero's *De Inventione* as one source of his treatment of invention, although the anonymous *Rhetorica ad Herennium,* which is almost as ancient as *De Inventione* and had for centuries been attributed to Cicero, was Wilson's more important source.[13] Now it must be conceded that *De Inventione* and the *Rhetorica ad Herennium* do not treat all details of inventional theory in the same way, but the differences between them are less significant historically than the similarities, and thus Wilson's special dependence upon the *Rhetorica ad Herennium* does not mean that he departs in any major way from the three phases just outlined.

Since Wilson's day, thanks to the influence of Bacon and Descartes, man has tended more and more to believe that his most important deliberations must be conducted in the light

[11] *Ibid.,* 1. 5. 7; 2. 4. 12; 2. 51–59.   [12] *Ibid.,* 1. 14–56.

[13] Russell Halderman Wagner, "Wilson and his Sources," *QJS,* XV (1929), 530–532. For an excellent discussion of the date, authorship, sources, and organization of the *Rhetorica ad Herennium* and its relation to *De Inventione,* see Harry Caplan, trans., *Ad C. Herennium de Ratione Dicendi,* Loeb Classical Library (Cambridge, Mass., 1954), pp. vii–xxxiv.

of all the particular facts that bear upon them. No longer does he feel that he can draw predominantly from common sense, general reason, or the wisdom that rests largely upon deductions from analogous past experience. When Descartes abandoned his belief in tradition and custom and decided to reconstitute his knowledge in terms of the direct observation of the great book of the world,[14] he not only took a decisive step toward the creation of modern science, but he also represented in his own personal life the change that was coming over the whole intellectual life of Europe. And that change was too vast to leave rhetoric unaffected.

The modern speaker may be said to approach the problem of content by undertaking to study as many of the facts as he can possibly locate. "The really difficult problem in the preparation of the case," says a distinguished twentieth-century advocate, "is to learn what the facts are, and no matter how long or conscientiously you work, you will never know them all." He adds:

The law seldom decides the issue, the facts do; and as contrasted with the ascertainment of the facts, the law is relatively easy to discover. There are a hundred good researchers of the law to one who has a genius, I may say a nose, for the discovery of the true facts.[15]

Later, when this same advocate is discussing the modern lawyer's closing speech to the jury, he likens the preparation of that speech to the preparation of a learned book:

The trial, for the lawyer, is what research is for the author. Histories and biographies, letters, memoirs, diaries, and the archives of great libraries are the material from which a book is made. The evidence, documents, and the demeanor of the witnesses are the stuff from which the advocate's summation must be constructed.[16]

[14] Gilson's ed., p. 51.
[15] Lloyd Paul Stryker, *The Art of Advocacy* (New York, 1954), p. 11.
[16] *Ibid.*, pp. 113–114.

These views emphasize that the modern speaker, whether in the law court or on the political platform, speaks less from the old method of armchair analysis than from the method of research into the realities of his case. Like Burke advocating conciliation with America, the modern speaker allows his speech to refer extensively and minutely to such concrete realities as population figures, trade statistics, and the amount of income from agriculture and fisheries. Like Webster answering Hayne, the modern speaker feels called upon to deal with such complex matters as the history of the federal land question, the tariff, consolidation of powers, internal improvements, and the issue of nullification. Like Lincoln at Cooper Union, he analyzes minutely such biographical and historical considerations as those relating to the individual attitudes of the constitutional Fathers toward slavery in the federal territories. Like Churchill in 1940, he discusses such facts as present military losses and gains on land, on the sea, and in the air. Today we consider such realities the building blocks of any serious and important speech, the grounds of any dependable induction; and our speakers, despite their frequent addiction to the trash and nonsense that clutter oratory no less than literature, adhere at their best to the principle that realities cannot be mastered except as speakers participate in the disciplines of the scholar and scientist.

In changing its predominant emphasis from mental interpretation to external realites, rhetorical invention has in our time simultaneously abandoned the historic distinction between artistic and nonartistic arguments. This distinction stemmed from Aristotle's *Rhetoric,* and upon it was based the concept of proof supplied by the classical system of invention as opposed to proof supplied by other means. Says Aristotle:

> Of the modes of persuasion some belong strictly to the art of rhetoric and some do not. By the latter I mean such things as

are not supplied by the speaker but are there at the outset—witnesses, evidence given under torture, written contracts, and so on. By the former I mean such as we can ourselves construct by means of the principles of rhetoric. The one kind has merely to be used, the other has to be invented.[17]

It is doubtful that Aristotle meant this distinction to be as heavy a commitment to mental interpretation, and as light a commitment to external realities, as later classical rhetoricians assumed. In one of the most important chapters of the second book of his *Rhetoric* he lays great emphasis upon facts as the starting point for the construction of arguments on any subject.[18] But, even so, the passage just quoted seemed to identify external realities with nonartistic arguments and to put them both beyond the pale of the principles of rhetoric. Today the emphasis is almost exactly the reverse. The same external realities that have become the focus of scientific investigation claim the center of interest in the modern concept of rhetorical invention, while mental interpretation is accepted as the means of making those realities humanly important and of deciding how best to present and use them.

5

Still another change in the theory of communication since the Renaissance concerns the method of arranging ideas for public presentation. In this field, the change has been one in which complicated structures have been abandoned and simpler structures adopted.

If we were to wake up tomorrow in the England of 1625 and were interested in studying what that period thought of the problem of organizing discourses, we would find that two distinct practices were then in evidence.

One practice, which was applied to what I have been calling

[17] *Rhetorica,* 1355[b] 36 ff., in *The Works of Aristotle,* ed. W. D. Ross, Vol. XI.
[18] *Ibid.,* 1396[a]–1396[b].

learned discourses, required such communications to be organized either in an ascending or a descending order of
generality. The ascending order, called the compositive, required an author to proceed from the smallest units of a subject to the whole, as when a treatise on logic would treat first
of words, then of propositions, and finally of syllogisms and
arguments. The descending order, called the resolutive, required an author to proceed from the whole to smaller and
smaller parts, until at length the indivisible units of the subject were reached.

The theory of learned presentation was not always treated
in these two divisions by the logicians of the early seventeenth
century. The Ramists, for example, believed that only the
descending order was legitimate in the field of learned writing.[19] The Systematics believed in the ascending as well as the
descending order, and occasionally one of them added a third
method to these standard two.[20] Bacon, who did not belong
to either of these schools, adhered to the theory that learned
discourse had two other major divisions, "whereof the one
may be termed Magistral, and the other of Probation." [21]
Bacon means his divisions to represent the difference between
elementary, dogmatic exposition and something more in-
quiring and philosophical; and it must be admitted that this
distinction, and his subsequent treatment of it, have greater
range and caliber than did the standard distinction, although
the latter was the more popular in its time.

The other practice of organizing discourses in the England
of 1625 was applied to popular address, and it consisted in
following the theory of the classical oration. Thus speakers
were taught to arrange their ideas so that there was first an
introduction, then a narration, and then a division or pre-

[19] For a discussion of this matter, see my *Logic and Rhetoric in
England*, ch. 4.
[20] *Ibid.*, ch. 5.   [21] *Works of Bacon*, VI, 289.

view, these parts being forerunners of the proof, refutation, and conclusion. Cicero was, of course, the great authority behind this theory, although sixteenth-century England knew it also from Thomas Wilson's *The Arte of Rhetorique* and by 1625 from Thomas Vicars's *Manuductio ad Artem Rhetoricam* and Thomas Farnaby's popular *Index Rhetoricus.*

It is obvious that modern rhetoric advocates a simpler and more natural organization than that represented by Renaissance theory. Our learned discourses rarely adhere with regularity to an ascending or a descending pattern. Scholarship, history, biography, scientific exposition, organize themselves unobtrusively into sequences suggested by the relations of their units in space, time, logic, or causality. On many occasions serious arrangement appears to be in the class of things that an author must avoid, at least in outward appearance, as if the learned reader would be insulted by clarity of form, and the layman's delicate interest would not survive in the atmosphere of system and order.

As for our oratory, we organize it theoretically into fewer parts than did Cicero, and we strive in practice for the simplest possible structure. In fact, when Aristotle, long before Cicero, said that a speech needed to have only two parts, the statement and argument, to which on occasion the speaker might want to add an introduction and an epilogue, but no other divisions,[22] he was closer to our current practice than the Roman or medieval rhetoricians are. And why? Perhaps because his times were much like ours in preferring subject matter to form, inquiry to communication, individuality to convention, and democratic procedures to authoritarian rituals. At any rate, it cannot be denied that we have moved away from the ceremonial organization advocated by Cicero toward the simpler theory of Aristotle.

[22] *Rhetorica,* 1414^a–1414^b.

6

The fifth, and for my present purposes the final, change that has come over rhetoric since the Renaissance concerns the theory of style. Style is often conceived as the dress our thoughts wear when they have been made ready to appear in good society. "Elocution," said Thomas Wilson, "getteth words to set forth inuention, and with such beautie commendeth the matter, that reason semeth to be clad in Purple, walking afore both bare and naked." [23] We may elaborate this image a bit and say that the great change in the theory of rhetorical style since Wilson's day has been a change from the convention of imperial dress to the convention of the business suit.

In the sixteenth century rhetorical style was largely, sometimes exclusively, taught in terms of tropes and schemes.[24] Tropes were what we call today figures of speech, including such devices as metaphor, synecdoche, metonymy, irony, and allegory. Schemes were unusual arrangements of language. Thus language arranged in rhymed verses was one sort of scheme, called in Latin *similiter desinens* and in English *like-ending*. Other typical schemes involved saying the same thing in many different ways (*expolitio*), dividing a whole into parts (*partitio*), and changing suddenly from the third person to the second in order to speak as if directly to a person or thing (apostrophe). The list of schemes and tropes was long in sixteenth-century textbooks, as English schoolboys knew to their dismay.[25]

The theory behind tropes and schemes was that men have one language for ordinary intercourse and another for formal

[23] Mair, p. 160.   [24] See my *Logic and Rhetoric in England,* ch. 3.
[25] Henry Peacham's *The Garden of Eloquence* (London, 1577, 1593) is one of the most complete of these lists. For a recent edition of this work, see William G. Crane's facsimile reproduction (Gainesville, Fla., 1954).

communication, and that the latter differs from the former by employing tropes and schemes throughout. Englishmen of the Renaissance did not believe the language of ordinary life to be suitable for formal discourse. They believed instead that formal discourse must be deliberately contrived to appear systematically unlike the language of ordinary life. The contrivances by which ordinary speech was transformed into proper oratorical or poetical speech were what the Renaissance understood tropes and schemes to be.

We all know that in present-day American education students no longer memorize tropes and schemes, nor do they use them as the official public language. Students are taught instead to speak a public language that corresponds to the best elements of the language of ordinary intercourse. Such public language is not unlike the poetic idiom identified by Wordsworth as "a selection of language really used by men." [26] Incidentally, Wordsworth's great contribution to English poetry has often been described as that in which poetry abandoned the stylistic conventions of the eighteenth century and learned to express itself in the speech of ordinary life. What could also be emphasized, however, is that Wordsworth's reforms in poetry were part of a great trend, begun in the Renaissance and constantly in evidence since, away from a contrived literary language and toward the idioms of everyday speech.

The tendency of modern rhetoric to recommend the speech of ordinary life as opposed to the artful and elaborate speech of the courtier reflects the change that has occurred since the Renaissance as political power and economic influence have been transferred from the aristocrat to the commoner. When

[26] In his celebrated "Preface to the Second Edition of Several of the Foregoing Poems, Published, with an Additional Volume, under the title of 'Lyrical Ballads.'" See *The Complete Poetical Works of William Wordsworth*, ed. Andrew J. George (New York [1904]), p. 791.

the aristocrat was the final source of both of these forms of
authority, ordinary language did not serve a decisive political
or economic purpose, and tropes and schemes, as the antitheses of that language, were the preferred means of communication. But when the commoner became politically powerful, and wealth began to center in his commercial enterprises
rather than as before in the aristocrats' estates, the tropes and
the schemes passed into history, except as a way of expressing emotional overtones of meaning, while the idiom of ordinary life, purified of its ordinary defects, assumed a new
and growing importance. In support of this same trend, the
new science found the fashions of aristocratic speech un-
suited to the expression of scientific subject matter and un-
responsive to the expectations of those seeking intellectual,
humanitarian, or commercial profit from the publication of
experiments and discoveries. Small wonder, then, that the
scientists of the seventeenth century evolved their new vocabulary from "the language of Artizans, Countrymen, and
Merchants, before that, of Wits, or Scholars." [27] Thus did the
scientific, the economic, and the political forces in the pattern of Western European culture conspire to produce for
the twentieth century a theory of rhetorical style quite different from that in vogue in the early Renaissance.

We should not say, however, that the rise of ordinary
speech to a position of prominence in rhetorical style represents a gain for rhetoric, nor that the decline in the importance of tropes and figures represents a loss. What we should
say is that ordinary speech as a medium of communication
better reflects the needs of a businessman's culture and that
tropes and figures were better for a culture of landed aristocrats. It is the business of rhetoric to react to the situation
in which it is used and to reflect in its theory the needs that

[27] See Thomas Sprat, *The History of the Royal-Society of London*
(London, 1667), p. 113.

it serves. Rhetoric does not deserve praise for evolving its present theory of rhetorical style, for that is not praiseworthy which is done as a matter of normal obligation. But rhetoric would deserve blame if it still sought to elevate tropes and figures into the exclusive language of public discourse. That sort of attitude would be in effect a declaration that a given set of means is of greater value than its presumed end—that the way in which a communication is phrased counts more heavily than does the possibility that it will not reach its audience.

7

Other changes have taken place in the theory of rhetoric during the past four centuries. Some of them have come with the development of mass media of communication, some with the application of the concept of propaganda to the fields of commerce, public relations, and statecraft. Some have come as rhetoric has stated its problems in terms of the principles of modern psychology, some as means have been developed to explore the state of public opinion and to measure the effect of communications upon the audience. These changes are of course vitally important in the growth of modern rhetoric. I have not treated them here because the impulses which produced them have originated within the past half-century and thus cannot be said to have deep roots in the ancient world as well as in our own.

What I have tried to do here is to discuss five problems which rhetoric has faced in antiquity and in the period since the Renaissance; I have tried to indicate that the solutions of those problems have changed as needs have dictated. The emphasis upon the theory of communication during the Middle Ages gave rhetoric and its allied arts a central position in the academic curriculum. As a result of that emphasis, grammar, rhetoric, and logic shared the responsibility for teaching communication and intelligently divided that responsibility among them. Grammar became the study of the medium of communication, rhetoric and logic the study of the means of reaching the two types of audience. As emphasis has shifted from the theory of communication to the theory of inquiry, rhetoric has lost in certain directions but has held its own in others. It has lost its central position in the curriculum; it has lost its productive association with logic; and although it has extended its scope to include a concern for the learned audience, it has failed to develop for modern learning what ancient logic developed in its time—a vocabulary by which specialists in one field can communicate with specialists in other fields. Meanwhile, however, rhetoric has developed a theory of invention that fits modern requirements, and it has adapted itself to new conditions in respect to the theory of arrangement and style. Certainly its future will mean further change; and perhaps it can recover some of the ground it has lost in the last four hundred years, if it endeavors always to see its present problems in the light of its long and illustrious history.

CHAPTER 5

The Declaration of Independence and Eighteenth-Century Logic

1

"When forced, therefore, to resort to arms for redress," wrote Thomas Jefferson in explaining what his most famous work was designed to do, "an appeal to the tribunal of the world was deemed proper for our justification. This was the object of the Declaration of Independence. Not to find out new principles, or new arguments, never before thought of, not merely to say things which had never been said before; but to place before mankind the common sense of the subject, in terms so plain and firm as to command their assent, and to justify ourselves in the independent stand we are compelled to take. Neither aiming at originality of principle or sentiment, nor yet copied from any particular and previous writing, it was intended to be an expression of the American mind, and to give to that expression the proper tone and spirit called for by the occasion. All its authority rests then on the harmonizing sentiments of the day, whether expressed in conversation, in letters, printed essays, or in the elementary books of public right, as Aristotle, Cicero, Locke, Sidney, &c." [1]

These serene and judicious words have been on occasion invoked not only to prove Jefferson's own full awareness that

[1] Letter to Henry Lee, May 8, 1825. See Paul Leicester Ford, ed., *The Writings of Thomas Jefferson* (New York, 1892–1899), X, 343.

the Declaration of Independence made use of familiar ideas but also to provide the opportunity to assert that the greatness of that document lies in its being a true and living reflection of what the men of its time accepted and believed. Thus Carl Becker, as he prepares to examine the antecedents of Jefferson's philosophy of natural rights, quotes part of the passage just cited to give weight to his own belief that Jefferson was right in drawing upon familiar sentiments and that "nothing could have been more futile than an attempt to justify a revolution on principles which no one had ever heard of before." [2] Thus also, having taken note of similarities between the Declaration and certain treatises by John Locke and James Wilson, Julian P. Boyd has this to say in justifying Jefferson's use of sources: "But even if Jefferson had 'copied from any particular and previous writing,' even if he had used an identifiable model—and his colleagues in Congress would have agreed as to the excellence of Locke—the most that would be proved by this is that he had failed to be original in an enterprise where originality would have been fatal. The greatness of his achievement, aside from the fact that he created one of the outstanding literary documents of the world and of all time, was that he identified its sublime purpose with the roots of liberal traditions that spread back to England, to Scotland, to Geneva, to Holland, to Germany, to Rome, and to Athens." [3]

For the student of eighteenth-century logic and rhetoric, Jefferson's statement of the object of the Declaration and of its conscious concern for accepted ideas is interesting in still another direction. So far as Jefferson intended the Declaration to appeal to the tribunal of the world, to command the

[2] Carl Becker, *The Declaration of Independence: A Study in the History of Political Ideas* (New York, 1940), pp. 24–25.

[3] Julian P. Boyd, *The Declaration of Independence: The Evolution of the Text as Shown in Facsimiles of Various Drafts by Its Author, Thomas Jefferson* (Princeton, 1945), p. 5.

assent of mankind, to justify the rebellion of the colonies against the British Crown, and to express the American mind in the proper tone and spirit called for by the occasion, he intended it to achieve logical and persuasive goals. Thus the question arises whether it conforms in these respects, as it so obviously does in political philosophy and liberal outlook, to the best traditions of its time—whether in so vital a matter as its actual capacity to influence men, to appeal to their reason, and to induce them to support the extreme alternative of civil disobedience and mutiny, it can be shown to follow the accepted persuasive principles of the eighteenth century and to rest consciously upon them rather than upon an uncalculated, an accidental, or perhaps even an original persuasive design.

The answer to this question is outlined in the following chapter. I shall attempt in it to show that an unmistakable parallelism exists between the argumentative structure of the Declaration and the theory of argumentative structure set forth in the most significant of the logics and rhetorics of Jefferson's time. In fact, I shall point to a particular logic that can be shown to have influenced the Declaration, and I shall explain how that influence made itself felt and under what auspices it reached Jefferson. This sort of analysis will indicate that, although all the authority of the Declaration rests, as Jefferson said, "on the harmonizing sentiments of the day," its ideas were given added persuasive power by their adherence to the best contemporary standards of mathematical and scientific demonstration and to what the best contemporary thinkers expected of proof before it could claim to convince the reason. This sort of analysis will also indicate the direction to be followed in supplementing Carl Becker's adroit critical appraisal of the literary qualities of the Declaration.[4] For the literary standards of Jefferson's era

[4] Becker, *Declaration,* pp. 194–223.

are stated more exactly in eighteenth-century logic and rhetoric than in the similar works of our time, and yet those logics and rhetorics are now so far forgotten or disparaged as unhappily to have lost their opportunity to teach us what we cannot afford to do without if we would fully understand the nonfictional literature of their time.

2

The chief logical treatises in England during the seventeen hundreds consciously followed the great *Port-Royal Logic* of the preceding century in dividing their subject into four parts, namely, perception, judgment, reasoning, and method, which were conceived as operations of the mind.[5] The theory

[5] In addition to *The Port-Royal Logic,* which was published at London in a total of 10 editions in French, Latin, and English between 1664 and 1717, the major logical works in England during the late 17th and most of the 18th centuries were the following (listed after each title are dates indicating editions that I have thus far been able to locate in surviving copies): John Wallis, *Institutio Logicae* (1687, 1702, 1715, 1729, 1763); Henry Aldrich, *Artis Logicae Compendium* (1691, 1692, 1696, 1704, 1723, 1750 [in English], 1771, 1793) (There were many 19th-century editions); Jean Pierre de Crousaz, *A New Treatise of the Art of Thinking. . . . Written in French. . . . Done into English* (1724); Isaac Watts, *Logick* (1725, 1726, 1729, 1733, 1736, 1740, 1745, 1751, 1763, 1779, 1786, 1789, 1792, 1793, 1797) (There were several 19th-century editions); William Duncan, *The Elements of Logick,* in Robert Dodsley's *The Preceptor* (1748, 1754, 1758, 1763, 1769, 1775, 1783, 1793), and as a separate work (1748, 1752, 1759, 1764, 1770, 1776, 1787, 1790, 1792) (There were several 19th-century editions).

Of these, Aldrich failed to adhere to the fourfold organization here described. He repudiated the Port-Royalists as innovators and went back himself to a conservative Aristotelianism. For his attack on the Port-Royalists, see the abridged (not the full) text of his *Artis Logicae Compendium* (Oxford, 1691), sig. G4^v–H2^r. But he did nevertheless treat method, even if he decided not to make it a formal division of logic. Wallis's *Institutio Logicae* treats perception, judgment, and reasoning, and places method as a subdivision of the latter topic.

For a discussion of *The Port-Royal Logic* as an offshoot of Descartes's *Discours de la Méthode* and a reform of the logic of Peter Ramus, see my *Logic and Rhetoric in England, 1500–1700,* pp. 342–363.

of perception involved not only the traditional doctrine of the logical term but also the emerging theories of sensations and images, later to be taken over by psychology. Judgment, the second part of logic, dealt with such matters as thoughts, ideas, statements, and intuitions, all of which amounted to a theory of terms connected into logical propositions. Reasoning in logic meant the combination of terms and propositions into syllogistic or inductive structures, and this part of logical theory blended traditional Aristotelian doctrine with insights from the philosophy of Francis Bacon, René Descartes, and Locke. As for the fourth part of eighteenth-century logic, it continued the practice, made popular by Peter Ramus in the sixteenth century, of insisting upon *dispositio* or method as a main division of logical theory; but it followed the reform of later logicians in giving method an investigative as well as a presentational aspect.[6]

Investigative arrangement in eighteenth-century English logic was called the analytic method, after the terminology endorsed by the Port-Royalists. This consisted in going from the known to the unknown over the route that an investigator would follow in proceeding from observed facts to a theory explaining them. It involved in the first instance the making of original discoveries in experimental science or in scholarship, and not unnaturally it was given such subordinate names as the method of inquiry, of invention, of discovery, and of resolution. The analytic method could of course be followed in acquainting someone else with a discovery after it had been made, and thus it had a presentational as well as an investigative aspect. But it owed its fundamental character to

[6] Howell, *Logic and Rhetoric*, pp. 146–172, 282–317. For the antecedents of Ramus's theory of method, see Walter J. Ong, S.J., *Ramus Method, and the Decay of Dialogue* (Cambridge, Mass., 1958), pp. 225–269; see also Neal W. Gilbert, *Renaissance Concepts of Method* (New York, 1960), pp. 3–128.

its use in research, whether employed for that purpose or for the business of teaching.

The reverse of the analytic method in eighteenth-century logic was called the synthetic method, and this was properly the instrument of instruction, exposition, communication, and proof. It too moved from the known to the unknown. But it did so over the route traveled by the teacher in giving his students knowledge to replace their ignorance rather than over the route of an investigator seeking to replace his own ignorance by knowledge. Thus the teacher would begin his demonstration by citing the established truths upon which his conclusion would later be made to depend, and he would proceed to connect that conclusion with the established truths by showing that a fundamental aspect of the latter was also a fundamental aspect of the former. The logicians called this procedure, not only the synthetic method, but also the method of doctrine, of instruction, and of composition. Like the analytic method, it too had a double function. It could be used for discovering new knowledge in certain fields, notably in mathematics; and it could be used for the presentation of the knowledge thus discovered. But in its fundamental character it was the method of instruction, communication, and conviction in respect to truths already known.

3

The discipline of rhetoric had traditionally dealt with *dispositio* or arrangement of discourse, along with the other rhetorical subjects of invention, style, memory, and delivery. Rhetorical *dispositio* was, however, a fully developed theory of the classical form of an oration; and this form, as described in the rhetorical writings of Cicero, and in various modified or extended ways by later rhetoricians, had consisted of six major parts—the exordium, the narration, the division, the proof, the refutation, and the conclusion. Within these six terms the theory of oratorical structure was comprised during the classical Roman era, the Middle Ages, the Renaissance, and the seventeenth century.

One obvious thing about the eighteenth century in England is that these six terms were no longer supreme in the theory of oratorical arrangement. Only John Ward among the major eighteenth-century rhetoricians used them in the manner advocated by Cicero and Quintilian.[7] His later contemporaries—George Campbell, Joseph Priestley, and Hugh Blair—recognized in varying degrees that the analytic and synthetic methods of the new logic were having a strong influence upon the dispositional theory of rhetoric and were threatening to crowd out the elaborate six-part oratorical structure of the past.

Campbell's great work, *The Philosophy of Rhetoric,* begun in 1750 [8] and first published in 1776, gives no place at all to the traditional six parts of the classical oration. In fact, it discusses only analysis and synthesis as terms for the theory of argumentative form. These two terms appear in the course of Campbell's treatment of subject matter and sense in discourse, where he associates rhetoric with logic and thus analyzes not only intuitive evidence and deductive evidence, as the bases of conviction, but also the methods by which argument is put together.[9] Campbell does not present analysis and synthesis as a fully developed formula for oratorical structure, but in the absence of such a formula, his use of these two terms indicates that his sympathies lie with the logical rather than the rhetorical antecedents of the doctrine of *dispositio:*

In moral reasoning we proceed by analysis, and ascend from particulars to universals; in syllogizing we proceed by synthesis, and

[7] John Ward, *A System of Oratory* (London, 1759), Lectures 12–18.

[8] See George Campbell, *The Philosophy of Rhetoric* (London, 1776), I, iii.

[9] *Ibid.,* I, 95–166.

descend from universals to particulars. The analytic is the only method which we can follow, in the acquisition of natural knowledge, or of whatever regards actual existences; the synthetic is more properly the method that ought to be pursued in the application of knowledge already acquired. It is for this reason it has been called the didactic method, as being the shortest way of communicating the principles of a science.[10]

If Campbell seems here to be advocating that rhetoric throw out its traditional theory of the six-part classical oration and substitute for it the logical theory of method, the same thing can be said of Priestley's *Course of Lectures on Oratory and Criticism.* These lectures, by the way, have the distinction of being a great scientist's contribution to a subject little cultivated in its theoretical aspects by the scientific community. And when Priestley comes to speak of rhetorical arrangement, his lectures also have the distinction of offering to oratory the logical as opposed to the rhetorical theory of *dispositio,* and of calling that theory "method," after its name in logic. "Logicians," says Priestley, "speak of two kinds of method in argumentative discourses, the *analytic* and the *synthetic;* and the distribution is complete and accurate. For, in all science, we either proceed from particular observations to more general conclusions, which is *analysis;* or beginning with more general and comprehensive propositions, we descend to the particular propositions which are contained in them, which is *synthesis.*" [11] Priestley goes on to emphasize that the analytic method is obligatory as the method of investigation but optional as a method of communicating truth to others, whereas the synthetic method is generally more convenient in explaining a science.[12] Speaking of the analogy between

[10] *Ibid.,* I, 165–166.

[11] Joseph Priestley, *A Course of Lectures on Oratory and Criticism* (London, 1777), p. 42. Italics are Priestley's.

[12] *Ibid.,* pp. 42–43.

geometry and oratory in respect to the synthetic method, he observes:

> Every proposition is, by geometricians, demonstrated either from *axioms,* that is, self-evident truths; or such as have been elsewhere demonstrated from those which are self-evident.
>
> In like manner, whatever we propose to demonstrate, the last appeal lies to *self-evident truths;* in moral subjects, to consciousness, or internal feelings; and in matters of revelation, to the plain sense of scripture: and it is very expedient and adviseable, in discourses upon important subjects of any kind, after the manner of geometricians, to premise these self-evident truths, beyond which no appeal can be admitted.[13]

Priestley's *Lectures* were not published until 1777, but he began to deliver them in 1762, when he was tutor in languages and belles-lettres in the academy at Warrington.[14] Three years before, in 1759, Hugh Blair, the last great British rhetorician of the eighteenth century, inaugurated at the University of Edinburgh his famous lectures on rhetoric and belles-lettres, which eventually were published in 1783.[15] As part of his subject Blair treated the theory of *dispositio.* Like John Ward in his earlier Gresham College lectures on rhetoric, which had been collected and published in the year in which Blair started his lectures at Edinburgh, Blair treated *dispositio* with the traditional parts of the classical oration in mind; and thus he speaks of the introduction, the proposition, the division, the narration, the argument, the pathetic part, and the conclusion.[16] But when it comes to argument or proof, says Blair, "two different methods may be used by Orators in the conduct of their reasoning; the terms of art for which are, the Analytic, and the Synthetic method." [17] Blair's

---

[13] *Ibid.,* p. 46.   [14] *Ibid.,* p. i.

[15] Robert Morell Schmitz, *Hugh Blair* (New York, 1948), 62, 142. See also Hugh Blair, *Lectures on Rhetoric and Belles Lettres* (Dublin, 1783), I, iii.

[16] Blair, *Lectures,* II, 359–416.   [17] *Ibid.,* II, 392.

explanation of these terms is brief and does not add to what has already been observed. But it might be added that he regards the analytic method as less suitable to popular speaking than is the synthetic. The latter consists in laying down the point to be proved, and making one argument after another bear upon it, "till the hearers be fully convinced." [18]

4

William Duncan, who was commissioned professor of natural philosophy at Marischal College in Aberdeen in 1752,[19] deserves a special place in the present discussion. His *Elements of Logick,* first published at London in 1748, and reprinted many times during the next half-century,[20] is the dominant logical treatise of its time and place. Moreover, although its contribution to the development of George Campbell's *Philosophy of Rhetoric,* itself a work of considerable stature, has never been worked out in detail, a mere reading of the two books will convince anyone that Campbell owes an important debt to Duncan. In this connection we might remind ourselves that both men graduated from Marischal College, Duncan in 1735 and Campbell in 1738, and that, during the last year of Duncan's term of service as member of the Marischal College faculty, Campbell was appointed the college principal.[21] No such ties link Duncan and Priestley; and yet it seems obvious that the latter's account of method in rhetoric owes its philosophical groundwork to the former's *Logick*—a point that probably has not been noticed since the eighteenth century.

But Duncan's *Logick* has much stronger claims than these to our present attention. It originally appeared as the first

[18] *Ibid.,* II, 393–394.
[19] Peter John Anderson, *Fasti Academiae Mariscallanae Aberdonensis* (Aberdeen, 1889–1898), II, 45.
[20] For details, see above, n. 5.
[21] Anderson, *Fasti Academiae Mariscallanae.* II, 29–30, 45, 308, 310.

treatise of the second volume of Robert Dodsley's *The Precep-tor,* a meritorious compilation in which, as its title page declares, "The First Principles of Polite Learning Are laid down In a Way most suitable for trying the Genius, and advancing the Instruction of Youth." Special prestige was given this collection by virtue of its containing a preface by Dr. Samuel Johnson.[22] Of profound interest to us, however, is that Thomas Jefferson's library contained the second volume of Dodsley's *Preceptor* and thus also Duncan's *Logick,* although the latter fact has hitherto not been noticed.[23] Nor has it been noticed that Jefferson must certainly have studied the *Logick* when he was enrolled at William and Mary between 1760 and 1762. Not only does the Declaration of Independence conform to the structure recommended by Duncan for works that seek to achieve a maximum degree of conviction and certainty, but also it contains an important verbal echo of the *Logick,* as I shall show later. Moreover, William Small, Jefferson's highly respected teacher at William and Mary, who, as Jefferson himself later testified, "probably fixed the destinies of my life," [24] had graduated from Mari-

[22] See *Boswell's Life of Johnson* (London, 1927), I, 129; also *The Works of Samuel Johnson* (Troy, New York, 1903), XII, 154–175.

[23] E. Millicent Sowerby, *Catalogue of the Library of Thomas Jefferson* (Washington, 1952–1959), I, 507.

Sowerby does not describe the contents of the second volume of *The Preceptor,* nor does she seek to identify the edition which Jefferson held. It can be established, however, that Jefferson owned a fifth or a later edition. The first and second editions were printed for R. Dodsley; the third and fourth, for R. and J. Dodsley; and the fifth, sixth, seventh, and eighth, for J. Dodsley. Since the edition in Jefferson's possession contained this last designation, it must have borne the date of 1769, 1775, 1783, or 1793. Thus Jefferson's copy was not the one that he would have used at William and Mary. His college copy may have been lost, and the copy in his library could have been purchased later to replace it.

[24] Herbert L. Ganter, "William Small, Jefferson's Beloved Teacher," *William and Mary Quarterly,* 3d Ser., IV (1947), 505. See also Dumas

schal College in 1755,[25] and thus had been a student under
William Duncan. To be sure, Small came to William and
Mary to teach natural philosophy, which was of course Duncan's own subject at Marischal College. But shortly after
his arrival at his academic post in Virginia, he was given the
temporary assignment of teaching moral philosophy as well
as natural philosophy, the former being at that time limited
by the statutes of the college to "Rhetorick, Logick, and
Ethicks," whereas the latter was made up of "Physicks, Meta-
physicks, and Mathematicks." [26] Small was evidently not a
man to take a temporary assignment lightly. He made such
substantial changes at once in the teaching of ethics and
rhetoric at William and Mary as to cause Jefferson to say
later that "he was the first who ever gave in that college
regular lectures in Ethics, Rhetoric & Belles lettres." [27] There
would have been every reason for Small to have given the
study of logic a new direction, too. For one thing, the statutes
of the college left it "to the President and Masters, by the

Malone, *Jefferson and His Time*, I, *Jefferson the Virginian* (Boston,
1948), pp. 49–61.

[25] Anderson, *Fasti Academiae Mariscallanae*, II, 323.

[26] *The Charter, Transfer and Statutes, of the College of William and
Mary, in Virginia: In Latin and English* (Williamsburg, 1758), p. 135.
Cited below as *The Charter and Statutes*.
Small attended his first faculty meeting at William and Mary on Oct.
18, 1758. At that time the Reverend Jacob Rowe, M.A., was professor
of moral philosophy, having occupied that post since the preceding
June 14. Rowe was expelled from his professorship on Aug. 14, 1760,
and his permanent successor, the Reverend Richard Graham, M.A.,
was not elected until June 12, 1761. Thus Small's term as temporary
professor of moral philosophy dated from the late summer of 1760 to
the middle of the following June, and coincided with the last seven
months of Jefferson's first college year and the opening three months of
his second. Small served on the faculty of William and Mary until 1764.
For the dates given here concerning him, Rowe, and Graham, see
William and Mary College Quarterly 1st Ser., III (1894–1895), 60–62,
130–132; XIV (1905–1906), 75–76; XXIV (1915–1916), 221–222.

[27] Ganter, "William Small," p. 505, quoting Jefferson's autobiography.

Advice of the Chancéllor," to feel no compulsion to follow "*Aristotle*'s Logick and Physicks, which reigned so long alone in the Schools," but "to teach what Systems of Logick, Physicks, Ethicks, and Mathematicks, they think fit. . . ." [28] For another thing, and this is crucial, we may be sure that Small, when forced by circumstances to add logic, rhetoric, and ethics to his teachings at William and Mary during Jefferson's first college year, would naturally remember the famous *Logick* that his own master had published in 1748, and would naturally recommend that work to young Jefferson, his daily companion and close friend.[29] Thus if the Declaration of Independence carries out the directions laid down by Duncan for discourse that would compel the assent of mankind, and if its cadences, in an outstanding instance, match one of Duncan's most important logical terms, there is every reason to believe that the influence of Duncan's *Logick* upon Jefferson is involved, and that his admired teacher, William Small, is the key figure in the transmission of that influence.[30] Indeed, there is every reason to suspect that, if

[28] *The Charter and Statutes*, p. 133.

[29] Ganter, "William Small," p. 505. Ganter quotes Jefferson's autobiography as follows on Small's relations with him: "He, most happily for me, became soon attached to me & made me his daily companion when not engaged in the school; and from his conversation I got my first views of the expansion of science & of the system of things in which we are placed."

[30] Duncan's *Logick* can be established on other grounds as part of the curriculum at William and Mary during the 18th century. In letters of Nov. 4 and Dec. 9, 1799, from J. Shelton Watson to his brother David, the former being an undergraduate of that era at the Virginia college, the *Logick* is unfavorably mentioned as one of Shelton's current academic assignments. See "Letters from William and Mary College, 1798–1801 . . . ," *Virginia Magazine of History and Biography*, XXIX (1921), 145–146, 148–149.

There is also some evidence of the general circulation of the *Logick* in 18th-century Virginia. For example, it is listed among 344 books that were being offered for sale in the printing office and bookshop of Dixon and Hunter in Williamsburg in 1775. See *Wm. and Mary College Qtly.*

Small fixed the destinies of Jefferson's life, William Duncan helped to fix the destinies of the Declaration of Independence.

Like all the progressive logics in England during the eighteenth century, Duncan's is arranged according to the four basic operations of the mind in discovering and ordering knowledge.[31] Thus Duncan successively treats perception, judgment, reasoning, and method. His basic thesis is that knowledge has three branches, each with a corresponding form of judgment and way of reasoning. These three branches, arranged in order of descent from absolute certainty to the lowest of the acceptable degrees of probability, are science, natural philosophy, and history. Perhaps the following quotation will best represent his basic view of them all:

> In *Scientifical* Knowledge, which regards wholly the abstract Ideas of the Mind, and those Relations and Connections they have one with another; our Judgments are grounded on *Intuition,* and the Manner of Reasoning is by *Demonstration.* In *Natural* Knowledge, respecting Objects that exist without us, their Powers, Properties and mutual Operations; we judge on the Foundation of *Experience,* and reason by *Induction* and *Analogy.* Lastly, in *Historical* Knowledge, which is chiefly conversant about past Facts and Transactions; *Testimony* is the Ground of Judgment, and the Way of Reasoning is by *Criticism* and *probable Conjecture.*[32]

1st Ser., XV (1906–1907), 109. For another example, it was one of the volumes in the library of John Parke Custis of Fairfax County, according to an inventory made in 1782. See "The Library of John Parke Custis, Esq., of Fairfax County, Virginia," *Tyler's Quarterly Historical and Genealogical Magazine,* IX (1927–1928), 101. Custis briefly attended King's College, now Columbia, in 1773.

The first American edition of the *Logick* was published at Philadelphia, Aug. 10, 1792, from the press of Mathew Carey. There is a copy in the Huntington Library, San Marino, Calif.

[31] All my references are to Duncan's *Logick* as it appears in [Robert Dodsley], *The Preceptor* (London, 1748), II. For Duncan's mention of the four operations of the mind, see that volume, pp. 3–6.

[32] *Ibid.,* p. 180. Italics and punctuation are Duncan's here and below.

So far as my present argument is concerned, the terms which have most importance in this statement are intuition, demonstration, and science. To Duncan, intuition is the immediate recognition that the ideas in a proposition are in fact related as the proposition declares them to be. "Thus, *that the Whole is greater than any of it's Parts*," he observes, "is an intuitive Judgment, nothing more being required to convince us of it's Truth, than an Attention to the Ideas of *Whole* and *Part.*" [33] Demonstration means syllogistic reasoning, as distinguished from induction and analogy; and it is the process by which intuitive judgments, as recognized truths in their own right, are made to yield derivative propositions that are themselves absolutely certain. Science is that which comes into being as a result of demonstration: "For whatever is deduced from our intuitive Perceptions, by a clear and connected Series of Proofs, is said to be demonstrated, and produces absolute Certainty in the Mind. Hence the Knowledge obtained in this manner, is what we properly term *Science;* because in every Step of the Procedure, it carries it's own Evidence along with it, and leaves no room for Doubt or Hesitation." [34]

Somewhat later Duncan clarifies still further the relation between the certainty produced by intuition and that produced by demonstration; and he identifies the intuitive judgment by calling it the "self-evident proposition or perception," this term being one that is repeated over and over again in the course of the *Logick*. Here are Duncan's own words:

When any Proposition is offered to the View of the Mind, if the Terms in which it is expressed are understood; upon comparing the Ideas together, the Agreement or Disagreement asserted is either immediately perceived, or found to lie beyond the present Reach of the Understanding. In the first Case the Proposition is said to be *self-evident,* and admits not of any

[33] *Ibid.,* p. 79.   [34] *Ibid.,* p. 80.

Proof, because a bare Attention to the Ideas themselves, produces full Conviction and Certainty; nor is it possible to call in any thing more evident, by way of Confirmation. But where the Connection or Repugnance comes not so readily under the Inspection of the Mind, there we must have Recourse to Reasoning; and if by a clear Series of Proofs we can make out the Truth proposed, insomuch that Self-evidence shall accompany every Step of the Procedure, we are then able to demonstrate what we assert, and the Proposition itself is said to be *demonstrable*. . . .

From what has been said it appears, that Reasoning is employed only about demonstrable Propositions, and that our intuitive and self-evident Perceptions, are the ultimate Foundation on which it rests.[35]

Mathematics offers to Duncan the purest example of science, the best illustration of first principles and self-evident truths, and the happiest models for demonstrations that produce absolute certainty. In fact, long before he explains the analytic and synthetic methods of logic, he outlines the steps by which the mathematicians arrive at truth: "First then it is to be observed, that they have been very careful in ascertaining their Ideas, and fixing the Signification of their Terms. For this Purpose they begin with *Definitions*. . . ."[36] "When they have taken this first Step, . . . their next Care is, to lay down some self-evident Truths, which may serve as a Foundation for their future Reasonings."[37] To the mathematician, self-evident truths are known as axioms and postulates, the former being self-evident speculative, the latter self-evident practical propositions, whereas demonstrable propositions are correspondingly known as theorems and problems. Having laid down his self-evident truths, the mathematician as his next step invokes corollaries, which are propositions flowing so immediately from the self-evident or demonstrated truths as to require no separate proof of their own. And finally, the mathematician uses scholia, which are inde-

[35] *Ibid.*, pp. 96–97.   [36] *Ibid.*, p. 98.   [37] *Ibid.*, p. 99.

pendently annexed to definitions, propositions, or corollaries, and serve the same purpose as annotations upon a classical text. "In a System of Knowledge so uniform and well connected," writes Duncan, "no wonder if we meet with Certainty; and if those Clouds and Darknesses, that deface other Parts of human Science, and bring Discredit even upon Reason itself, are here scattered and disappear." [38]

As if fascinated by self-evident truths more than by anything else in logic, Duncan adds that they cannot be detected by external marks or characteristics. Nothing in them more striking than their self-evidence can be used to identify them. With a touch of poetic fervor, he declares: "Intuitive Judgments need no other distinguishing Marks, than that Brightness which surrounds them; in like manner as Light discovers itself by its own Presence, and the Splendor it universally diffuses." [39]

The immediate authority behind Duncan's regard for mathematical method is John Locke. This fact is plainly established when Duncan discusses reasoning as the third part of logic. Speaking of the studies that will help the beginner to master the art of reasoning, he mentions that for such a purpose no science is better than mathematics:

Not that we look upon it as necessary, *(to use the Words of the great Mr.* Locke) that all Men should be deep Mathematicians, but that, having got the Way of Reasoning which that Study necessarily brings the Mind to, they may be able to transfer it to other Parts of Knowledge, as they shall have Occasion. For in all sorts of Reasoning, every single Argument should be managed as a Mathematical Demonstration, the Connection and Dependence of Ideas should be followed, till the Mind is brought to the Source on which it bottoms, and can trace the Coherence through the whole Train of Proofs. . . . Nothing does this better than Mathematicks, which therefore I think should be taught all those, who have the Time and Opportunity, not so much to

[38] *Ibid.,* p. 102.   [39] *Ibid.,* p. 103.

make them Mathematicians, as to make them reasonable Crea-
tures.[40]

One other aspect of Duncan's treatment of reasoning should
be given attention at this time to emphasize his conception of
demonstration or proof and its origin in self-evident truths
and syllogistic order. After his discussion of the forms, figures,
and moods of the syllogism, during which he refers his readers
to *The Port-Royal Logic*,[41] he speaks briefly of induction, and
then devotes a chapter to the standards that must be met in
proving a proposition. His doctrine is not original, but his
emphasis and wording give it a special attractiveness:

> When a Proposition is thus by means of Syllogisms, collected
> from others more evident and known, it is said to be *proved;* so
> that we may in the general define *the Proof of a Proposition,* to
> be a Syllogism, or Series of Syllogisms, collecting that Proposi-
> tion from known and evident Truths. But more particularly, if
> the Syllogisms of which the Proof consists, admit of no Premisses
> but Definitions, self-evident Truths, and Propositions already es-
> tablished, then is the Argument so constituted called a *Demon-
> stration;* whereby it appears, that Demonstrations are ultimately
> founded on Definitions, and self-evident Propositions.[42]

As for the standards finally to be met in achieving certainty
in a demonstration, Duncan finds them in the rules governing
syllogisms of the first figure. "For since all the Syllogisms
that enter the Demonstration," he remarks, "are reducible to
Syllogisms of some one of the four Figures, and since the Syllogisms of all the other Figures are farther reducible to
Syllogisms of the First Figure, it is evident, that the whole

---

[40] *Ibid.,* pp. 121–122. The whole quotation from Locke occupies 33
lines of Duncan's text. Duncan credits it to Locke's essay, "Of the Conduct of the Understanding." For the first 11 lines of the quotation, see
Posthumous Works of Mr. John Locke (London, 1706), pp. 30–31; for
the rest, *ibid.,* pp. 26–27. Duncan's quotation is not entirely faithful to
Locke's original text, but he does not change Locke's meaning in any
real sense.

[41] *The Preceptor,* II, 124.   [42] *Ibid.,* pp. 134–135.

Demonstration may be resolved into a Series of these last Syllogisms." [43] The universal principles of certainty in all syllogisms of the first figure, the great laws of deductive reasoning, the self-evident truths of logic itself, are what the logicians call the *Dictum de omni* and the *Dictum de nullo,* respectively defined by Duncan as follows: *"Whatever may be affirmed universally of any Idea, may be affirmed of every or any Number of Particulars comprehended under that Idea,"* and, *"Whatever may be denied universally of any Idea, may be in like Manner denied, of every or any Number of it's Individuals."* [44]

Duncan's discussion of method as the fourth part of logic constitutes an important statement of the accepted distinction between the analytic and the synthetic methods. He recognizes the two established methods of arranging and communicating thought, he gives each its conventional terminology,[45] and he makes a contribution of his own to the theory of synthetic method by urging that it be called the method of science, "not only as in the Use of it we arrive at *Science* and Certainty, but because it is in Fact the Method, in which all those Parts of human Knowledge, that properly bear the Name of *Sciences,* are and ought to be delivered." [46]

Above all, he emphasizes the essential identity between the method used by mathematicians and that required in any other field where abstract ideas of the mind are involved. The last words of the *Logick* lay stress upon this important fact, so central to his whole design:

It is true the Method here laid down, hath hitherto been observed strictly, only among Mathematicians; and is therefore by many thought, to be peculiar to Number and Magnitude. But it appears evidently from what we have said above, that it may be equally applied in all such other Parts of Knowledge, as regard

[43] *Ibid.,* p. 135. [44] *Ibid.,* p. 137. [45] *Ibid.,* pp. 148–149.
[46] *Ibid.,* p. 149.

the abstract Ideas of the Mind, and the Relations subsisting between them. And since wherever it is applied, it necessarily be-
gets *Science* and *Certainty,* we have hence chosen to denominate
it the *Method of Science,* the better to intimate its true Nature
and Extent.[47]

5

Even if we did not know that Thomas Jefferson owned a
copy of Duncan's *Logick,* and that his beloved teacher, William Small, who taught him rhetoric, logic, and ethics during his first year at William and Mary, had been a disciple of
William Duncan at Marischal College, and would have been
certain to transport to Virginia his own master's logical as
well as scientific teachings—even if we were not sure of these
facts, we would nevertheless suspect, upon examining Duncan's *Logick* in relation to the Declaration of Independence,
that the former influenced the latter. The nature of that influence must now be briefly examined.

As the Declaration is usually printed, its second paragraph
begins with the famous words, "We hold these truths to be
self-evident, that all men are created equal, that they are en-
dowed by their Creator with certain unalienable Rights, that
among these are Life, Liberty and the pursuit of Happiness." [48]
It is difficult to believe that the word "self-evident" appears at
this point in the Declaration by mere chance. Jefferson is here

[47] *Ibid.,* p. 192.
[48] In Jefferson's original draft, this passage begins thus: "We hold
these truths to be sacred & undeniable; that all men are created equal &
independant. . . ." See Boyd, *Declaration,* 19. The words "sacred & undeniable" were crossed out later, and "self-evident" was written above
them. Boyd feels that this correction, as written upon Jefferson's
original draft, is in Jefferson's own handwriting and therefore originated with him (*ibid.,* 22, 24). Becker, *Declaration,* 142, 198, thought
that the correction is in Franklin's handwriting or that it comes from
Adams. This seems to me to be a case in which the physical evidence
cited by Boyd to link Jefferson with the correction is squarely cor-
roborated by all the evidence linking Jefferson with Duncan's *Logick.*

laying down the major premise of the syllogism that constitutes the whole demonstrative strategy of the Declaration, and
is here thinking in terms of the need to make that syllogism
command the assent of mankind. It was Duncan who repeatedly insisted, as we have seen, that for a syllogistic argument
to achieve certainty, to compel assent, to reach the highest
status in philosophy, it must be founded upon a self-evident
major premise, that is to say, upon a proposition that would
be equivalent to axioms and postulates in mathematics, and
that would convince any reasonable man of its truth if he
merely gave his attention to the ideas making it up. In other
words, "self-evident" as it appears in Duncan's *Logick* has a
precise technical meaning and is used in a stable, precisely defined context. As it appears in the Declaration, does it not
have the same technical meaning, and the same exact context,
except that it is being used in an operational as distinguished
from a doctrinal sense? A parallelism of this sort could of
course be attributed to accident, and perhaps it should be.
But a reader of Duncan's *Logick* is strongly inclined to feel
otherwise.

Again, it does not seem to be merely the result of accident
that the Declaration turns out in fact to be a perfect example
of the method of science as described so convincingly by Duncan. To be sure, this method, under its older rubric, synthesis,
was a fixed part of eighteenth-century logical doctrine, and
there are descriptions of it in *The Port-Royal Logic,* in Crousaz's *Art of Thinking,* and in four of the seven logical treatises
that were in Jefferson's library and could have been read by
him before 1776.[49] But of all the logics that flourished in

---

[49] Sowerby, *Catalogue,* V, 13–15, lists eight logics in Jefferson's library,
as follows: Abraham Fraunce's *The Lawiers Logike* (London, 1588);
Aristotle's *Logica,* in . . . *Opervum Aristotelis . . . Noua Editio, Graece
et Latinè* [ed. J. Pacius] ([Lyon], 1597); Richard Crakanthorp's
Logicae Libri Quinque, 4th ed. (Oxford, 1677); Wallis's *Institutio*

England during the first two-thirds of the eighteenth century, only Duncan's can be said to elevate the theory of method into a vital role in the philosophy of knowledge and in the strategy of scientific proof. Thus it would appeal above all to a mature writer or speaker seeking a persuasive formula more compelling and more fateful than any that would be merely prescribed in college exercises in composition.

If we may consider that the beginning words of Jefferson's immortal document have the effect of a logical definition, so far as they bring his present purposes into relation with a specific series of disruptive events, on the one hand, and with a generalized "respect to the opinions of mankind," on the other, then it is obvious that the Declaration as a whole fits Duncan's recommended plan for demonstrative proof. For after that opening, almost as if he were following Duncan's own prescription, Jefferson undertakes next "to lay down

---

Logicae (Oxford, 1702); Aldrich's *Artis Logicae Compendium* (Oxford, 1723); Watts's *Logick,* 8th ed. (London, 1745); Etienne Bonnot de Condillac's *Logica* (Madrid, 1794); Joseph Neef's *The Logic of Condillac* (Philadelphia, 1809). To this list must be added Duncan's *Logick* as printed in the second volume of *The Preceptor.*

Of these nine logics, Aristotle's *Logica* does not deal with what was later called the synthetic method, although his *Topica,* as one of his logical writings, provides the basis for the later division of dialectic into invention and *dispositio;* Crakanthorp's *Logicae Libri Quinque* does not recognize method as a part of logic, and thus remains thoroughly traditional in an age that was intent upon reforming the dialectical system of Ramus; Fraunce's *Lawiers Logike* treats methods in the manner of a devout Ramist, and thus does not include refinements introduced by Crakanthorp's contemporaries; Condillac's *Logica* and Neef's *The Logic of Condillac* were published too late to have influenced Jefferson in writing the Declaration; but the remaining four (Wallis, Aldrich, Watts, and Duncan) discuss the synthetic and the analytic methods in some detail.

There were other logics in Jefferson's library in volumes not devoted exclusively to that subject. For example, John Brightland's *Logic* accompanied his *Grammar* and other works in a volume held by Jefferson. See Sowerby, *Catalogue,* V, 116. But such elementary treatises as that do not require attention in this study.

some self-evident Truths," [50] which will serve as the foundation of his future reasonings; and he then proceeds syllogistically, so as to meet the requirements for a necessarily valid conclusion, while corollaries flow "naturally and of themselves," and particulars needed to illustrate the subject and to complete the reader's information are thrown in as scholia.

The argument of the Declaration falls naturally into the form of a categorical syllogism of the first figure. One attempt to reconstruct the propositions making up this syllogism will inevitably differ from another, as the critics' interests shift from politics to logic. Although Carl Becker's reconstruction is lucid and graceful, he states the syllogism from the point of view of its political implications,[51] and thus he does not reproduce the contours of Jefferson's own logical structure. In contrast, I should like to propose that we visualize Jefferson's argument in the following terms: [52]

Major Premise: All governments denying that men are created equal and that mankind therefore have inalienable rights to life, liberty, and the pursuit of happiness, may be altered or abolished at the hands of the people, from whose consent alone can governments derive their just powers.

Minor Premise: The history of his present majesty is a history of unremitting injuries and usurpations having in direct

[50] The source of this quotation is given above in n. 37. For the quotation immediately following, see Duncan's *Logick* in *The Preceptor*, II, 102.

[51] Becker, *Declaration,* pp. 203–204.

[52] In framing this syllogism I have worked, not from the accepted official text of the Declaration, but from Jefferson's own original draft before it was revised by Adams and Franklin, by the Committee of Five appointed to draw the document up, or by Congress itself in the process of giving it final form. I could not have done so with any confidence, however, if it had not been for Boyd's excellent study of the evolution of the text of the Declaration, to which I have earlier referred, and to which I now pay grateful tribute. For a reconstruction of Jefferson's original draft, see Boyd, *Declaration,* pp. 19–21.

object the establishment of an absolute tyranny over the American states.

Conclusion: All allegiance and subjection of these states to the kings of Great Britain and all others who may hereafter claim by, through, or under them, are therefore rejected, renounced, dissolved, and broken off.

The corollaries stated in the course of framing these propositions flow "naturally and of themselves," as Duncan says they should; [53] and their effect is to create the positive counterpart of the main syllogism, or to reinforce its conclusion. For example, a corollary of the right of the people to destroy a tyrannous government is their right "to institute new government, laying it's foundation on such principles & organising it's powers in such form, as to them shall seem most likely to effect their safety & happiness." [54] Thus it is later possible for Jefferson to declare, as a corollary of his conclusion, that the colonies are "free and independant states, and that as free & independant states they shall hereafter have full power to levy war, conclude peace, contract alliances, establish commerce, & to do all other acts and things which independant states may of right do." [55] For another example, a prudent people asserting their right to destroy a tyrannous government acknowledge as a corollary their duty to be patient under trivial and temporary political evils; thus governments abrogating the fundamental rights of the governed have to acknowledge in turn that such an action frees their people from the obligations of patient sufferance and places upon them the duty to revolt. Jefferson memorably develops these corollaries as follows: "Prudence indeed will dictate that governments long established should not be changed for light & transient causes: and accordingly all experience hath shewn that mankind are more disposed to suffer while evils are suf-

[53] See above, n. 50.   [54] Boyd, *Declaration,* p. 19.
[55] *Ibid.,* p. 21.

ferable, than to right themselves by abolishing the forms to which they are accustomed. But when a long train of abuses & usurpations, begun at a distinguished period, & pursuing invariably the same object, evinces a design to subject them to arbitrary power, it is their right, it is their duty, to throw off such government & to provide new guards for their future security." [56]

As for scholia, they appear in the Declaration, not as marginal glosses or footnotes, to be sure, but as if they were otherwise intended to conform to Duncan's requirement that they should illustrate the subject and complete the reader's information in the manner of annotations upon a classical text.[57] One such annotation occurs when, after commenting upon the native reluctance of mankind to revolt against oppression, Jefferson calls attention to the situation facing the American people: "Such has been the patient sufferance of these colonies; & such is now the necessity which constrains them to expunge their former systems of government." [58] Another annotation occurs after the minor premise has been stated: "To prove this, let facts be submitted to a candid world, for the truth of which we pledge a faith yet unsullied by falsehood." [59] Indeed, the list of eighteen specific injuries and usurpations alleged against the King as proof of the minor premise is a series of annotations upon Jefferson's text to complete the information of the reader. And his later notations concerning the cold reception of the petitions and remonstrances that the colonies had addressed to the King have precisely the same character and function.

6

Those who approach the Declaration in the belief that the principles of rhetoric are timeless and unchanging, and that

[56] *Ibid.,* p. 19.
[57] See Duncan's *Logick* in *The Preceptor,* II, 101–102.
[58] Boyd, *Declaration,* p. 19.   [59] *Ibid.*

the Declaration, or any other major persuasive work of any
period or place, should of course conform to those unchanging principles, or else be judged inartistic, are at once confronted by a paradox. For the Declaration is obviously persuasive in purpose and effect; but it does not conform to what
would have been called in its own time the principles of traditional rhetorical theory. For example, it does not follow the
prescriptions so fully described in John Ward's early eighteenth-century lectures at Gresham College on the classical
rhetorical system of Aristotle, Cicero, and Quintilian. Ward
emphasizes persuasion, not pre-eminently conviction, as the
end of oratory; he makes probability, not certainty, the orator's
normal attainable goal; he stresses appeals to passion and interest, not alone the appeal to reason, as the orator's means;
he points to the enthymeme and the example rather than to
the syllogism as the usual types of oratorical argument; he
discusses the topics of proof rather than the axioms of politics
and morality and the facts of contemporary life as the source
of oratorical materials; he recommends the classical form of
the oration rather than the form of mathematical demonstration as the proper structure of persuasive discourse; and he
prefers appropriate amplification and ornament to the short
dry way of logic as the accepted standard of oratorical style.
According to these principles, which Jefferson could have
read in his own copy of Ward,[60] the Declaration seems anti-
rhetorical. Yet it stands as one of the most persuasive and
influential discourses of the modern world. How then do we
explain this apparent contradiction?

The answer is, of course, that rhetoric is not fixed and
changeless. It changes as the culture around it does. Thus the
Declaration is an expression, not of traditional eighteenth-
century rhetoric, as expounded by Ward, but of a newly

[60] See Ward, *Oratory*, Lectures 2–4, pp. 10–19. See also Sowerby,
Catalogue, V, 17.

emerging rhetoric that was influenced by Locke and by Duncan and that would be fully expressed later in the century by Priestley and above all by Campbell. This new rhetoric was created out of new attitudes toward science, toward knowledge, toward reason, and toward man. There is hence no real strangeness involved in finding that the Declaration is not only in accord with the principles of Duncan's *Logick* but is also by that very fact a better specimen of effective rhetoric than it would have been if Jefferson had written it with the formulas of John Ward in mind. It delivered its ideas by the method of science to a generation which greatly respected scientific standards of thought and expression. In a century which revered John Locke, it followed Locke's dictum that "in all sorts of Reasoning, every single Argument should be managed as a Mathematical Demonstration, the Connection and Dependence of Ideas should be followed, till the Mind is brought to the Source on which it bottoms, and can trace the Coherence through the whole Train of Proofs." It employed the forms of philosophical address at a time when such forms were believed equal to the tasks of persuasion and appropriate as the means of expressing the doctrine of human rights. According to Jefferson's own intention, as expressed in the quotation with which this paper opened, it sought "to place before mankind the common sense of the subject, in terms so plain and firm as to command their assent, and to justify ourselves in the independent stand we are compelled to take." If anyone says that a discourse written to conform to these requirements is not a good example of rhetoric, he is saying in effect that rhetoric is the art of ignoring the sources of effectiveness in literary composition, and is the art of producing something beneath the status of good literature.

Jefferson's preference for a logical rhetoric as distinguished from a rhetoric of probability and ornamentation is rooted no more deeply in his devotion to the ideals of the Enlightenment than in his abiding admiration for the classics of Greek and Roman antiquity. One good expression of that admiration is found in his letter to Joseph Priestley on January 27, 1800; another, in his letter of July 1, 1814, to the Reverend Jason Chamberlayne; and still another, in his letter to David Harding on April 20, 1824.[61] As president of the Jefferson Debating Society of Hingham, Harding had written to notify Jefferson that the Society was being given his name. Jefferson's reply reads in part as follows:

The object of the institution is laudable, and in a republican nation whose citizens are to be led by reason and persuasion and not by force, the art of reasoning becomes of first importance. In this line antiquity has left us the finest models for imitation, and he who studies and imitates them most nearly will nearest approach the perfection of the art. Among these I should consider the speeches of Livy, Sallust and Tacitus as pre-eminent specimens of logic, taste, and that sententious brevity which using not a word to spare, leaves not a moment for inattention to the hearer. Amplification is the vice of modern oratory. It is an insult to an assembly of reasonable men, disgusting and revolting instead of persuading. Speeches measured by the hour die with the hour.

These sentiments indicate that Jefferson saw no contradiction between logic, taste, and brevity, on the one hand, and perfection in the art of persuasion, on the other. That such a contradiction seems inherent in the culture of twentieth-century America is a sign, not that wisdom has increased since Jefferson's day, but that superficiality and confusion have come upon us.

[61] For the letter to Priestley, see Ford, ed., *Writings of Jefferson*, VII, 413–416. The letters to Chamberlayne and Harding are as yet unpublished, but they will appear in due course in a future volume of Julian P. Boyd's great work, *The Papers of Thomas Jefferson* (Princeton, 1950—). Boyd kindly furnished me with the complete text of the letter to Harding, and my excerpt comes from that source. A shorter excerpt and a brief quotation from the letter to Chamberlayne are printed in Sowerby, *Catalogue*, V, 13.

CHAPTER 6

De Quincey on Science,
Rhetoric, and Poetry

1

De Quincey's famous distinction between the literature of knowledge and the literature of power is considered by Charles Sears Baldwin to confirm the ancient Greek distinction between rhetoric and poetics.[1] Baldwin expresses this opinion without any attendant elaboration or analysis; he is merely interested at the moment in pointing to a few modern examples of the sort of critical thinking that had been prevalent in antiquity. It doubtless seemed obvious to him that his casual reference to De Quincey was sufficiently clear in its context and needed nothing in the way of specific explanation. At any rate, we have no recourse but to examine that context as best we can and make it say whatever Baldwin allows it to suggest, if we are properly to evaluate his statement about De Quincey.

Not long before he mentions De Quincey, Baldwin speaks of rhetorical theory and poetical theory in ancient Greece as presupposing that "the art of speaking and writing is not throughout its various phases single and constant, but distinctly twofold"; he says further that "the ancients discerned and developed an art of daily communication, especially of public address, τέχνη ρητορική, ars oratoria, rhetoric; on the other hand, an art of imaginative appeal, τέχνη ποιητική, ars

[1] Baldwin, *Ancient Rhetoric and Poetic*, p. 4.

poetica, poetic"; and he refers, moreover, to Aristotle's *Rhetoric* and *Poetics* as the only ancient works to define sharply and elaborate fully the distinction between these two grand divisions of discourse.[2] Hence, when he goes on almost at once to identify De Quincey's distinction with that of the ancient critics, we must assume—must we not?—that to him De Quincey voiced opinions closely similar to those of Aristotle.

Baldwin is completely right in insisting that the distinction between rhetoric and poetics is a fundamental postulate of Aristotle's literary theory and is so pervasive in Greek and Roman criticism that its latent presence is everywhere discernible. But he ought to have emphasized that the ancient critics considered dialectic and rhetoric, rather than rhetoric alone, to have pre-eminent jurisdiction over the rhetorical, or better, the nonimitative branch of literature. His failure to stress this fact and to explain that in the Aristotelian view dialectic was what we would call today the theory of formal scientific writing, while rhetoric was what we call the theory of popular argumentation, makes his analysis of Aristotle's theory of nonimitative discourse incomplete and to some extent misleading.[3] Somewhat misleading, also, is his account of the ancient theory of poetical or imitative literature. He says that poetry and its companion forms were considered by the ancients to be "primarily imaginative, a progress from image to image determined emotionally." [4] Such language as this he did not borrow from Aristotle's *Poetics* but from much later works. What he does—and this deserves stress—is to superimpose upon his account of ancient poetical theory a terminology in which severe cleavages between intellect and imagination, reason and emotion, are more consciously pre-

[2] *Ibid.,* pp. 1–4. The direct quotations are from p. 1.

[3] For a discussion of the relations between dialectic and rhetoric in antiquity, see my *The Rhetoric of Alcuin and Charlemagne* (Princeton, 1941), pp. 33–64.

[4] Baldwin, *Ancient Rhetoric and Poetic,* p. 3; see also pp. 134–135.

supposed than they were by Aristotle. But, despite these two weaknesses in his analysis of ancient rhetorical and poetical theory, his emphasis upon the tendency of Greek criticism to presuppose or even to acknowledge explicitly the existence of two great families of discourse, one different in fundamental ways from the other, is both necessary and significant.

It is my purpose in this chapter to inquire into the propriety of Baldwin's remark that De Quincey's distinction between the literature of knowledge and the literature of power supports and strengthens Aristotle's distinction between rhetoric and poetry. What I shall do is to examine first of all De Quincey's opinions on rhetoric and eloquence, in an attempt to show that he and Aristotle have little in common so far as these subjects are concerned. Then I shall examine De Quincey's distinction between the literature of knowledge and the literature of power and compare it with Aristotle's conception of the relations between nonimitative and imitative literature. It will, I hope, become obvious as I proceed that De Quincey did not design his theory of the two great classes of discourse as Aristotle designed his. And it will probably be obvious, too, that in my opinion De Quincey's distinction is less satisfactory than Aristotle's as a way of accounting for the major difference between nonpoetical and poetical literature.

2

In the year 1828, De Quincey contributed to *Blackwood's Magazine* a review of Whately's *Elements of Rhetoric,* in which he sought not so much to evaluate the work of his learned contemporary as to set forth at some length his own theory of the difference between rhetoric and eloquence. Nowhere else in his writings does he afford us a better opportunity to understand his own conception of these two subjects or his own knowledge of Aristotelian rhetoric. Therefore, to his review I shall now devote some attention.

At an early stage of his review,[5] De Quincey mentions that
Coleridge was "in the habit of drawing the line with much
philosophical beauty between Rhetoric and Eloquence." Ad-
mitting, however, that he had never been so fortunate as to
hear Coleridge explore this topic, he proceeds to distinguish
the two terms in his own way. To him, eloquence is "the overflow of powerful feelings upon occasions fitted to excite
them," whereas "Rhetoric is the art of aggrandizing and
bringing out into strong relief, by means of various and striking thoughts, some aspect of truth which of itself is supported
by no spontaneous feelings, and therefore rests upon artificial
aids." These, I repeat, are De Quincey's own definitions. Certainly he intended them to limit eloquence to the type of discourse in which an appeal is made to the passions; and to divorce rhetoric, as a theory of composition, from any interest
in the methods of conviction and demonstration. This intention is fully clarified when he remarks, as a prelude to these
definitions, that "where conviction begins, the field of Rhetoric ends; that is our opinion; and, as to the passions, we con-
tend that they are not within the province of Rhetoric, but of
Eloquence." [6]

"In this view of Rhetoric and its functions," De Quincey
observes, "we coincide with Aristotle; as indeed originally we
took it up on a suggestion derived from him." [7] This avowal
by De Quincey of his direct indebtedness to Aristotle's *Rhetoric* led David Masson, the editor of De Quincey's collected
writings, to explain in a detailed footnote some of the meanings that the word *rhetoric* had acquired since the time of

[5] The text to which I refer throughout this study is in *The Collected
Writings of Thomas De Quincey,* New and Enlarged Edition, ed. by
David Masson, 14 vols, (Edinburgh, 1889–1890), X, 81–133. The reference to Coleridge and the definitions of eloquence and rhetoric are on
page 92. In subsequent notes "De Quincey" will stand for this edition.
[6] De Quincey, X, 82.   [7] *Ibid.,* p. 83.

Aristotle, and to set forth those points in Aristotle's doctrine that De Quincey had imperfectly remembered or wrongly understood. But such explanations need not enter our present discussion. It is for the moment sufficient to emphasize that eloquence designated to De Quincey the sort of discourses which Aristotle would have regarded as the typical products of rhetorical theory, and that rhetoric meant to De Quincey all of the typical products of that narrow, unphilosophical rhetoric which Aristotle did so much to condemn. Perhaps we should add that the conception of rhetoric constructed by De Quincey under the authority of Aristotle is so attenuated, so unreal, so far divorced from actual human experience, so completely devoid of connection with the urgent issues of politics and law, that we can only wonder why De Quincey would think it worth while for Aristotle or any serious-minded person to bother with it in any theoretical or practical way.[8]

The narrowness of De Quincey's idea of rhetoric is apparent throughout his review of Whately's *Elements*. Sketching the history of rhetoric, and accounting for its periods of popularity and oblivion, he has something to say of the rhetorics of Greece, Rome, England, France, Germany, Italy, and Spain. At one point he remarks:

Rhetoric, in its finest and most absolute burnish, may be called an *eloquentia umbratica;* that is, it aims at an elaborate form of beauty which shrinks from the strife of business, and could neither arise nor make itself felt in a tumultuous assembly.[9]

A moment later, he observes that "all great rhetoricians in selecting their subject have shunned the determinate cases of

[8] For a more favorable view than mine of De Quincey's theory of rhetoric, see H. H. Hudson, "De Quincey on Rhetoric and Public Speaking," *Studies in Rhetoric and Public Speaking in Honor of James Albert Winans*, pp. 133–151. See also above, pp. 28–29.

[9] De Quincey, X, 93.

real life." This remark leads him to speak of rhetoric in Greece. He says:

> We can readily understand, therefore, why the fervid oratory of the Athenian assemblies, and the intense reality of its interest, should stifle the growth of rhetoric: the smoke, tarnish, and demoniac glare of Vesuvius easily eclipse the pallid coruscations of the aurora borealis. And, in fact, amongst the greater orators of Greece there is not a solitary gleam of rhetoric. Isocrates may have a little, being (to say the truth) neither orator nor rhetorician in any eminent sense; Demosthenes has none.[10]

If it seems strange to us that not a solitary gleam of rhetoric is to be found among the greater orators and the great orations of Greece, especially when we remember that Aristotle, writing what he conceived to be the theory of what orations are and what orators do, called that theory rhetoric, De Quincey's treatment of the rhetoricians in Rome seems even stranger, even more capricious. He includes among them Livy and Ovid, the two Plinys, Lucan, Petronius, Quintilian; above them all he places the two Senecas.[11] He does not mention Cicero—Cicero, a great speaker, who almost alone among the great speakers of Western Europe interested himself in the theory of his art and wrote treatises on rhetoric which constitute in sum the most enlightened of such works in the Roman period and the best synthesis of Aristotle's *Rhetoric* ever attempted. De Quincey is not interested in the theory that would give an explanation of the orations against Catiline; to him rhetoric grows out of society's sterility and defeat, and out of the rhetorician's preoccupation with language when language is used without reference to the things it symbolizes. In fact, he clearly suggests this view when he says:

> To hang upon one's own thoughts as an object of conscious interest, to play with them, to watch and pursue them through a maze of inversions, evolutions, and harlequin changes, implies a

[10] *Ibid.,* p. 94.   [11] *Ibid.,* p. 95.

condition of society either, like that in the monastic ages, forced to introvert its energies from mere defect of books (whence arose the scholastic metaphysics, admirable for its subtlety, but famishing the mind whilst it sharpened its edge in one exclusive direction); or, if it implies no absolute starvation of intellect, as in the case of the Roman rhetoric, which arose upon a considerable (though not very various) literature, it proclaims at least a quiescent state of the public mind, unoccupied with daily novelties, and at leisure from the agitations of eternal change.[12]

Small wonder that, in De Quincey's view, "the age of Rhetoric, like that of Chivalry, has passed amongst forgotten things"![13] Even eloquence, he observes, has suffered an eclipse in the modern world. He adds, however:

Eloquence is not banished from the public business of this country as useless, but as difficult, and as not spontaneously arising from topics such as generally furnish the staple of debate. But rhetoric, if attempted on a formal scale, would be summarily exploded as pure foppery and trifling with time.[14]

Inconsistencies in De Quincey's conception of rhetoric begin to show when he names the English authors who qualify as eminent masters of that art. Foremost among these he places Donne. Opposing Dr. Johnson's designation of Donne as a "metaphysical poet," De Quincey remarks that Donne is better described as "rhetorical." "In saying *that,* however," he hastens to add, "we must remind our readers that we revert to the original use of the word *Rhetoric,* as laying the principal stress upon the management of the thoughts, and only a secondary one upon the ornaments of style."[15] Is not De Quincey's reminder perplexing in the extreme? Up to this point he has been treating rhetoric as the art of stylistic ornamentation, or as that kind of composition in which an author eddies about his own thoughts, allows his fancy to move "self-sustained from its own activities," and indulges in a "flux and

[12] *Ibid.,* p. 97. [13] *Ibid.,* p. 97. [14] *Ibid.,* p. 100.
[15] *Ibid.,* p. 101.

reflux of thought, half meditative, half capricious"; [16] and he has claimed for this conception the authority of Aristotle. Now he emphasizes that rhetoric is something more than mere verbal intricacy—that it is the art of managing thoughts and by extension the art of coming to terms with the objective realities to which thoughts and words ultimately refer. Would Aristotle prefer this latter view to the former? De Quincey does not openly say he would. But the fact that the two views are not identical, and that De Quincey has both in mind, may account for his inclusion of the names of Burton, Milton, Jeremy Taylor, Sir Thomas Browne, Bolingbroke, Canning, and (with some qualifications) Burke among the great English rhetoricians. Hailing Burke as "the supreme writer of his century, the man of the largest and finest understanding," De Quincey adds that he was not the one "to play with his fancy for the purpose of separable ornament," and that only in rare cases did he "indulge himself in a pure rhetorician's use of fancy." [17]

In these remarks, **and** in others about Burton, Milton, Taylor, and Browne, De Quincey may be said to preserve his conception that rhetoric is the art of dressing thoughts *en grand costume;* but if he had explicitly to alter this view in order to make Donne a respectable rhetorician, we cannot be too sure that he did not implicitly alter it in giving his other authors that same title.

3

Our survey of De Quincey's opinions on rhetoric and eloquence indicates that the second of these terms, and on rare occasions the first, meant to him what the first meant to such

[16] These phrases appear later in the work under consideration; see De Quincey, X, 121.

[17] For the references to Burke, see De Quincey, X, 114–115. The discussion of English rhetoricians begins on p. 100 and extends to p. 121.

writers as Aristotle and Cicero. As we turn now to De Quincey's discussion of the literature of knowledge and the literature of power, we ought to keep in mind that, if these large classes of discourse are to be regarded as parallel to the rhetorical and the poetical branches of ancient theory, then we would expect to find De Quincey classifying what he called eloquence, and perhaps what he called rhetoric, within the scope of the literature of knowledge. In other words, we would expect that De Quincey's distinction between the one sort of literature and the other would not place the oration and the sermon within the field of poetry. But our expectation is not fulfilled by De Quincey. He visualizes sermons, orations, and that curious kind of word-play which he calls rhetoric, as more nearly akin to poetry than to scientific writing. Emphasizing that the literature of power, or literature properly so called, includes works printed in books and works published by other means—by oral communication, for example—he remarks that "much literature, scenic, forensic, or didactic (as from lecturers and public orators), may never come into books, and much that *does* come into books may connect itself with no literary interest." [18] Somewhat earlier he said:

> The weekly sermons of Christendom, that vast pulpit literature which acts so extensively upon the popular mind—to warn, to uphold, to renew, to comfort, to alarm—does not attain the sanctuary of libraries in the ten-thousandth part of its extent. The Drama again,—as, for instance, the finest of Shakespere's plays in England, and all leading Athenian plays in the noontide of the Attic stage,—operated as a literature on the public mind, and were (according to the strictest letter of that term) *published* through the audiences that witnessed their representation some time before they were published as things to be read.[19]

If these positive statements are not in themselves sufficient evidence of De Quincey's intention to regard orations and ser-

---

[18] De Quincey, XI, 54.   [19] *Ibid.*, pp. 53–54.

mons as part of the literature of power, they tend at least in
that direction. So also do the remarks that he makes when he
describes the actual specimens of the literature of knowledge.
To this class he assigns no work that he would call rhetorical
or oratorical. To this class, instead, he assigns such books as
dictionaries, encyclopedias, grammars, spelling-books, the
Court Calendar, and the parliamentary reports, these being
the humbler examples, while histories, biographies, travels,
and works like Newton's *Principia* and those of Laplace, he
specifies as higher examples and warns that they are sometimes confused with true literature by unperceptive critics.[20]

It ought to be remarked at this point that De Quincey's
distinction between the literature of knowledge and the literature of power exists in two versions, one of which was published in 1823, when he was 38 years of age, and the second in
1848, when he was 63.[21] The first version appears in a work
entitled "Letters to a Young Man whose Education has been
Neglected," published in several installments in the *London
Magazine*. Advising his readers upon the question of selecting
foreign languages for a coherent plan of education, De Quincey remarks that a particular language ought to be chosen
after one has decided whether his inclinations lie in the direction of science or in the direction of literature. How can
one make this decision? De Quincey's answer, which he credits
in its broad outline to many years' conversation with Wordsworth,[22] is given as a distinction between what he calls books
of knowledge, or antiliterature, or *literae didacticae*, or παιδεία,
on the one hand, and literature, or *literae humaniores*, on

[20] He mentions in several places the types of works which belong to
the literature of knowledge; see especially De Quincey, X, 47, and XI,
57, 59.

[21] For the text of the first version, see De Quincey, X, 33–52; for that
of the second, see De Quincey, XI, 51–97.

[22] De Quincey, X, 48, note. For the terms used by him in this first
version, see *ibid.*, pp. 47, 49.

the other. The terms "literature of knowledge" and "literature of power," as a way of expressing this distinction, appear in the second version, which was published in the *North British Review* for August, 1848, in connection with De Quincey's critical estimate of Roscoe's edition of the works of Pope.

The first version provides two criteria which the critic may use in determining whether a given work justly belongs to science or to literature. One criterion involves certain realities in the given work itself. If it is a work, says De Quincey, "in which the matter to be communicated is paramount to the manner or form of its communication," [23] then it belongs to science—it is a book of knowledge. He does not state what the relation of matter and form would have to be in the work of literature. But he is thinking of one class as the logical antithesis of the other, and we may therefore assume that in his view the literary work would be that in which form or manner of communication is paramount to the matter. The second criterion involves the effect of the given work upon the reader. "All that is literature," says he, "seeks to communicate power; all that is not literature, to communicate knowledge." [24] What, then, we ask, is power? De Quincey's answer is explicit. Reduced to its simplest terms, his idea is that power is a personal possession of the reader of a literary work when that work has so affected him as to make him conscious of unhabitual emotions and of their organization. De Quincey's own definition of power is as follows:

Now, if it be asked what is meant by communicating power, I, in my turn, would ask by what name a man would designate the case in which I should be made to feel vividly, and with a vital consciousness, emotions which ordinary life rarely or never supplies occasions for exciting, and which had previously lain unwakened, and hardly within the dawn of consciousness—as

[23] *Ibid.,* p. 47.　　[24] *Ibid.,* p. 48.

myriads of modes of feeling are at this moment in every human mind for want of a poet to organize them? I say, when these inert and sleeping forms *are* organized, **when** these possibilities *are* actualized, is this conscious and living possession of mine *power,* or what is it? [25]

A consciousness of unhabitual emotions and of their organization, their structure—this, then, is the state of mind of the reader of a great poem. De Quincey illustrates this effect by describing with warmth and skill how *King Lear* and *Paradise Lost* affected him. Unfortunately he does not turn then to give a parallel definition of knowledge, conceived as the effect of a good work in science upon the mind of a reader. Remembering, however, as we did a moment ago, that he is thinking of books of knowledge as the logical antithesis of literature, and reminding ourselves that in the old psychology *thought* was regarded as a kind of antithesis of *emotion,* we may assume that to De Quincey *knowledge* is a consciousness of new thoughts and their structure.

Is there not a fundamental inconsistency between the two criteria proposed by De Quincey as a means of determining whether a book is literary or scientific? If a scientific work is such that in his view the matter to be communicated is paramount to the manner or form of the communication, then the reader of that work must be conscious of matter rather than form. That is to say, the formal aspects of that work, the structure and organization of its parts, will not appear in the reader's consciousness as configurations of his awareness of substance. Yet, if our statement of the effect of that kind of work upon the reader is a true antithesis of De Quincey's definition of power, then he himself would declare that the reader of a scientific work would be conscious not only of new thoughts, but also of their organization, their structure. In short, according to De Quincey's second criterion, the

[25] *Ibid.,* p. 48.

reader of a work in science would have that very consciousness of manner or form which the first criterion seeks to deny
to him. Would not De Quincey have been wise to discard
altogether his first criterion, and to recognize explicitly that
scientific works have a system of forms or structures suitable
to themselves, and literature has a different system of structures to complement and administer its different procedures?

Another difficulty arises even when we abandon De Quincey's first criterion. His second criterion implies that the literature of power gives us no values except those associated
with our consciousness of unhabitual emotions and their organization. Yet it is fair to insist that literature has something
to do with our thoughts—that literature may make us aware
no less than science of new thoughts and their organization.
Once we admit this, we have destroyed much of the validity
of De Quincey's second criterion; but we have prepared the
way for a distinction between science and literature that will
limit neither to an exclusive preoccupation with some one
faculty of the mind, conceived as having power to operate
more or less independently of other faculties. Perhaps it is
because we can no longer believe in the validity of such a
conception of the mind that we cannot accept De Quincey's
definition of power as a full account of the happenings within
ourselves when we read some great work like *King Lear* or
Paradise Lost.

Twenty-five years after De Quincey formulated his distinction between science and literature, he stated it again, this
time in the form which most scholars and critics associate
with his name. Perhaps he felt that some of the inconsistencies in his earlier version should be eliminated; perhaps he
had changed his mind on some details; perhaps he had even
forgotten exactly what he had previously said. At any rate,
his second account differs markedly from the first.

Whereas in the earlier version he had alluded with some

contempt to the vulgar antithesis between instruction and pleasure as the determining factor in the distinction between the two kinds of discourse, and had dismissed it with the remark that "this wretched antithesis will be of no service to us," [26] he now uses a modification of it as the entering wedge for his dichotomy. He observes:

> In that great social organ which, collectively, we call literature, there may be distinguished two separate offices that may blend and often *do* so, but capable, severally, of a severe insulation, and naturally fitted for reciprocal repulsion. There is, first, the literature of *knowledge;* and, secondly, the literature of *power.* The function of the first is—to *teach;* the function of the second is—to *move;* the first is a rudder; the second, an oar or a sail. The first speaks to the *mere* discursive understanding; the second speaks ultimately, it may happen, to the higher understanding or reason, but always *through* affections of pleasure and sympathy.[27]

Involved in these words is one set of terms which may need a bit of explanation. The "mere discursive understanding," to which the literature of knowledge speaks, is probably to be accepted as De Quincey's term for man's intelligence; the "higher understanding or reason," to which speaks the literature of power, is his term for man's intuitive faculty. Something of the force of these terms within the framework of his whole distinction can be gathered from what he himself says a moment later:

> It [that is, the literature of power] is concerned with what is highest in man; for the Scriptures themselves never condescended to deal by suggestion or co-operation with the mere discursive understanding: when speaking of man in his intellectual capacity, the Scriptures speak not of the understanding, but of *"the understanding heart,"*—making the heart, *i.e.* the great *intuitive* (or non-discursive) organ, to be the interchangeable formula for man in his highest state of capacity for the infinite.[28]

[26] *Ibid.,* p. 47.   [27] *Ibid.,* XI, 54.   [28] *Ibid.,* p. 56.

In De Quincey's review of Whately's *Elements,* he has something to say which further clarifies the meaning he assigns to the intuition and the ordinary intelligence. There he observes:

An *intuition* is any knowledge whatsoever, sensuous or intellectual, which is apprehended *immediately:* a notion, on the other hand, or product of the discursive faculty, is any knowledge whatsoever which is apprehended *mediately.* All reasoning is carried on discursively; that is, *discurrendo,*—by running about to the right and the left, laying the separate notices together, and thence mediately deriving some third apprehension.[29]

These words, it may be observed, are written by De Quincey in order that he may deliver a reprimand to Milton for degrading the fallen angels in *Paradise Lost* by making them debate with the ordinary instruments of the discursive faculty. Arguing that spiritual beings must share with God the ability to see the whole argument in a flash of intuition, not in a slow development of intermediate propositions, and that Milton had violated this propriety, De Quincey calls the Second Book of *Paradise Lost* a descent from poetry into rhetoric, and suggests that Milton doesn't do any better in his logic than would the House of Commons. Be that as it may. What is of interest to us at this moment is that to De Quincey the process of mediate inference in logic, with its concern for the fully articulated syllogism, is characteristic of man's reasoning faculty, whereas the immediate inference of logic, with its mode of inferring one proposition directly from another without the use of a middle term, is the instrument of man's intuition.

It is now clear that De Quincey's second version of the distinction between the two kinds of literature involves in the last analysis not so much the terms *teaching* and *moving* as the terms *intelligence* and *intuition.* What he has to say about

[29] *Ibid.,* X, 103.

the difference between scientific truth and literary truth illustrates this point. A scientific truth he describes as a truth
which a person may be absolutely unconscious of before he
learns it. "To be capable of transplantation," he observes, "is
the immediate criterion of a truth that ranges on a lower
scale." [30] That is to say, a man may not know that a stone is
hard; but the knowledge can be given him, either by direct
experience with a stone, or by words from somebody who
transplants the notion in his consciousness. When man first
acquires such notions as these, they are new to him, or at
least, as De Quincey says, they are "connected with something
of absolute novelty." But literary truth is that of which a person is never, at any time in his life, wholly unconscious. De
Quincey says:

> It is the grandeur of all truth which *can* occupy a very high
> place in human interests that it is never absolutely novel to the
> meanest of minds: it exists eternally by way of germ or latent
> principle in the lowest as in the highest, needing to be devel-
> oped, but never to be planted.[31]

This higher truth is connected with man's innate ideas.
"Tragedy, romance, fairy tale, or epopee," declares De Quincey, "all alike restore to man's mind the ideals of justice, of
hope, of truth, of mercy, of retribution, which else (left to
the support of daily life in its realities) would languish for
want of sufficient illustration." [32]

In De Quincey's view, the literature of power not only presents higher truth but also creates in the reader a deep sympathy for it. Indeed, he finds a parallel between the effect of
literature and the effect of children or of direct experience
upon the individual or society. In one of his most attractive
passages he says:

> What is the effect, for instance, upon society, of children? By

[30] *Ibid.,* XI, 55.   [31] *Ibid.,* p. 55.   [32] *Ibid.,* p. 56.

the pity, by the tenderness, and by the peculiar modes of admiration, which connect themselves with the helplessness, with the innocence, and with the simplicity of children, not only are the primal affections strengthened and continually renewed, but the qualities which are dearest in the sight of heaven,—the frailty, for instance, which appeals to forbearance, the innocence which symbolizes the heavenly, and the simplicity which is most alien from the worldly,—are kept up in perpetual remembrance, and their ideals are continually refreshed. A purpose of the same nature is answered by the higher literature, viz. the literature of power.[33]

And again he speaks to the same purpose:

Were it not that human sensibilities are ventilated and continually called out into exercise by the great phenomena of infancy, or of real life as it moves through chance and change, or of literature as it recombines these elements in the mimicries of poetry, romance, etc., it is certain that, like any animal power or muscular energy falling into disuse, all such sensibilities would gradually droop and dwindle.[34]

As he completes his second version of the distinction between science and literature, De Quincey remarks upon the provisional character of the one as contrasted to the permanent character of the other:

The very highest work that has ever existed in the Literature of Knowledge is but a *provisional* work: a book upon trial and sufferance, and *quamdiu bene se gesserit*. Let its teaching be even partially revised, let it be but expanded,—nay, even let its teaching be but placed in a better order,—and instantly it is superseded. Whereas the feeblest works in the Literature of Power, surviving at all, survive as finished and unalterable amongst men.[35]

De Quincey provides an illustration of this statement by comparing Newton's *Principia* with such works as the *Iliad* and

[33] *Ibid.*, p. 55.   [34] *Ibid.*, p. 56.   [35] *Ibid.*, p. 57.

Hamlet. The former survives, he observes, only so far as it can continue to surpass the rival works of Laplace in respect to exact truth and felicity of arrangement; but the *Iliad* and *Hamlet* survive without vying with each other—they survive because each is unique, self-sustained, triumphant for ever.

4

In this analysis of De Quincey's thinking upon the subject of science, rhetoric, and literature, we have seen that rhetoric, conceived by him to be stylistic virtuosity, lies within the province of literature properly so called, near the subdivision of eloquence, and not far from the subdivision which contains the highest poetry. There can be little or no doubt that he would tend to identify poetry, on the one hand, with oratory and verbal ingenuity, on the other; for poetry, in his view, is directly concerned with an emotional effect, so far, at least, as it operates through affections of pleasure and sympathy, whereas rhetoric aims at an elaborate form of beauty, and eloquence is an overflow of powerful feelings. We have also seen that the literature of knowledge is coextensive in his thinking with all sorts and degrees of scientific writing, and that his theory of the division of discourse into two classes makes one class rather small and narrow and definite, the other being wide and strangely assorted and blurred in its internal groupings. We have looked closely at his two versions of this theory. The first, as we have indicated, affords two criteria for discerning whether a book belongs to science or to literature. The second criterion, which identifies function with a reader's consciousness of emotions and their organization or of thoughts and their organization, seems to us to contradict the first, in which De Quincey states that matter is paramount in science, form in literature. The second criterion, moreover, because it implies that man's emotions and his thoughts can be, as it were, dissociated, and can respond as separable units of consciousness, without close organic interconnection, seems today to be questionable. What, now, of the second version of De Quincey's theory? That, as has been pointed out, depends upon a third criterion—the difference between man's faculty of intuition and his faculty of reason. If we accept this criterion as a way of establishing a scheme of values for scientific writing and poetry, we may often wonder how far it is allowable for us to exclude intuition from science or reason from literature. We may also wonder why, if De Quincey makes a distinction at one time between two things in terms of emotion and thought, and a later distinction in other terms, it is not incumbent upon him to explain rather than to ignore this change in his basic terms. It would seem, therefore, that De Quincey's two attempts to distinguish between science and literature are not of the highest value, when we judge them in and for themselves. He poses a very important question in criticism; he raises essential issues. But his answer to the question is vitiated by an inconsistency and founded upon a psychological theory that denies the possibility of interconnections between emotional and intellectual experience.[36]

5

The question whether De Quincey's theory of the divisions of discourse corroborates that of Aristotle need not concern us at great length. The chief resemblance between the two is that each postulates two main families of discourse and seeks

[36] J. H. Fowler, in *De Quincey as Literary Critic*, The English Association, Pamphlet No. 52 (July, 1922), pp. 4–8, finds De Quincey's distinction between literature of knowledge and literature of power to be unhelpful, false, harmful. In making this appraisal, Fowler only examines the second version of the distinction, and does not press his analysis of it to the point where he perceives the importance of the issues raised by De Quincey. See also above, pp. 27–29, 191–193.

to explain the differences between them. But here close resemblance ends. And it may at once be anticipated that a correspondence based upon a postulate of this sort need not be extensive or systematic, and would not in itself establish Baldwin's statement that De Quincey's theory confirms Aristotle's.

To Aristotle, the two main families of discourse embrace on the one hand scientific writing, historical writing, and oratory, and on the other drama, epic poetry, and lyric poetry. That is to say, he does not draw the line between the two families in such a way as to place oratory in the class of poetical compositions; rather, he places oratory in the other class, no doubt in the belief that the oral utterance in the law court and the public legislative body has somewhat the same ultimate relation to the realities with which it deals as does the oral or written utterance in the philosophical academy or the historical seminar. Nor does he draw the line between the two families in such a way as to suggest a severe insulation, a reciprocal repulsion, between the mental faculties to which scientific discourse and poetical discourse are sometimes considered respectively to relate. Had he drawn both of these lines, his theory would have anticipated De Quincey's, and De Quincey's would have supported his. But his real distinction is made with other postulates in mind.

The works of Aristotle to which we must refer in determining the main outlines of his whole theory of discourse are the *Topics,* the *Rhetoric,* and the *Poetics.* At least, these are to be regarded as his major contributions to literary speculation. It may be said that each of these works focuses attention upon one of the three chief activities in the field of discourse, and that, taken together, the three works cover the field.

The reader of the *Topics* and the *Rhetoric* does not need to be reminded that these two works are interconnected at many points. Indeed, the *Rhetoric* begins with the statement that

"Rhetoric is the counterpart of Dialectic," [37] dialectic being of course the true subject of the *Topics;* and the cross references between the former work and the latter are frequent and suggestive. When Aristotle's thinking upon these two subjects has been explored, the conclusion is plain that he intended dialectic to be the theory of the formal scientific utterance, in an age when scientific procedures were in the hands of philosophers and dialecticians, and rhetoric to be the theory of popularizing and defending truth or good probability. Although rhetoricians might seem at times to be using verbal deception and fraudulent statements as a substitute for accurate expression, and to be therefore adhering to a theory that contradicts good procedures in scientific and historical writing, yet Aristotle, particularly in his analysis of the four uses of rhetoric, insists upon the superior persuasiveness of true statements over false,[38] and thus clearly recognizes the correspondence between truth in scientific writing and persuasiveness in oratory.

In sum, Aristotle's *Topics* and *Rhetoric* offer together a theory of one of the two main families of discourse. Aristotle gives no name to this family. But might we not say that his treatises on scientific writing, or dialectic, and oratorical expression, or rhetoric, constitute a kind of theory of the literature of statement? That is to say, these treatises investigate the relations between statements, as verbal phenomena, and the facts to which words refer—these treatises investigate the degrees and kinds of correspondence that must exist between verbal descriptions of reality and reality itself, if those descriptions are to convince people, as in the case of science, or persuade people, as in the case of oratory.

[37] Lane Cooper, *The Rhetoric of Aristotle: An Expanded Translation* (New York, 1932), p. 1.

[38] *Ibid.*, pp. 5–6. See also Plato's *Phaedrus,* where the same theory of persuasion is advanced.

Looking now at Aristotle's theory of the other main family of discourse, we observe that in the *Poetics* he states very explicitly the principle which differentiates poetry and science. He says:

Turning first to the conception of poetry in general, we may follow the natural order, and begin with what is fundamental, the principle of artistic imitation. Epic Poetry and Tragedy, as well as Comedy and Dithyrambic Poetry, and for the most part the music of the flute and lyre, in their general nature are forms of imitation; that is, they represent, or imitate, something through an arrangement of words or notes.[39]

Here then, is the underlying poetic principle—the principle that forms of poetry are forms of imitation, with words as the medium. Elsewhere in the same chapter, Aristotle applies this principle to a case in which scientific writing might be confused with poetry, and shows how the principle operates to preserve the separate identity of these two kinds of discourse. Empedocles had written versified natural science; Homer, too, had written in verse. But should Empedocles and Homer both be called poets, their work poetry? No, says Aristotle. And why not? Because such terminology would be accurate only "if it were not the principle of imitation that characterized the artist"; and he adds, "hence, if it is proper to style Homer a poet, Empedocles must be classed as a natural scientist rather than a poet."[40]

What Aristotle says later about the difference between the historian and poet is an elaboration of the distinction between scientific writing and poetry, history being scientific in the sense that historians seek to state accurately in words the events that once actually transpired. Says Aristotle:

[39] Lane Cooper, *Aristotle on the Art of Poetry: An Amplified Version* (New York, 1913), p. 2.
[40] *Ibid.*, p. 4.

The essential distinction [between history and poetry] lies in this, that the Historian relates what has happened, and the Poet represents what might happen—what is typical. Poetry, therefore, is something more philosophic and of a higher seriousness than History; for Poetry tends rather to express what is universal, whereas History relates particular events as such.[41]

The universals expressed in poetry are of course conceptions —conceptions about actual human life and actual human behavior. These conceptions direct the poet in his selection of a story that will reveal them; these conceptions dominate the story, give it unity, mood, purpose. But the story is partly or wholly invented. It is the process of using such stories and episodes to embody the meaning and the purpose of human life as the poet has actually observed it round about him that suggests what Aristotle means by "imitation" or "representation." In other words, the poet gathers his conceptions from his own observation of human situations in his experience; but he transmits these conceptions to other men by telling a story or presenting a dramatic action that stands by analogy for his own observation and experience. The historian, however, transmits to other men a consciousness of events that once transpired, by means of words that stand directly—not by way of symbol and analogy—for those actual events. Whereever the historian's method is at work—and it is at work in science and in oratory as in history—we may call it the method of statement, and its products, the literature of statement. Wherever the poet's method is at work, we may call it the method of representation, and its products, the literature of representation. At any rate, Aristotle would seem by express statement and by implication to lend support to such a way of describing the differences between the two great families of verbal compositions.

[41] *Ibid.,* pp. 31–32.

6

We may conclude, therefore, that Aristotle's distinction would place rhetoric within the province of De Quincey's literature of knowledge, whereas De Quincey himself would place rhetoric within the province of the literature of power. We may also conclude that De Quincey bases his distinction upon an assumption of a sharp separation between the faculties of reason and emotion, or (in his second version) reason and intuition, whereas Aristotle bases his upon the assumption that truth finds its way from one man to another either by words that directly convey it or by words that represent it by means of symbols. Thus Baldwin would appear to have little basis for his statement that De Quincey confirms Aristotle. But what is more important is that if criticism is to provide an accurate description of the difference between rhetoric and poetry, Aristotle would seem to establish a better foundation than does De Quincey.

CHAPTER 7

Literature as an Enterprise in Communication

Mais si les vrais orateurs sont poètes, il me semble aussi que les poètes sont orateurs; car la poésie est propre à persuader.
—Fénelon, *Dialogues sur l'Éloquence*

1

My purpose in this chapter is to examine the relation of the artistic enterprise to the communicative enterprise, in an effort to find what bearing the former has upon communication and social action. Enlightened social action may well be considered the necessary condition of our survival as human beings. Communication is without question the great enterprise by which enlightened social action is determined. This enterprise consists in the transfer of truth and opinion from one person to another through the channels provided by our educational institutions, our books, periodicals, newspapers, radios, television sets, political campaigns, and legislative processes, our pulpits, our courts, our mediation boards, our conventions of scientists and scholars. I propose to inquire whether or not the artistic enterprise is to be considered a part of this enterprise of communication; and if so, whether it is therefore in danger of losing its identity and of being confused with what we popularly regard as the more practical and more pedestrian arts of the orator, the propagandist, and the popularizer of knowledge.

This inquiry can hardly be ignored, so important has it

become in the twentieth century. The status of the fine arts has been vigorously debated throughout the course of recorded history, but at no time has this debate been more acrimonious than it is at present. Oppressed by the fear that the artistic enterprise may become a mere tool of the party in power, and may be forced to parrot the insidious and soul-destroying ideologies that issue from the ministry of propaganda, some recent critics have taken the position that the fine arts are not a means of communication and persuasion. This school of criticism identifies the fine arts with pleasure rather than instruction, with beauty rather than utility, with imagination and taste rather than reason and judgment, and with aesthetic needs rather than practical daily necessities. Meanwhile, other critics, recognizing the persuasive value of the work of art, have said in effect that art is nothing but propaganda; and that, when artists deliberately assert the contrary, they are influenced, not by the facts of artistic effect, but by their class-conscious aversion to standards by which some of them would be judged failures, or by their snobbish unwillingness to renounce their long associations with the rich and the aristocratic. The truth seems to lie somewhere between these two rival positions, once each has been stripped of the eulogistic or vituperative language in which it is usually expressed. The truth seems in short to be that a genuine work of art and a genuine specimen of propaganda are not alike in all respects, but that each has nevertheless a social purpose that can be connected with the elaborate process by which human beings adjust themselves to each other and to their environment in the eternal quest for security and survival.

Verbal utterances, spoken or written, occupy a central position among the products of the communicative enterprise, and a no less central position among the products of the artistic enterprise. The specialists in propaganda, oratory, and popularization necessarily use words in disseminating information and in seeking to influence the attitudes of great masses of men, although pictures and other devices are important parts of the machinery of communication. The verbal utterances used by these specialists have many names, but as a matter of convenience they may all be called rhetorical. The poet, the dramatist, and the novelist use the same medium of words, now and then in combination with pictures, musical notes, painting, dances, and the like. Verbal utterances created by these men and women—by artists, as distinguished from rhetoricians—may all be called poetical. How words behave in the rhetorical and the poetical enterprises would seem to be an inquiry that might lead to a possible clarification of the differences between propaganda and art. It is this inquiry which will occupy us here.

In the ensuing discussion I shall consider three main propositions. The first is that the poetical utterance belongs to the enterprise of communication by virtue of the fact that it does actually convey to readers a something that they did not have before. What this something is has been variously described. To some it is a feeling, an attitude, a mood; to others, a meaning or a complex of meanings; to others, an idea, an ideology, a truth; to others, an insight, an intuition, an imaginative view of the world. The history of criticism abounds in terms to be applied to what it is that a poetic utterance gives its readers, but there has never been a movement in criticism that holds to the notion that poetry is devoid of all power to give anything to anybody. Nevertheless, as I mentioned earlier, attempts have been made to say that the poetical utterance is not primarily communicative, and thus my first proposition requires some discussion. My second proposition is that the poetical utterance differs from the rhetorical utterance by virtue of the fact that the words used in the latter refer directly to states of reality, and that the

words used in the former refer directly to things that stand
by deputy for states of reality. These things that stand by deputy for other things I shall call symbols. Symbolism is characteristic of poetical representation; it is not the primary
characteristic of rhetoric, as I shall endeavor to explain later.
My third proposition is that the poetical, like the rhetorical,
utterance persuades those who come in contact with it, and
thus affects social action. Some will of course have an initial
impulse to feel that the term *persuasive* cannot with propriety be applied to poetry; but I hope to show that it can,
and I hope to suggest that, when it is placed there, it will
give poetry no inferiority of status in human affairs, but on
the contrary a status that poetry ought not willingly to disavow.

2

Critics who detach poetry from the enterprise of communication usually base their thinking upon the assumption
that the absence of a desire to communicate is what gives the
poetical utterance its unique characteristics, and that the
presence of this desire makes any utterance rhetorical. They
argue that the personal lyric is the purest form of poetry,
and that the other types of literature—the narrative, the tragedy, the comedy, the satire—are progressively less pure as
they manifest an increasing intention to reach and impress
an audience; whereas in oratory and propaganda, where the
communicative intention of an author is developed to its
farthest extent, poetical qualities vanish altogether. But these
critics do not as a rule deny that the lyric poem has the capacity to transfer some mood or attitude from the poet to his
readers. What they do deny is that the lyric is produced for
the sake of the impression it is to make. They say that it must
exhibit within itself no evidence of a communicative purpose
—that it must be created for the sake of expression, not im-

pression. Since expression is considered by them to be a private need of the poet, of no primary concern to the adjoining populace, their dialectic reduces the social function of the lyric to a secondary, almost to an accidental, status.

This view of poetry and rhetoric has twentieth-century adherents.[1] I should like to examine it, however, not in its more recent formulations, but in the version that its adherents cite as one of their chief sources. That version is found in John Stuart Mill's "Thoughts on Poetry and Its Varieties," published originally in *The Monthly Repository* in 1833. Early in that essay, Mill distinguishes science from poetry by saying that "the one addresses itself to the belief, the other to the feelings." This differentiation prepares the way for his discussion of the line of division between the oration and the poem. As he knew, oratory had traditionally been regarded as having to do both with belief and feeling. Thus it seemed to him to be in a position where it could claim affiliations with science and with poetry. In an effort to show how the oration and the poem could alike address the feelings, and yet remain distinct from each other, Mill remarks that the former bears within itself visible evidences of its author's awareness of his intention to communicate, whereas the latter does not.

Poetry and eloquence [he states] are both alike the expression or utterance of feeling. But if we may be excused the antithesis, we should say that eloquence is *heard,* poetry is *over*heard. Eloquence supposes an audience; the peculiarity of poetry appears to us to lie in the poet's utter unconsciousness of a listener. Po-

[1] See, for example, H. H. Hudson, "Rhetoric and Poetry," *The Quarterly Journal of Speech Education,* X (April, 1924), 143–154; and, by the same author, "The Field of Rhetoric," *Ibid.,* IX (April, 1923), 167–180. For less formal presentations of this view, see Marchbanks's speech to Proserpine in Bernard Shaw, "Candida," in *Plays Pleasant and Unpleasant* (London, 1957), II, 105; and also B. L. Smith, H. D. Lasswell, and R. D. Casey, *Propaganda, Communication, and Public Opinion* (Princeton, N.J., 1946), pp. 1–2.

etry is feeling confessing itself to itself, in moments of solitude, and embodying itself in symbols which are the nearest possible representations of the feeling in the exact shape in which it exists in the poet's mind. Eloquence is feeling pouring itself out to other minds, courting their sympathy, or endeavouring to influence their belief or move them to passion or to action.[2]

Mill immediately adds that "all poetry [i.e., all lyric poetry] is of the nature of soliloquy." Not wishing, however, to imply that poets are eccentrics who talk aloud to themselves and do not know of the other means of publication, he goes on to show that, while they may print for others what they have said to themselves, no trace of consciousness that any eyes are upon them "must be visible in the work itself." The poet's "act of utterance," continues Mill, must be "itself the end"; when it becomes the means to an end, "when the expression of his emotions, or of his thoughts tinged by his emotions, is tinged also . . . by that desire of making an impression upon another mind, then it ceases to be poetry, and becomes eloquence."

In criticism of Mill's view it must be emphasized that a consciousness of the impulse to communicate cannot be affirmed or denied to exist in the poet's mind at the moment of poetic creation without assuming that we know for a fact what is in effect only a speculation on our part. If we cannot be sure that we actually see what happens in the poet's mind when he is producing a poem, if we can be sure only that the happenings in that mind bear an analogy to normal mental experience, and are simply intenser configurations of that normal experience, then we could not go so far as to say that an impulse to communicate is totally absent from the poet's consciousness at the instant when an impulse to express something is present there. Mill's later hypothesis, which he

[2] I cite the text as it appears in J. S. Mill, *Dissertations and Discussions* (London, 1859), I, 71. The quotations that follow are from pp. 71 and 72.

explains at some length in the closing pages of his essay, is that the poetic nature differs fundamentally from the scientific or philosophical nature. Differences there are, to be sure, as one persons's heart action differs from another's. But it seems unwise to describe them in such a way as to eliminate from the poet's consciousness at a given moment a communicative impulse that, for all we know, is there present in some complex association with the expressive impulse.

A further weakness in Mill's position is apparent if we try to prove that the lyric utterance contains no evidence of its author's intention to communicate. The fact that words are the chief medium of human intercourse, and that the laws of grammar, logic, and rhetoric have shaped language so as to render it more communicative than a lawless medium would be, gives any utterance, poetical or rhetorical, predominantly communicative traits. In his *Counter-Statement,* Kenneth Burke has shown that these traits are everywhere apparent in the structural arrangements of poetry, in a chain of events arranged, for example, in the order of climax; and that these arrangements always betray the poet's communicative intention. Burke argues, indeed, that since the poetic utterance is designed to produce effects upon an audience, and since rhetoric aims at the same goal, effective literature can be nothing else but rhetoric.[3] This is an extreme position. It suggests that there is no major difference between the oration and the poem; by implication it denies the possibility of difference between producing effects upon an audience by direct statements about reality and producing effects upon an audience by deputies or symbols of reality. But it nevertheless has value in calling attention to the communicative function of poetry, and to the objective evidences of this function in any poem's structure. If we preferred the alternative view of Mill, we would find it hard to point out in a

[3] *Counter-Statement,* pp. 265–266. Also below, Chapter 8, *et passim.*

poem any evidences that it was purely expressive. Sooner or later we would have to admit that Mill's view allows poetry to be merely communicative for the sake of expression as its purer aim, and requires rhetoric to be only communicative for the sake of communication as its entire aim. Such an admission would make it clear that, if the distinction between poetry and rhetoric can only be expressed in terms of the difference between the soliloquy and the direct address, then it is not a very satisfactory distinction. A better one, indeed, is suggested by Mill's surprisingly incidental statement that the poetic utterance achieves its uniqueness by "embodying itself in symbols which are the nearest possible representations of the feeling in the exact shape in which it exists in the poet's mind." Here he implies the importance of the symbol in artistic representation. But he prefers, I think unwisely, to treat the symbol as a minor aspect of his theory, and to place major emphasis upon shadowy and unverifiable assumptions about the presence of uncommunicative characteristics in poetical utterances and the absence of communicative impulses in the poet's mind.

For actual proof that poetry conveys something to its readers, we must turn from the examination of the weakness of such a theory as Mill proposes and consider our own experiences with poetic utterances. We would acknowledge that the plays of Shakespeare and Ibsen and Shaw really said something to us when we witnessed their production in the theatre. We might disagree with each other in our attempts to state what a given one of these plays had to say; we might even dislike what we thought any one of them said; but our disagreements and our dislikes would indicate that something had been transferred to our minds as a result of our contact with its author's words. We would also acknowledge that great epic poems—*The Divine Comedy* and *Paradise Lost* are excellent examples—communicated something to us when we read them. Prose fiction from the pen of Dickens, Thackeray, Hardy, Conrad, Hawthorne, Melville, Tolstoy, Manzoni, Flaubert has excited so much interest and such lively controversy that it could hardly be called uncommunicative or incapable of saying anything. Even lyric poetry, although it does not have as many willing readers as do the forms just mentioned, produces vivid and lasting effects upon those who submit themselves to its exacting disciplines. I. A. Richards observes: "But poetry itself is a mode of communication. What it communicates and how it does so and the worth of what is communicated form the subject-matter of criticism." [4] Indeed, anyone who wishes an empirical demonstration of the communicativeness of lyric poetry has only to turn to the book just cited. It describes Richards's procedure in assigning thirteen lyrics to students in his classes at Cambridge University and elsewhere, and in requiring those students to write a critique of each poem. By printing the poems and the comments elicited by each, Richards shows not only that poems transfer something to readers, but that the responses to a given poem display wide variety, and that the systematic study of these responses is a useful means of charting the course to be followed by teachers in giving students a more perfect control over poetry as one of the great modes of communication.

3

Although the poetical utterance shares with the rhetorical utterance a communicative function, the two differ from each other in an important way. The simplest way to describe this difference, as I have already indicated, is to say that the words which make up the rhetorical utterance lead the reader to states of reality, whereas the words making up the

[4] *Practical Criticism: A Study of Literary Judgment* (London, 1929), p. 11.

poetical utterance lead the reader to things which stand by deputy for states of reality. These things which stand by deputy for states of reality are, as I earlier said, the poet's symbols. Thus lyric poetry, drama, and fiction may collectively be called the literature of symbol; expository prose, journalistic writing, oratory, and all the verbal utterances designed to deal directly with factual states and conditions in human experience, may collectively be called the literature of statement.[5]

In thus making symbolism the key term in the differentiation of poetry from rhetoric, I should like to guard myself against the inference that I am asserting the symbolist school of art to be superior to the rival schools of realism and naturalism. The symbolist school of art has claimed symbolism as its own peculiar property, and has made it appear that this term is out of place unless it is used to designate an artistic procedure that this school believes in and that the naturalists and realists do not believe in. Since the closing years of the nineteenth century, the symbolists have taken the position that realistic fiction or drama or poetry conveys what it has to say by literal means, by direct statements, for example, whereas the proper method is to use suggestion and indirection. It is true, of course, that there are differences between the detailed and the abstract methods of presentation, as can be seen if we compare a realistic play like Elmer Rice's *Street Scene* with Maeterlinck's symbolical *Blue Bird*. But as I use the term, symbolism would designate a common characteristic of these two plays, not a characteristic which the latter has and the former does not have. Thus realism and naturalism, on the one hand, and romance and allegory, on the other,

[5] For a discussion of these terms in relation to De Quincey's distinction between the literature of knowledge and the literature of power, see Chapter 6.

would designate alternative ways or methods of presenting the things chosen by the author to stand by deputy for other things. The realist would treat a situation in such minuteness of detail that it would seem as if his purpose were that of a scientist describing a phenomenon; the allegorist would treat a situation in terms of a few of its salient characteristics. But the realist would be an artist, not a scientist, because his fully drawn situation would stand as the deputy of broadly analogous situations in a reader's experience; and the allegorist would be an artist, not a dreamer or schizophrenic, because his abstract situation would likewise stand as the delegate of parallel happenings in human life. Thus, it is of the symbol as a characteristic of artistic representation of any sort that I propose to speak; and this use of the term is amply justified by its accepted primary meaning.

We can see the difference between statement and symbolism if we regard readers as travelers going from one country to another far away, and utterances as the signposts along the road. The rhetorical signpost, we may say, contains the name of the country to which the traveler is going, and a number to indicate the number of miles to be covered before he reaches his destination. Names of real countries, and numbers to represent real distances, are characteristic of rhetorical signposts. The poetical signpost, we may say, contains the name of the winter season of the year, and a number to indicate the stages in the span of human life. It seems uncommunicative in any practical way; its words appear strange and obscure. Such strangeness and obscurity, such an apparent lack of practical application, are traits of a poetical signpost. But suppose our traveler had the good sense to reflect that its words might have a bearing upon his journey. Suppose he understood the words to mean that when he arrived at his distant destination, the season of his life would be winter, and the total number of stages in that life would thus have been mainly devoted to the conquest of the space that stretched out beyond the signpost. Here would be information about his journey; and it might be as accurate as that on the other signpost. It might be more useful, too. For it would tend to place upon the journey a greater value, a greater significance in human terms, than the rhetorical signpost does. It would, for example, make the journey mean that the traveler would have no time for other things when it was over—that he would be old, then, and spent. Thus the accuracy and the utility of the one signpost in relation to the other are not grounds for determining the difference between them. The difference between them is that the poetical signpost gives direction about places and relations in space, not in words that refer to exact spatial relations and real places, as does the rhetorical signpost, but in words that (so far as my illustration is concerned) refer to temporal relations that stand by deputy or symbol for spatial relations. How it is that the words of a poem can concretely designate one thing, and can make a reader see that thing as the delegate of a constituency of other things, is to be explained by the fact that words carry literal and associative meanings, and that the poet can by his allusive yet concrete manner of presentation make us see in one conscious instant the thing directly named by his words, and related things suggested by that thing.

My illustration is of course subject itself to the hazards of metaphor. A metaphor says something about a given thing by asserting its significant likeness to something else, as when, in saying that a ship plows the sea, we lend meaning to a naval implement by giving it a characteristic of an agricultural implement. My metaphor tries to say something about poetry by likening it to a signpost, and there is danger that my comparison will say too little or too much or something untrue or partial. Hence, I should like, by attempting a more objective description of the relation between rhetoric and poetry, to guard against being misunderstood.

As I said before, the rhetorical utterance and the poetical utterance are both made up of words. Everyone will agree that words are arbitrary signs affixed by common consent to things, to activities of things, to characteristics of things, in our complex environment. Everyone knows that, by manipulating these arbitrary signs, he can show to himself and to others what relations and differences, what consequences to himself, he perceives among those things. If we think, then, of words as the signs of things, and of things as the "referents" of words, we can accept the notion that the meanings we assign to words are a reflection of the meanings we assign to their referents.

The problem of assigning a meaning to a rhetorical utterance would therefore appear to be the problem of determining what referents that utterance has—what things it designates, and what those things actually mean in our experience. The words, as we read them, call up in our mind the things to which they refer. Our experience has already to a degree made us familiar with those things, and has given us conceptions and ideas about them. As we read on, we find ourselves moving among our experiences with things because the words before us stand for those things. Our transaction with the rhetorical utterance is complete when we have fully connected its words to their referents in our experience, and have, by this traffic with signs, extended our experience with things, or modified or rejected parts of it, or fully verified it, or perhaps not altered it at all.

The problem of assigning a meaning to a poetical utterance is also that of finding the referents for the words used in it. But the things to which a poetical utterance refers may be, for example, the events set forth in Shakespeare's *Hamlet,* and thus Shakespeare's words have these events as primary referents. We may read of these events, and then say that we are not princes, that our mother did not marry our paternal uncle just after our father died, and that our uncle did not then conspire to kill us. In other words, we may find no secondary referents in our own experience for the words in Shakespeare's play. We may even like *Hamlet,* nevertheless, for its exciting action and its memorable language. But as our own experience with life and with people deepens and grows, we may come to see that *Hamlet,* even without literal analogies in our own life, is in a sense our story, the story of everyman. The problem of Hamlet's delay, of his tormented unwillingness to take sides until it was too late, is not unlike that presented to all sensitive men in the eternal struggle against the evil of this world. At any rate, our problem in reading *Hamlet,* or any work of fiction or of poetry, becomes that of finding the second set of referents for its words.

The difference between this problem and that presented by the rhetorical utterance can be shown diagrammatically by letting W stand for the words we read, E stand for our experience with the things of our world, and S stand either for the experience that people like ourselves have with the things of their world, or for the things that are linked by convention, by association, by accidental or pertinent resemblance, to other things. In reading the rhetorical utterance, we go from W to that part of E which W is dealing with; in reading the poetical utterance, we go from W to S and thence onward by complex processes of association to that part of E which is relevant to S.

I do not mean to imply that the reader of either kind of utterance solves the whole problem of interpretation only by studying an author's words. The reader must of course seek assistance from other sources: from the study of the author's life and of his times; from the study of historical changes in the uses of words; from the study of the contemporary audience that the author addressed; from the study of the whole climate of opinion in which the author dwelt. Thus biography, history, linguistics, philosophy, must be brought to bear upon the problem of understanding what a given text, rhetorical or poetical, means. But the major clues to an author's meaning are his own words, and it is in studying them that we must proceed with an eye to the difference between statements and symbols.

4

If it is right to say that the words which make up rhetorical and poetical utterances lead us to things in our own experience, and induce us either to consider those things directly or to consider them through intermediaries, then it is difficult to believe that the poetical utterance has none of the persuasive force universally admitted to be characteristic of the rhetorical utterance. Either of these two forms of language has the power to make us see the things around us in a new way—to make us formulate new evaluations of our own experience, or to confirm us in our own previously formulated evaluations. Once we have changed or modified or verified or not changed the ideas which we inevitably and necessarily bring with us into our transaction with any author's words, we are in possession of a mental outlook that tends to have its own inexorable consequences in our future action. It is what we conceive things to be that determines how we act towards them, or how we fail to act. Our beliefs, our prejudices, our inhibitions, our complex orientations, toward the bewildering variety of things that make up our environment, force us to project those attitudes into our behavior and conduct. Thus, action is a consequence of something that happens within our consciousness or our subconsciousness as a result of our construct of interpretations, evaluations, insights, revelations, fears, hopes, about the things of our world. To deny to poetry its consequences in action would be to assert that poetry makes nothing happen within us when we read it or that the happening has nothing to do with the processes by which we reduce the things in the world to coherence and meaning. Neither of these assertions, as I have already shown, could be verified by the experience of the thoughtful reader of poetry. Some readers may say that poetry makes nothing happen to them, and in this case, at any rate, we can be sure that their subsequent action would not be appreciably influenced. But other readers have spent much time and ingenuity in describing what happenings are induced in them by poetry. We may accept their testimony as evidence of the reality of the happenings, and we may verify this evidence against the testimony of our own experience. Having done so, we would not be inclined to doubt that poetry brings to us a sense of the order and significance of things around us, and thus induces the outlook that, once it is accepted by us as true, determines our action.

The aesthetic factors in a poem and the rhetorical factors in a speech or piece of exposition are not to be interpreted to imply a difference between our sense of delight in the harmony of a work of art and our sense of conviction of the truth of a more practical communication. We ordinarily associate delight with a sense of harmony, and conviction with a sense of truth; but our delight is an aspect of conviction, as conviction is an aspect of delight. What I mean is that the sense of harmony which produces our delight in a poem is a correlative of the sense of truth which leads us to be convinced by an oration. Harmony may be said to be a correspondence between the realities of human life and the equivalent symbol, projected into language. The poet works to achieve this correspondence, the reader to perceive it.

Truth may be said to be a correspondence between the realities of the objective world and the equivalent verbal statement. The scientist and orator work to achieve this correspondence, their audience to accept or perchance to reject it. Considerations like these, placed in a somewhat different context, led Walter Pater, in his celebrated essay, "Style," to affirm the resemblance between truth in science and beauty in literature. Said he:

> In the highest as in the lowliest literature, then, the one indispensable beauty is, after all, truth:—truth to bare fact in the latter, as to some personal sense of fact, diverted somewhat from men's ordinary sense of it, in the former; truth there as accuracy, truth here as expression, that finest and most intimate form of truth, the *vraie vérité*.[6]

Pater conceived of the scientific utterance as one in which truth was achieved when the author's words accurately fitted the facts under his observation, without any intrusion of his own personality; the poetical utterance, in his view, achieved its truth or harmony when the author's words accurately accorded with his own peculiar imaginative sense of the facts under his observation. The difference between facts as transcribed with rigorous objectivity and facts as transcribed with a high degree of subjectivity led Pater to classify all verbal utterances into one or the other of two groups, which he respectively named the literature of fact and the literature of the imaginative sense of fact. His theory deserves careful study. It seems questionable in its assumption that complete objectivity is possible of attainment in scientific writing.[7] It seems questionable, too, in its assumption that oratory and poetry as subjective modes of discourse are to be considered

[6] *Appreciations, with an Essay on Style,* p. 34.

[7] For a good examination of this assumption from the point of view of the historian, see C. L. Becker, "Everyman His Own Historian," *The American Historical Review,* XXXVII (1932), 221–236.

essentially identical. But in its insistence upon the similarity of the concept of truth and that of literary beauty or harmony, it invites us to see the alliances and affiliations between the rhetorical and the poetical utterance, and to reexamine suspiciously the conventional dichotomies that would deny beauty to the one and persuasiveness to the other.

5

It would therefore appear that rhetoric and poetry, as the two chief modes of communication and persuasion, diverge from each other because the one uses words to illuminate factual matters, and the other uses words to illuminate things that in turn illuminate factual matters. This major difference explains others. It explains why it is that narration is the dominant pattern of the poetical utterance. Narration, with its elements of plot, setting, and characterization, enables the poet to represent human beings in action, and to draw together in the representation those diverse factors of environmental influence and individual predisposition that give meaning to conduct. Narration permits the reader to understand the particulars of his own situation by seeing them objectified as a meaningful fusion of analogous particulars. Narration uses analysis for the sake of synthesis. On the other hand, the dominant patterns of the rhetorical utterance are argument and exposition. These patterns proceed by generalization and division; these patterns permit the reader to understand a situation by seeing it as a complex fusion of its own particulars, temporarily isolated from analogous things; these patterns use synthesis for the sake of analysis. Without the poetical and the rhetorical modes of communication, or more broadly, without these two modes of understanding, human society would not exist. Rhetoric and poetry are as it were two equal ministers in the communicative structure of human affairs. Each has its own method of operation.

ach has its own subjects of major interest. Society does not
ave to choose between them. Society needs only to use both,
nd to come to understand how both are most effectively to
e used.

CHAPTER 8

Kenneth Burke's "Lexicon Rhetoricae": A Critical Examination

1

The most influential modern critical treatment of the relations between rhetoric and poetics was formulated by Kenneth Burke in his well-known work, *Counter-Statement*. First
published in 1931, and given other editions in 1953 and
1957, *Counter-Statement* has set a contemporary fashion in
criticism and has been instrumental in inducing academic
critics to write on such subjects as the rhetoric of fiction, the
rhetoric of tragedy, or even the rhetoric of irony. Indeed, if
the present discussion did not begin with a reference to
Counter-Statement, it would not be easy to convince the
American literary establishment that the relations between
rhetoric and poetry have been anything more than an occasional minor topic in twentieth-century aesthetics, and I
might have to resort to the expedient of going back to Aristotle's *Rhetoric* and *Poetics* for some adequately recognized
doctrine that could now be invoked in getting the connection between these two arts in shape for analysis. It would
not be objectionable to me, at any rate, to return to Aristotle
on the present occasion, and I shall certainly do so before this
chapter is finished. But I should like first to comment upon
Burke's more fashionable theory of the place of rhetoric in
literary criticism.

Burke's basic conclusion, which was not derived from Aris-

otelian sources, consists in his asserting that rhetoric is " 'the
se of language in such a way as to produce a desired im-
ression upon the hearer or reader,' " and that therefore
'effective literature could be nothing else but rhetoric." [1]
This proposition plainly means, of course, that drama, prose
iction, and lyric and narrative poetry, as well as the various
ypes of nonfiction, lie within the proper jurisdiction of
hetorical theory. In fact, many of the illustrations used by
Burke to establish rhetoric as the art of producing a calcu-
ated response in an audience are taken from Shakespeare,
nd these belong as convincingly to his argument as do his
nany other illustrations from Mark Twain, Gustave Flau-
ert, Thomas Mann, André Gide, or T. S. Eliot. [2] As a crucial
ndication of the primacy assigned by Burke to rhetoric in the
vhole scheme of critical theory, it should be noted that he
ises the phrase "Lexicon Rhetoricae" to name the dictionary
of essential terms in literary and dramatic criticism. [3] It should
lso be noted that, in an effort to overcome the prejudice
ncountered by a serious critic who attempts to make rhetoric
a respectable term in the literary world, Burke considers the
wentieth-century distrust of rhetoric in aesthetic circles to
e in fact a revolt against its mundane functions—a revolt in
vhich the art of appeal is disparaged in its totality because
hat art is affiliated with the endeavors of oratory, journalism,
ropaganda, publicity, and public relations. [4] As a corrective
of this distrust. Burke would ask the literary critic to accept
he art of appeal as an indispensable general procedure hav-
ng a practical focus in the devices of the orator, the editorial

[1] *Counter-Statement* (1931), p. 265. I cite this edition through this
chapter.
For an account of the source of Burke's definition of rhetoric, see
above, pp. 37–42.
[2] For Burke's reference to these authors, see *Counter-Statement*, pp.
3–14, 38–40, 43–48, 50–53, 68–69, 74, 116–135, 158.
[3] *Ibid.*, pp. 156–232.   [4] *Ibid.*, p. 266.

writer, and the publicist, and an artistic focus in the work o
the playwright, the novelist, and the poet.

In applying his theory of rhetoric to the task of criticism
Burke makes it plain that the rhetorical element shared ir
common by nonpoetic and poetic utterances is bound up ir
their form; and to him all formal considerations not only
constitute, as he says, "a major portion of the rhetorician'
lore," [5] but also are to be conceived as verbal indications o
any author's attempt to create an appetite in the auditor and
then adequately to satisfy that appetite. "This satisfaction—
so complicated is the human mechanism—at times involves a
temporary set of frustrations," remarks Burke, "but in the
end these frustrations prove to be simply a more involved
kind of satisfaction, and furthermore serve to make the satis
faction of fulfilment more intense." He adds:

If, in a work of art, the poet says something, let us say, about a
meeting, writes in such a way that we desire to observe that
meeting, and then, if he places that meeting before us—that is
form. While obviously, that is also the psychology of the audience, since it involves desires and their appeasements.[6]

2

At first glance, of course, the scholar-rhetorician is grateful
to Burke for his obvious success in having made rhetoric a
more respectable term than it was in the years preceding
1931. During the seventeenth and eighteenth centuries, this
term began to lose its traditional reference to the whole
sweep of Aristotelian and Ciceronian rhetorical doctrine, and
it came to be used indiscriminately to designate either the
art of arguing by commonplaces rather than by facts, or of
using a heavily ornamental rather than a plain manner of
speaking and writing, or of delivering a passage in the accents
of the theatre rather than in the voice of ordinary life. Out

[5] *Ibid.*   [6] *Ibid.*, p. 40.

of these contradictory meanings emerged a later disposition to regard rhetoric with contempt. It was characterized in some quarters as the art of avoiding rather than meeting the facts of public life. It was thought in other quarters to mean pomposity and false impressiveness in style. And in still other quarters it was counted pretentious declamation. Anyone who has conscientiously tried to take rhetoric seriously as a historical phenomenon or as a scholarly discipline knows how frustrating it is even yet to be associated with some of the degraded aspects of the rhetorician's procedures, and to be assumed in teaching those procedures to emphasize only what the pejorative senses of the term rhetoric would seem to allow. It is undoubtedly true, by the way, that many of those who are active participants in the twentieth-century revival of rhetorical training in American universities are themselves under the influence of one or more of the degraded meanings to which rhetoric is subject. It is also true that the unfortunate example which these modern rhetoricians have set is used by their detractors as proof that the discipline of rhetoric does not deserve a full share of academic respectability and honor. Burke has at least helped to correct the impression that rhetoric comprises only the abuses of discourse. At most he has made rhetoric a stylish (if somewhat mystical) term in the modern critical establishment. For these benefits, and they are in fact estimable, the scholar-rhetorician may properly express his thanks.

The rhetorician has every reason, moreover, not to object to that form of Burke's thesis in which rhetoric would be authorized to study the effects that have been or may be produced upon listeners whenever they are addressed by direct statements; and he also has reason to agree with Burke that any author whatever will "seek to produce such effects as appeal to a large audience, or to a small audience, or to a particular kind of audience (as an audience of working-men, or an audience of scholars)." [7] In short, linguistic utterances of all sorts must be said to create responses in hearers or readers. An aesthetic or a rhetorical theory that did not recognize this basic law would be untenable, and Burke is amply justified in making it a central doctrine in his system.

But Burke develops this law in such a way as to indicate that it makes the poetical utterance and the rhetorical utterance specifically alike, and that their common capacity to produce effects argues their identity in method and structure. Thus he makes syllogistic progression a major aspect of literary form, and he declares that, "in so far as the audience, from its acquaintance with the premises, feels the rightness of the conclusion, the work is formal." [8] He means here that the premises arouse expectations in the audience, and the conclusion satisfies those expectations. "The arrows of our desires," he adds, "are turned in a certain direction, and the plot follows the direction of the arrows." And he finds syllogistic form to be illustrated in a demonstration by Euclid no more truly than in a story of ratiocination by Poe. This sort of reasoning leaves us wondering whether, if Euclid is a rhetorician-poet because he arouses and satisfies expectations by using syllogistic progression in geometrical proof, and if Poe is a poet-rhetorician because he uses the same means to the same end in a fiction, there can ever be any way of accounting for the differences that readers and hearers feel to exist between a theorem in geometry and an imaginative story. It is because Burke does not appear interested in accounting for such differences that his identification of rhetoric with poetry opens itself to objection.

3

In constructing a critical system that on the one hand will allow rhetorical and poetic utterances to be designed to pro-

[7] *Ibid.*, p. 241.   [8] *Ibid.*, p. 157.

duce effects upon an audience, and on the other will be fully responsive to the differences between the rhetorical, as distinguished from the poetic, means of producing these effects, we might begin by calling attention to a former tendency in criticism to distinguish between the two literatures. Aristotle was the earliest major critic to recognize that two literatures do in fact exist. His own way of calling attention to the essential differences between them involved his celebrated distinction between imitative and nonimitative art and his attendant illustrative definition of the respective provinces of poetry and history.[9] The same distinction was in his mind when he took notice of the tendency to call Empedocles a poet, not by reason of any imitative dimension in his work, but because he composed natural philosophy in hexameters. "Homer and Empedocles, however, have really nothing in common apart from their metre," he insisted; "so that, if the one is to be called a poet, the other should be termed a physicist rather than a poet." [10] Other critics, much nearer the outlook of the twentieth century than Aristotle is usually counted to be, have followed his example in emphasizing the existence of the two literatures, although their respective ways of differentiating one from the other have not made direct use of Aristotle's perceptive formula. Thus Fénelon, believing that an oration and a poem are at their best both persuasive and delightful, found the distinction between them by saying that good oratory is almost poetry—that "poetry differs from simple eloquence only in this: that she paints with ecstasy and with bolder strokes." [11] Thus Wordsworth drew a careful distinction between matter of fact or

[9] Aristotle, *Rhetoric* (trans. W. Rhys Roberts), *Poetics* (trans. Ingram Bywater), Modern Library (New York, 1954), pp. 223–224, 234–235.

[10] *Ibid.*, p. 224.

[11] See my *Fénelon's Dialogues on Eloquence,* p. 93. For an analysis of Fénelon's view of the relations between oratory and poetry, see above, Chapter 3.

science and poetical composition.[12] Thus De Quincey evolved his celebrated but cloudy differentiation between the literature of knowledge and the literature of power.[13] Thus also, in a particularly influential contribution to the philosophy of the two literatures, John Stuart Mill thought of the rhetorical utterance as exhibiting everywhere within itself the visible evidence of its author's intention to communicate with an audience, whereas the poetic utterance, the lyric poem in particular, betrays the poet's complete lack of awareness of a listener, and is of the nature of soliloquy.[14] And thus again, having this same basic problem in mind, Walter Pater offered yet another solution, even more penetrating than that of Mill, by developing a theory of the literature of fact as contrasted to the literature of the imaginative sense of fact.[15]

These prominent critics have had their twentieth-century counterparts, one of whom is Charles Sears Baldwin. Baldwin wrote what amounts to a three-volume history of rhetoric and poetics from ancient times to the end of the sixteenth century,[16] and of course he could not avoid dwelling upon the basic traditional distinction between these two types of literary endeavor. In one place he said that the rhetorical discourse, being primarily intellectual, involves "a progress from idea to idea determined logically," while po-

[12] "Preface to the Second Edition of Several of the Foregoing Poems, Published, with an Additional Volume, under the Title of 'Lyrical Ballads,'" in *The Complete Poetical Works of William Wordsworth* (Boston, 1904), p. 793, note.

[13] Details are given above, pp. 199–214.

[14] See Mill's essay, "Thoughts on Poetry and Its Varieties," in his *Dissertations and Discussions* (London, 1859), I, 71–72. Also above, p. 219.

[15] See his *Appreciations, with an Essay on Style*, pp. 5–38. Cited below as *Essay on Style*. Also above, pp. 34, 231, *et passim*.

[16] The titles of two of these works are given above, Introduction, p. 27. The third is entitled *Renaissance Literary Theory and Practice* (New York, 1939).

ctical discourse, as primarily imaginative, involves "a prog-
ess from image to image determined emotionally." [17] In
another place he elaborated this line of analysis as follows:

Rhetoric meant to the ancient world the art of instructing and
moving men in their affairs; poetic the art of sharpening and expanding their vision. To borrow a French phrase, the one is
composition of ideas; the other, composition of images. In the
one field life is discussed; in the other it is presented. The type
of the one is a public address, moving us to assent and action;
the type of the other is a play, showing us in action moving to
an end of character. The one argues and urges; the other represents. Though both appeal to imagination, the method of rhetoric is logical; the method of poetic, as well as its detail, is
imaginative. To put the contrast with broad simplicity, a speech
moves by paragraphs; a play moves by scenes. A paragraph is a
logical stage in a progress of ideas; a scene is an emotional stage
in a progress controlled by imagination. [18]

Another twentieth-century critic to give effective thought
to the problem of distinguishing the two literatures is Hoyt
H. Hudson. His approach owed a heavy and respectfully
acknowledged debt to John Stuart Mill, and accordingly he
developed the thesis that rhetoric is given its essential character by reason of the dominance of its intention to make an
impression on others, and poetry, its essential character by
the dominance of its intention to seek expression for its own
sake. [19] Thus form and style in one of the two literatures
differ from form and style in the other even as truth made
persuasive for an audience on a specific occasion is not shaped
or verbalized in the same way as truth is when it is made

[17] *Ancient Rhetoric and Poetic*, p. 3.
[18] *Ibid.*, pp. 134–135. Baldwin indicates that the French phrase is
taken from G. Renard, *La méthode scientifique de l'histoire littéraire.*
[19] See Hudson's fine essay, "Rhetoric and Poetry," to which I have
made reference above, p. 219. See also Raymond F. Howes, ed., *Historical Studies of Rhetoric and Rhetoricians* (Ithaca, N.Y., 1961), pp.
369–379.

expressive for the poet's satisfaction alone. Said Hudson in these latter connections:

> The writer in pure literature has his eye on his subject; his subject has filled his mind and engaged his interest, and he must tell about it; his task is expression; his form and style are organic with his subject. The writer of rhetorical discourse has his eye upon the audience and occasion; his task is persuasion; his form and style are organic with the occasion.[20]

Baldwin is quite right in observing that none of the attempts to establish a viable distinction between the two literatures has controlled any consecutive movement in modern criticism.[21] But whatever any present or future critic may say in endorsing or opposing one or more of the distinctions just enumerated, he must admit that the two literatures exist as hard realities in the world of letters, and that much ingenuity, perceptiveness, and divergence have already been displayed in working out the nature of the relation between them. He must also admit upon careful reflection that Kenneth Burke, in bringing all effective literature within the sphere of rhetoric, has not only ignored the existence of a long contrary tradition, but has constructed a critical apparatus which makes it difficult to distinguish the rhetorical from the poetic utterance so as to allow them to share what they unmistakably have in common and to diverge when each sets out to accomplish its particular and unique destiny. That an interesting difference exists between good rhetoric and good poetry seems disturbingly evident. It is certainly an important task of criticism to decide what the basis of that difference is.

[20] This remark occurs in one of his other essays, "The Field of Rhetoric." See above, p. 219. See also Howes, *Historical Studies of Rhetoric and Rhetoricians*, pp. 3–15. The quotation given here appears on p. 13.

[21] *Ancient Rhetoric and Poetic*, p. 4.

4

Perhaps the groundwork of the distinction between the two literatures can best be laid by considering it as it primarily underlies oratory and drama, one of which is a good representative of the rhetorical utterance, and the other, a good representative of poetry, while each of them in its separate capacity reaches fulfillment in the actual presence of a living audience. Drama may be said to pass judgment upon some aspect of human life by providing an occasion in which that judgment works itself out in terms of a fictitious dramatic action presented to spectators in the theatre. On the other hand, oratory may be said to pass judgment upon some aspect of human life by speaking directly of that aspect in the presence of listeners. In more traditional terms, drama allows its comment to remain latent and prospective in a fictitious plot, in character, in thought, in diction, in melody, and in spectacle, whereas oratory makes its comment overt by uttering a statement formulated through the process of rhetorical inquiry into the available means of persuasion, through the process of rhetorical arrangement that may and often does create and satisfy the desires of the audience by means of syllogistic progression, and through the process of rhetorical style, where words are used, not to deal with reality in terms of the analogous situations invented by the poet, but to deal with reality as directly as may be possible in terms of the signs of speech. These rhetorical processes, to which we should add delivery or oral utterance, are of course the chief heads of the theory of rhetoric, according to the Aristotelian and Ciceronian view; and plot, character, thought, diction, melody, and spectacle will be remembered as the chief heads of the theory of poetry in Aristotle's celebrated analysis of Greek tragedy. Thus the present definition of

the relations between rhetoric and drama would seem to involve somewhat more of Aristotle than of Burke, and would
seem to bring into focus a well-developed ancient tradition
that Burke has not sought to incorporate into his critical
system.

In attempting to show wherein that ancient tradition offers some prospect of effective critical use in regard to the
judging of the two literatures, I should want to stress that
the rhetorical utterance is a transcript of reality as reality is
envisaged in the consciousness, the ambitions, the desires, the
insights, even at times the prejudices and distortions of the
speaker, and that a poetical utterance, on the other side of the
literary world, is a transcript of an imagined situation which
stands by deputy for some significant aspect of experience
retrospectively envisaged by the poet and prospectively to be
recognized by the audience. In other words, the difference
between a verbal parallel of a pattern of fact or experience
and a verbal parallel of an imagined pattern that mirrors
actual experience would thus seem to be the crucial difference between the two literatures. The imagined pattern is
the poetic fiction—the story of Hamlet or Lear, the biography that is not a factual biography, the history that is
feigned and supposed rather than documented and actual.
This fiction or fable is at the heart of the poetic utterance.
But it is not at the heart of the rhetorical utterance, where
the author's words, whether intended as history or biography
or oratory or science, lead the reader or listener directly to
the realities that the author is discussing. If it is permissible
to call the poetic fiction a symbol, in the sense in which it
stands for or suggests the parallel situation in the experience
of the poet and his public, then it is permissible to call the
poetic utterance an example of the literature of symbol; but
it would not be permissible to apply the same terms to the
rhetorical utterance, since that kind of discourse lacks the

dimension of symbol and deals instead with reality by means of direct assertions. It would therefore seem necessary to call the rhetorical utterance an example of the literature of statement in order to show what its method of dealing with reality is, and how its method differs from that of the other literature.[22]

Actually, of course, both literatures make statements about reality, and the recognition by the hearer or reader that the statements and the reality correspond with each other, and that the statements are therefore true, and therefore to be heeded, is the very essence of the effect that any rhetorical or any poetic utterance has.[23] But the rhetorical statement consists of converting reality directly into the signs of speech in accordance with the author's estimate of the meaning of that reality, and of using those signs in such a manner that in the end he and his audience will agree upon the meaning which the reality has for them. On the other side of the dividing line, the poetic statement consists in converting reality into a symbolic action, and in using the signs of speech so as to con-

[22] These terms for the two literatures are proposed and explained above, pp. 223–229.

[23] My thinking upon this matter has been deeply influenced by Walter Pater's *Essay on Style,* where he lays down what he considers to be the basic law of literary effort in rhetorical and in poetic writings. For this law, see above, p. 231. To it Pater adds: "And what an eclectic principle this really is! employing for its one sole purpose—that absolute accordance of expression to idea—all other literary beauties and excellences whatever: how many kinds of style it covers, explains, justifies, and at the same time safeguards!" There is no better guide to good writing and speaking than this. My chief reservation about Pater's whole theory of the two literatures is that, although he judiciously makes scientific writing and poetry into natural opposites, he tends to allow oratory to rest between them in a position closer to poetry than to scientific discourse. Thus he fails to observe the essential distinction between an oration and a poem, and indeed between the two literatures. His emphasis upon the principle of truth as the essential criterion for either kind of discourse is a brilliant modern application of the basic law of rhetoric as given in Plato's *Phaedrus.*

vert that symbol into something capable of carrying within it
to an audience the significance that it has in relation to itself
and to the reality behind it. The poet may hope but will
never really expect that his own understanding of the symbolic action and his hearers' understanding of it will be
identical. But he postulates that the two understandings will
approximate each other—that the hearers will see things
more or less as he did, after they have contemplated the relation of the symbolic action to their own particular lives; and
he is aware that the great advantage of his utterance over the
rhetorical utterance consists in its having the power to convey to his own generation a multidimensional rather than a
single comment upon reality, and to transmit to posterity the
sort of expanding comment which can wondrously illuminate
the spiritual crises of a later time.

The poetical utterance is always attended by an aura of
ambiguity, by an appearance of having said more than one
thing. Thus it would indeed be a confusing instrument in
business transactions, in legal documents, in courts of law, in
senatorial debates, in historical writing, and in scientific exposition. But businessmen, lawyers, politicians, historians,
and scientific writers have nevertheless some capacity for
confusing rather than clarifying the realities with which they
deal, even if the rhetorical enterprise, to which they are com-
mitted by profession, offers them a greater opportunity for
precision of meaning than poetry could. Thus they sometimes speak before they have understood the facts, or they
sometimes speak after they have misunderstood or ignored
or distorted them, and in any of these instances they fail to
achieve what rhetoric exists to foster—the transfer of accurate
evaluations of reality to an audience in such a way that, without needing to construe them by analogy, the audience ac-
cepts them as direct guides to conduct and life. The poet can
fail, too. He fails, however, not when he says more than one

thing at a time, but when he frames his fiction so as to impose upon it those meanings which are specious or redundant, which cannot enlarge the imaginative resources of the human spirit, which cannot make men and women more aware of their essential humanity than they had ever been before.

Kenneth Burke recognizes the symbolic aspect of poetry, and it would be a gross misstatement of his critical theory to imply that he does not.[24] But he defines the symbol merely as "the verbal parallel to a pattern of experience," [25] and thus he makes no allowance for the fact that a historical work or an oration fits that particular definition quite literally and completely, whereas a drama or novel of any artistic stature needs to be described as the verbal parallel to an emblematic situation conceived by the poet to stand for a pattern of experience in his own life and in the life of humanity. In other words, the verbal construct that we call an oration takes the audience to the realities with which it deals, but the verbal construct that we call a drama takes the audience to an imagined reality which fulfills itself by becoming a parallel of realities in the spectator's experience. Burke says almost this very thing when he illustrates symbolism (even if his previous definition of symbolism says significantly less than the illustrations do):

The poet, for instance, may pity himself for his undeserved neglect, and this self-pity may colour his day. It may be so forceful, and so frequently recurrent as to become selective, so that he finds ever new instances of his unappreciated worth. Self-pity assumes enough prominence in his case to become a pattern of experience. If he converts this pattern into a plot, The King and the Peasant (about a King who has but the trappings of kingliness and a Peasant who is, in the true sense, a King) he has produced a Symbol. He might have chosen other Symbols to ver-

24 For his discussion of symbolism in art, see *Counter-Statement* pp. 71–78, 193–204.
25 *Ibid.,* p. 193.

balize the same pattern. In fact, if his pattern continues to ob-
sess him, he undoubtedly will exemplify the same pattern in
other Symbols: he will next produce The Man Against the Mob,
or A Saint Dying in Neglect. Or he may be still more devious,
and finding his own problems writ large in the life of some historic figure, he may give us a vigorous biography of the Little
Corporal.[26]

Perhaps Burke is too much inclined in these examples to reduce artistic achievement to the sole motivation of self-pity
and egotism, as if a poet might not have other causes of concern than his own unappreciated worth. But at any rate
Burke's essential analysis seems valid enough, and it indicates
that the poet does not directly discuss unappreciated worth
as an orator would necessarily do, but instead he translates
unappreciated worth into an emblem of the worthless king
admired for the external appearance of merit, and of the no-
ble peasant despised for the external appearance of worthless-
ness. This emblem is the poet's fiction; it is his characteristic
way of dealing with unappreciated worth and unsuspected
depravity in actual human experience. This emblem is also
the poet's symbol. And as a symbol it is not a verbal parallel
of actual human experience, but a verbal parallel of a depu-
tized experience that through its imagined reality utters
deep truths about the reality felt by actual people in the here
and now.

The difference between the historical narrative and the
fictitious narrative is the difference that Burke ignores, and
this is the essence of the distinction between the two literatures. Historians would agree that there is on the one hand an
actual series of human events filling every hour of past time,
and on the other hand a parallel series of past events that
man has chosen to remember. "The two series correspond
more or less," said Carl Becker, "it is our aim to make the

[26] *Ibid.*, pp. 193–194.

correspondence as exact as possible; but the actual series of events exists for us only in terms of the ideal series which we affirm and hold in memory." "This is why I am forced," Becker added, "to identify history with knowledge of history. For all practical purposes history is, for us and for the time being, what we know it to be." [27] Becker's provocative line of analysis leads us to see that historical narration is a context of verbal statements standing in relation to a context of past realities and seeking to introduce a reader or student to the historian's own understanding of the realities which those statements represent. Historical truth is achieved when the historian's statements correspond to those realities in a way which other historians can verify. Fictitious narrative, however, does not seek to reproduce a context of events that have actually occurred in the past; or, if the fiction is based upon fact, as historical dramas are, the poetic narrator does not seek to reproduce the facts for the sake of their factual order and significance. Instead, the poet tells a story of events that he may imagine in their entirety or take from happenings known to have taken place; and he tells this story in such a way as to make his hearers or readers identify themselves with it and see themselves doing or suffering what the characters in the story do and suffer, while at the same time, through their own actual existence outside the story, the audience has some glimpse of what those doings and sufferings mean in the realm of human choice and avoidance. Poetic truth is achieved when the poet's symbol—the fable, say, of Hamlet or Lear—affords the spectator in the theatre the opportunity to see the realities of his own life in terms of the imagined realities on the stage and to understand that what happened to Hamlet or Lear is happening here and now to himself and to every man, not so much in a literal as in a figurative and

[27] See his address, "Everyman His Own Historian," *The American Historical Review,* XXXVII (1932), 222.

analogous way. The points of similarity between the spectator's sense of the meaning of life and the poet's sense of it as
revealed in his story must outweigh the points of difference
in order for the poetic analogy to be valid and true for the
hearers. Thus poetic truth is more complicated than historical
truth. After all, the historian, as Aristotle said, tells us what
has happened, and the poet, what might happen; and it is
obvious that the historian's narrative can be verified or disproved by taking it to the actual record, whereas the poet's
narrative can only be verified or disproved by taking it to a
record that in each individual human being is written only
in terms of his deep awareness of the potentialities of his
own restless human soul. Who is there, then, but the individual man and woman to decide whether the events in a
poem correspond to the inherent powers of his own spiritual
life? But the decision, once made, can be communicated to
others and tested against the parallel decisions that others
have made, and when it is widely shared and successfully re-
tested time and again, it begins to have as much validity, as
much truth, as much universality, as man can expect his most
personal self-awareness to achieve.

5

Oratory belongs on the side of history rather than of
poetry. One movement of the classical oration was termed
narratio, or narration, and it fell in the speech at that point
where the speaker was to tell the story of events that had
occurred or might be supposed to have occurred in bringing
up for discussion the issue to which he had to address himself. The theory of *narratio* in classical rhetoric was not only
designed to help the orator pleading a case in court or arguing the merits of national policy before a parliamentary assembly; it was also designed to help all tellers of imaginary
or real tales, and in particular the writers of history. Perhaps

it was partly with this latter consideration in mind that
Cicero has Antonius declare rhetoric alone to be the art in-
herently qualified to teach historians and all other writers
how to be eloquent.[28] In this connection it is instructive to
remember that Edward Everett's speech at the consecration
of the Gettysburg national cemetery—the forgotten oration,
one might say, in contrast to the memorable address given
by Lincoln on the same occasion—contained a detailed sketch
of the entire military campaign surrounding what Everett
himself called the battles of Gettysburg, and that Everett so
carefully checked the details of this history against his own
actual study of the battlefield itself and against the special
information made available to him by General Meade and
other participants as to have his speech considered by a com-
petent historian to be "the best contemporary account" of
the engagement that it describes.[29] Here, in other words, is
oratorical narration considered worthy to be accepted as
history, and this merger of two important forms of the literature of fact should surprise no one, despite the absurd tendency to think that oratory and history are on the same plane
of excellence only when the oration rises above itself and
takes on the qualities of poetry. An oration that took on the
symbolic quality that a poem must have would be ridiculous,
and without that particular quality it must remain in the
other category of literature. In short, the oratorical utterance
should never be confused with the poetic utterance, no matter how full it may be of the content indiscriminately asso-

[28] See Cicero, *De Oratore,* 2.9.36–38. On this same point, we should
also remember that other rhetoricians have joined Cicero in aligning
historical composition with rhetoric. See, for example, Thomas Gale,
Rhetores Selecti (Oxonii, 1676), p. 199, where, in a treatise entitled "De
Rhetorica" and attributed to "Anonymous Sophista," the four species
of rhetoric are listed as follows (my translation): judicial, deliberative,
encomiastic, historical.

[29] See William E. Barton, *Lincoln at Gettysburg* (Indianapolis, 1939),
p. 211.

ciated only with poetry—truth deeply loved, and fiercely sought, and lovingly spoken against the fury of animality and brutishness. This kind of content makes an oration eloquent, but eloquence is not poetry. As for the true poetic narration, it tells its story, not solely to express the poet's understanding of the events within it, but rather to call attention to the understanding we must all have of parallel events within the consciousness and experience of humanity as it gropes for a clue to its own identity.

If history and oratory (and biographical writing, too) belong to the literature of statement, what Wordsworth called matter of fact or science would belong even more unmistakably there. Indeed, in all accounts of the two literatures, scientific writing is always made the true opposite of poetry. For example, Pater, having mentioned Pascal as an author caught between the world of fact and the world of imagination, said: "In science, on the other hand, in history so far as it conforms to scientific rule, we have a literary domain where the imagination may be thought to be always an intruder." And in that domain, he added, "the functions of literature reduce themselves eventually to the transcribing of fact." [30] Thus a theorem in Euclid would have to be taken as a transcript of reality, and it would have to be counted an example of the literature of statement, and it would have to be judged true or false and hence good or bad according as it could be shown to convey its author's sense of fact to an audience in such a way as ultimately to make agreement upon that fact possible between them. Euclid's theorems have form, and that form is rhetorical, in the broad way in which rhetoric should now be accepted not only as the theory of all types of popular discourse within the province of the literature of statement, but also as the theory of all types of learned discourse formerly regarded as belonging to dialectic and

[30] *Essay on Style*, p. 9.

philosophy.[31] Euclid's theorems also involve syllogistic progression, as Burke observes, and this progression has about it a rhythm or movement that begins in a sense of anticipation on our part and ends for us in a sense of fulfillment. But the theorems are not stories. The lines and figures of geometry are not human lineaments and features. They do not stand before us as a Macbeth tortured by a forbidden ambition, as a Hamlet commanded to do what is at once hateful and necessary. Thus the theorems lack the dimension of poetry and are carefully to be distinguished from examples of the literature of symbol.

There are some utterances which would have to be counted as rhetorical even if they seem to conform to some of the conventions widely held to belong exclusively to poetry. Aristotle gave an example of one of them when he denied that Empedocles was a poet even if he did compose natural philosophy in epic metre. The versified botany of Erasmus Darwin is another example of the same sort. The fiction that seems to limit itself to the conveying of biographical or historical information about men or times—a fiction that is presented merely as biography or history—would have no poetic value, although it might be highly interesting, widely read, and factually correct. Popular songs, patriotic songs, even prayers and hymns, are rhetorical in intent, and I trust that, at this point in the present discussion, they may be classed in this way without disparaging them in any respect. There are lyric poems which, highly colored and figurative as they may be in style, say nothing that has a symbolic dimension, and thus they must be regarded as rhetorical. But most lyric poetry is episode as well as outburst, and the episode can be seen not only as a symbol of the reality behind it in the poet's imagination but of the reality ahead of it in the reader's awareness of his world. Most lyrical poetry would be truly poetical, not

[31] An elaboration of this view is given above, pp. 144–150.

because of its rhyme scheme, not because of its images and figures, not because it departed from the conventions of ordinary prose, but because it conveyed what it had to say by using the emblem, the analogous situation, as its vehicle.

6

At the center of the modern province of the literature of symbol is prose fiction, as epic poetry and drama were at the center of the province of imitative art in Aristotle's scheme. Pater recognized the actuality of this shift in taste when he called imaginative prose "the special and opportune art of the modern world." [32] Fielding did as much as any writer to bring this shift about—we need recall not only the nature of his fiction but also his famous Preface to *Joseph Andrews*, where he describes that work as a comic epic poem in prose. It would be possible to account for this shift by relating it to the growth of modern empirical science, modern historical scholarship, and modern biography. These forms of the literature of statement have disciplined the expectations of present-day men toward a prevailing but not exclusive preference for the realistic symbol as distinguished from the allegorical, the heroic, the legendary, or the supernatural symbols of former times. But in the hands of great writers like Fielding or Dickens or Henry James or Tolstoy or Faulkner the realistic symbol has all the power that any one of the older symbols had to convey to its public a sense of the humanity inhering in the structure of man's existence.

7

In sum, it is the multidimensional plot and the multidimensional character that make the story by Poe differ from the unidimensional proposition in Euclid. The story, the dramatic action, the novel, deal with the desires and satisfactions

[32] *Essay on Style,* p. 11

of an audience so far as hearers or readers can be made to see the private surface of their own experience mirrored in the predicament which confronts fictitious characters before them; but the propositions in Euclid, like learned debate, or oratory, or history, or scientific prose, deal with the lines and figures of reality and with man's craving for satisfaction in understanding the public surfaces of his experience. The latter utterances are best called examples of the literature of statement, and the former utterances, examples of the literature of symbol. The theory of rhetoric, purified of some of the rhetorical mechanisms which no longer meet the needs of the modern world—invention by resort to commonplaces, for example, or style that grows from the exploitation of the tropes and the figures—is still properly to be regarded as the organon of the literature of statement, while the organon of the literature of symbol is properly to be regarded as poetics. It seems confusing and unwise to merge poetics and rhetoric, even though both must be accepted as arts of appeal, and both must make use of common underlying principles of form and style.[33] It is Burke's weakness that, despite the many positive advantages which his system of criticism affords, his view of rhetoric fails to preserve the niceties of the inherited view, and thus it represents a retreat rather than an advance in this one aspect of critical theory.

[33] A discriminating and productive program that can be used by the literary critic who must occasionally deal with oratorical and argumentative prose in connection with his presumably major concern for poetry, and that can also be used by the rhetorical critic so far as he profits by understanding the difference between poetic and rhetorical composition, is set forth in Herbert A. Wichelns's classic essay, "The Literary Criticism of Oratory," in *Studies in Rhetoric and Public Speaking in Honor of James Albert Winans*, pp. 181–216. This essay is reprinted in Bryant, *The Rhetorical Idiom*, pp. 5–42, and in abridged form in Howes, *Historical Studies of Rhetoric and Rhetoricians*, pp. 217–224.

Index of Names, of Topics, and of Works Cited

Bacon, Sir Francis, (*cont.*)
Augmentis Scientiarum, 94; *Works,*
see Spedding, James, *et al.*
Bacon, Sir Nicholas, 79
Bain, Alexander, 146
Baldwin, Charles Sears, *Ancient Rhet-*
oric and Poetic, 27, 72, 191-193, 210,
214, 240-241, 242; *Medieval Rheto-*
ric and Poetic, 27, 149, 240; *Renais-*
sance Literary Theory and Practice,
240
Balkanized learning destructive of
culture, 150
Balzac, Honorè de, 18
Barton, William E., *Lincoln at Gettys-*
burg, 251
Basilius Magnus, 88; *De Legendis*
Gentilium Libris, 89
Bastier, P., *Fénelon: Critique d'art,*
126
beauty as truth, 138-139
Becker, Carl, *Declaration of Indepen-*
dence, 164, 165, 182, 185; "Every-
man His Own Historian," 231, 248-
249
Beëlzebub, 113
Black, Max, *Labyrinth of Language,*
25
Blackwood's Edinburgh Magazine, 27,
39, 193
Blair, Hugh, 169; *Lectures on Rheto-*
ric and Belles Lettres, 33, 171-172
Bolgar, R. R., 8, 9
Bolingbroke, Viscount, 198
Booth, Wayne, *Rhetoric of Fiction,* 42
Borgerhoff, E. B. O., *Freedom of*
French Classicism, 126
Bossuet, Jacques Bénigne, 124
Boswell, James, *Life of Johnson,* 173
Bovary, Emma, 110
Boyd, Julian P., *Declaration of Inde-*
pendence, 164, 182, 185, 186; *Papers*
of Thomas Jefferson, 190
Brightland, John, *Logic and Gram-*
mar, 184
Browne, Sir Thomas, 198
Brun, F., *Fénelon, critique d'art,* 125
Brutus, 61
Bryant, Donald C., ed., *Papers in*

Rhetoric and Poetic, 72, 110; ed.,
The Rhetorical Idiom, 9, 255
Burghley, Lord, see Cecil, William
Burke, Edmund, 36, 154, 198; speech
on conciliation with America, 154
Burke, Kenneth, 10, 11; *Counter-*
Statement, 36-40, 72, 221, 234-255
Burton, Robert, 198
Bywater, Ingram, see Aristotle, *Poetics*

Caecilius, comic poet, 66
Cambrai, 123, 124
Cambridge University, 223
Cambridge University Press, 9, 101
Campagnac, E. T., 142
Campbell, George, *Philosophy of*
Rhetoric, 19, 34, 169-170, 171, 189
Can Grande, Lord, 93
Canning, George, 198
Caplan, Harry, 10; "Decay of Elo-
quence at Rome," 149; "Four Senses
of Scriptural Interpretation," 93; *Of*
Eloquence, ed. Anne King and
Helen North, 93; trans., *Rhetorica*
ad Herennium, 152
Carcassonne, E., *Etat présent des*
travaux sur Fénelon, 123
Carmak, Paul A., ed., *Readings in*
Rhetoric (with Lionel Crocker), 9,
10
Cascellius, 66
Casey, R. D., 219
Catiline, 196
Cato, 66
Cecil, Robert, 79
Cecil, William, Lord Burghley, 79
Center for Medieval and Renaissance
Studies, University of California,
Los Angeles, 10
Cethegus, 66
Cherel, A., *Fénelon au XVIII*ᵉ *Siècle,*
124
Chicago school of Aristotelians, 45
Choerilus, epic poet, 66
Chremes, 66
Churchill, Winston, speeches in 1940,
154
Cicero, 23, 24, 113, 116, 126, 132, 135,
146, 157, 163, 168, 169, 188, 196,